W9-DFP-407

Tage Frid Teaches Woodworking

Book 1: **Joinery**
Book 2: **Shaping, Veneering, Finishing**

Tage Frid Teaches Woodworking

Book 1: **Joinery**
Book 2: **Shaping, Veneering, Finishing**

The Taunton Press

Cover illustrations: Hand dovetails with a compound miter (top);
using hex clamps to bend wood around a small form (bottom).

The Taunton Press
Inspiration for hands-on living™

10 9 8 7 6

Printed in the United States of America

A Fine Woodworking Book

Fine Woodworking® is a trademark of The Taunton Press, Inc., registered in the
U.S. Patent and Trademark Office.

The Taunton Press, 63 South Main Street, Box 5506, Newtown, CT 06470-5506
e-mail: tp@taunton.com

Distributed by Publishers Group West

Library of Congress Cataloging-in-Publication Data

Frid, Tage.
      Tage Frid teaches woodworking.
         p.   cm.
      ISBN 1-56158-068-6
      1. Woodwork. I. Title.
TT180.F77   1993   93-23053
684'.08—dc20   CIP

Book 1: **Joinery**

Contents

Foreword

In 1977, a little more than a year after Tage Frid began writing articles as contributing editor to Fine Woodworking magazine, it became apparent that those articles would make only an insignificant dent in the vast woodworking knowledge Frid had accumulated in his 50 years of cabinetmaking.

Frid learned cabinetmaking as an apprentice in his native Denmark, a country long noted for its strong woodworking tradition. After World War II, the American Crafts Council asked Frid to transfer some of this lore by establishing a woodworking program at the School for American Craftsmen, which was then at Alfred University but soon to be at Rochester Institute of Technology, where it remains today.

Frid set up the program and stayed 14 years at RIT until 1962, when he joined the faculty at the Rhode Island School of Design as professor of woodworking and furniture design, a position he still holds.

Over the years, Frid has taught a multitude of students to be well-versed in the many ways of working wood. Check the furniture conservation and restoration departments of major American museums, or the faculty of college-level woodworking and furniture design programs in this country, and likely as not you'll find a former Frid student. And of course, many other students have become commercially successful woodworkers.

The Frid hallmark is to teach virtually all the techniques and tools available to the woodworker. Thus his students are able to tackle any woodworking assignment under any shop conditions. This approach is also crucial to furniture design, where Frid's motto is to design around the construction. When one knows all the ways of making furniture, one also knows how to design furniture without falling into the trap of designing a piece that cannot be successfully made.

Frid's students come out of his courses able to design and build furniture in any style, though most naturally prefer the contemporary idiom, as does Frid. But even here, Frid encourages students to go their own way in design — so much so that it's impossible to tell what Frid's own design style is by looking at the work of his pupils.

Frid also believes his students should know how to make a living from working with wood, so he stresses the production techniques individual designer-craftsmen will need to know if they are to turn out work that is both well designed and efficiently produced — in other words, work that is many cuts above mass-produced furniture, but still competitively priced.

Frid himself has kept in touch with the commercial aspects of woodworking by accepting a string of commissions that range from kitchen cabinets to corporate boardrooms to church interiors, as well as difficult restorations like the 19th-century ship interiors at Mystic (Conn.) Seaport. And just this year, the Boston Museum of Fine Arts commissioned Frid to create some public seating that will become part of its permanent collection.

As his former students and clients can easily attest, Frid has much to teach, and thus we decided to do a series of three books on everything Frid knows about woodworking, structured in the same way as the courses he has taught. The first book would be about joinery and tools, for that's where woodworking must begin; the second about bending, turning, shaping, veneering and otherwise working with wood. The third volume would put these techniques all together into one book on the design and construction of furniture.

Frid's woodworking shop behind his farmhouse in Foster, Rhode Island, was converted to a photo studio. A former student, Rosanne Somerson, signed on for a time as scribe and photographer. And Frid's wife, Emma, kept things organized and flowing smoothly. This first volume is the result.

This book has been organized around processes, and it has been designed more as a shop manual than as a text or craft book. Each page or spread is self-contained—the text accompanying pictures is usually right alongside the pertinent pictures. Boldface numbers set into the text refer to the appropriate illustration. Where necessary, cross references to other parts of the book are included.

Sections of the book that deal with cutting joints usually end with a series of sequential drawings that recap the cutting of the joint. The color in each drawing highlights the cut being made at that time. The result is shown in black in subsequent drawings.

Because each section deals with a single subject, the table of contents also serves as an index.

A word about the photos: Most were taken in Frid's own shop. In the interest of clarity, safety guards were sometimes removed from machines, and scribed lines were sometimes darkened with a pencil.

This book is intended for the woodworker who wishes to learn how to select the best joints for the job at hand, and how to lay them out and cut them more accurately and efficiently. Novices will be able to follow Frid's step-by-step instructions; intermediates will improve their techniques and certainly pick up many tips; advanced woodworkers will be challenged by the more difficult joinery.

Newtown, Conn.
July 28, 1979

Paul Roman, Editor-in-Chief
The Taunton Press

Acknowledgments

My original agreement with the Taunton Press was to write three woodworking books in 1½ years, which I was sure I could do. Now, two years later, book one is finally finished. I had no idea how much work goes into writing a book and neither did Rosanne Somerson, who took most of the photographs and typed the whole manuscript from tapes, which was certainly not easy, if you have ever heard me talk. But being one of my former students, she managed. A special thanks to her for her great help.

I also want to thank Hank Gilpin for reading the first galley and offering many useful suggestions, and Roger Birn for taking some of the pictures.

If it had not been for my wife, this book would never have been written. Before Fine Woodworking *was established, the publisher, Paul Roman, asked me to write some articles. I was not interested at all. Never having written an article before, I felt I was not qualified, but my wife finally talked me into it. In thanks to her, I dedicate this book to my wife, Emma.*

Introduction
Chapter 1

This book is intended for small professional shops, schools and hobbyists. There are many ways to do some of the things I have described, and these are the ways that I have found to be the easiest and best through many years of experimenting. I have taught many of the woodworkers in this country who are now teachers, as well as many of the individual craftsmen. Most of them still use the methods that I taught them.

Many woodworking books have information that I find unnecessary. If I didn't need that information in the 50 years that I have been working with wood, I am sure that you won't either. There will be no charts for nail and screw sizes, sandpaper grits and the like. No industrial production machines will be covered. But each technique and every joint will be explained and demonstrated. I will describe how to perform various operations by hand, using small electric hand tools, and the small machines that a craftsman or hobbyist is likely to have access to. Each tool, material and machine will be introduced as it is needed to accomplish a specific operation.

You may notice that some of the machinery and tools in the photographs look worn and old. In many cases they are. I have had a good working relationship with all of these tools for many years; and I wouldn't feel right about ignoring this relationship by buying shiny new tools just for the photographs. You may have tools that you feel this way about now. If not, assuming that you care for your tools, you probably will someday. I will not go into too great detail about all the adjustments on the machines, because machines vary so much from brand to brand. But special tricks for operating them will be covered.

Most of what is in this book, I learned from older craftsmen when I was young. They, of course, were taught by some other craftsmen, so the trade has been passed on from generation to generation. A few things in this book I feel I have improved on, but the foundation is still what I learned when I was young. One thing I can't stand is when people who went through the same learning as I, won't pass it on to the younger generation. They keep it a secret as if it belonged only to them and seem to forget that they learned it from someone else.

The purpose of this book is to help you do things right. The easiest thing in the world is to make mistakes. The difficult thing is to know how to get out of those mistakes. In many instances you can't afford to throw out the piece with the mistake on it. You might be working on something where you have carefully matched the grain. Or you might be working with a special wood that is scarce and expensive. As well as teaching you how to do a certain technique, I will try in many cases to tell you what to do if you make a mistake.

I hope you will enjoy this book and learn enough to make beautiful, lasting pieces of furniture.

Some thoughts on being a woodworker   I have chosen to be a designer-craftsman. Most of my life I have concentrated on designing and working only with wood, and, having spent more than 50 years with that one material, I am still learning through experimentation and looking for new techniques and forms.

The only trouble with designing and working in wood is that it has the advantage – or disadvantage, however you look at it – of being beautiful in itself. It is not like metal. A piece of metal by itself is very cold and has to be hammered, shaped and polished before people will even look at it. A piece of clay, which is really dirt, must be shaped, fired and glazed. But take a piece of wood – plane, sand and oil it, and you will find it is a beautiful thing. The more you do to it from then on, the more chance that you will make it worse. Therefore, working with a material of such natural beauty, I feel that we have to design very quietly and use simple forms.

On being an apprentice   I was born in Denmark, so therefore my background for furniture is a little different from that of most American furniture designers. That may be the reason that I view design from a slightly different angle and feel strongly about the background that a furniture designer should have. I started as an apprentice in a cabinetmaker's shop in Copenhagen when I was very young. Because I was not what you would call an outstanding student in school, I decided that the best thing for me to do was to serve an apprenticeship.

When you become an apprentice in Denmark, you sign a five-year contract, which is binding on both parties. Those were five of the longest years that I have ever spent! The working hours were from 7 AM to 5 PM, and I was required to attend technical school at night, where drawing and a knowledge of the materials were taught. The salary was one dollar a week and the guarantee that I would be a journeyman at the end of five years. I did not learn very much about design, but I did learn a good deal about wood as a material – its strength, its limitations and how it is put together.

In many ways I still think the apprenticeship system is one of the best ways to learn about a material and the craft of working with it, but it is just about impossible to get a situation like that here. In Europe, craftsmen enjoy the recognition they deserve. Here, an effort should be made to put more respect into vocational training. A student taking vocational training may be just as intelligent as a student enrolled in a college program. The only difference is that the student has a different goal. I think it is better to be a good craftsman and happy than to be a doctor or lawyer and unhappy just to satisfy mom and dad.

I think we have to start with the teachers of vocational subjects in high schools by giving them a better background. Instead of teaching them a little of each craft and having them become jacks-of-all-trades, they should be taught one craft so that when it is mastered they can teach students in that particular field. I think also that they should be furnished with a better design background themselves in order to be able to guide the students in making their own designs. Now, a student who wants to make a coffee table is told to go to drawer #3 and pick a design, usually from some popular magazine, which certainly does not help the student to understand good design. A vocational student should be instructed in design and art history, as well as mechanical drawing, materials and processes.

Educators today like to talk about the spiral where the student knows a little bit about everything before finally reaching perfection. I think it would be much better to turn the spiral upside-down and learn one thing well, and, as you go on and improve, spread yourself out to other fields. However, I believe students should make up their mind at an early point what their major will be and spend much more time in it. I'm afraid the present educational system, where the students spend a few hours in one field and the next few hours in another, leads only to confusion, and they are unable to decide what they really want to do.

Knowledge of materials In 1948 I started teaching in the School for American Craftsmen, now located in Rochester, N.Y. When I arrived at the school, the students and some of the teachers kept talking about the "freedom of the material." This sounded interesting to me, and I could hardly wait to find out what it was all about. It didn't take me very long to find out when I started teaching. They did not have control of the material, so many of the things made were actually accidents.

I do not think that all furniture designers should be craftsmen first, but I certainly am convinced that designers should know the material in which they are going to design. I really do not see how designers can go in cold and design something in a material about which they have no knowledge. Even for a professional, it is extremely difficult to switch from one material to another and do a good job.

Design and construction If you combine technique and knowledge of the material, you certainly should be able to design and make some interesting and beautiful furniture, because if you have this background, you will automatically design around the construction, and not construct around the design. You will combine technique and form when you are designing—as construction becomes second nature. I am sorry to say that many times a different approach is used—that is, to construct around the design. Many designers are so worried about the looks and the sculptural qualities of the piece that they first think about the beauty of the piece and later worry about how it is put together. I strongly believe that this is the wrong approach to take when you are designing furniture. When people buy furniture, they are very practical—they want a chair they can sit on and a bed they can sleep in. Customers may, for example, buy a sterling-silver coffeepot that will tarnish and be unsafe to use to show that they can afford expensive items, or for whatever personal reason. They may buy a vase for its beauty even though it may have a crack in it. But when they are buying furniture, they want something they can use.

Furniture I feel that a piece of furniture should be in proportion to the size of the buyer and reflect his or her own personality. I don't think that anything can make a small person look more ridiculous—and perhaps make him feel smaller—than disappearing into an oversized, upholstered chair; or the reverse of a large person sitting on a delicate chair in which the chair disappears, and the person seems to be sitting on four legs. Furniture should be proportioned to the person who uses it. For example, there are certain requirements a chair must have. It should be designed so that it looks inviting to sit on, you should be able to sit in various positions, and it should be able to take the sitter's weight under stress circumstances. A chair is difficult to design because it has to fit the contours of the body, which haven't changed much since people started sitting on chairs. At the same time, a chair has to look good from all angles.

The furniture I have been talking about is the more functional type. There are others, for instance, the type that you are supposed to "discover," where the sculpture of the piece becomes more important than the function. A few designers and craftsmen can make this type, but one could not start an industry based on it. A designer-craftsman would have to design and make it because it would be so personalized that it would be impossible to make a working drawing, or to get anyone else to make it. But it would be very refreshing to have a few pieces of this furniture in your home. A limited number would be fine, because I don't want to spend half of my time trying to discover where I am going to sit in my own home. I am in favor of individual furniture, make it quite often myself and encourage my students to do so. It is fun to make a piece of sculpture that you can also sit on.

Designer-craftsmen If you study the older furniture designers, you will find that they were craftsmen, and they all designed around the construction. For that reason, we still enjoy their furniture today, and it mixes very well with well-designed contemporary furniture. The good furniture designer of today uses the same techniques, and those pieces will later become classical furniture. But in many cases the designs are copies, and to cut costs, shortcuts are taken. This is why we have some of the miscarriages we see today. Of course, I am fully aware that the high cost of material and labor and the shortage of skilled labor have a big influence on today's designs. But I still don't believe an inexpensive piece of furniture has to look cheap. The disappearance of the designer-craftsman was one of the prices we had to pay here in America for having mass production. In Europe they are specializing also, and the decline in the crafts field is noticeable, too. But it does not mean that it is dying. We don't need as many craftsmen as we once had because we have machines.

Many people think that the craftsman makes everything by hand. He does not, of course. He takes advantage of all the machines and techniques that are available. Some people think it is wonderful that something is made "by hand." I don't care how it is made—he can make it with his teeth or a machine—it is still the final product that counts. A craftsman is very flexible and it does not cost much to switch from one design to another; therefore he is able to combine machine work and handwork to get more individual pieces. Even in a small production line, each piece can still have its own individuality. I think a designer-craftsman can compete in price with factory-made furniture because people usually go directly to him, and the dealer's in-between costs are cut. The craftsman can customize the furniture to fit the customer's taste. He can alter a piece of furniture, making it slightly larger or smaller to fit in a particular place without having to increase the cost. Without the tremendous overhead the factory carries, the price will be pretty close to what a factory-made piece of the same quality would cost. So I believe there is a great opportunity and a great need for designer-craftsmen today, and that most clients are looking for something with a more personal touch and of better quality than is available in stores. □

The Material
Chapter 2

1

2

Wood

Trees A woodworker must have a basic understanding of the growth and structure of trees in order to design with an understanding of what can and cannot be done with wood. Only a few of the many trees that grow in this country and in other parts of the world ever reach the cabinetmaker in lumber form. Some woods warp and twist too much to be of practical use; others are too colorless or lack variety of grain; others are too soft. But all woods, regardless of their different characteristics, are subject to the stresses and strains inherent in their structure.

Wood is divided into two groups, hardwoods and softwoods. This has nothing to do with whether the wood is hard or soft — some softwoods are harder than hardwoods. The division into the two categories is by the type of leaves of the tree. Softwoods are generally evergreens, coniferous trees, and usually do not shed their leaves in the fall. Deciduous trees, which shed their leaves in the fall, make up the group of hardwoods.

Both the cell and the cell walls of a living tree are filled with moisture, or sap. When a tree is felled, the moisture in the cells, called free moisture, is the first to drain out or evaporate. Once the cells are free of moisture, the cell walls gradually give up the moisture that has soaked into them. It is this drying process that causes the stresses that result in warpage, twisting, checking and shrinking. This is true in all types of lumber. The moisture content of wood is of prime concern to anyone designing or constructing furniture and cannot be ignored.

Logs I don't think I have to explain about the birds and the bees. We all know that the seed gets into the ground and the sapling gets started and each year puts a new year ring on. A tree grows from the inside out, which means that the closer you get to the center, the older the wood.

(1) Let's examine the end of a cherry log after it is cut. Notice the dark heartwood and the light sapwood. Each year a new ring is added to the sapwood, and one sapwood year ring on the inside dies and gets added to the heartwood. The tree does not grow at the same rate during the year — it grows faster in the spring and slower in the summer. The faster spring growth is softer and lighter than the slower summer growth. And the tree does not grow the same size annual rings each year: It all depends on the weather.

(2) This log was plainsawn, or cut tangentially to the annual rings. The cut angles in to make the figure more apparent. Since the color differs from spring to summer growth, very beautiful and interesting patterns result. You can see how the grain of the sliced vertical section relates to the rings on the end.

Many times you hear people who have turned or carved a bowl saying, "I studied the grain before I started shaping the wood." This is a good sales pitch, but it is a lot of baloney. When you carve or turn a bowl the rings follow the shape as you cut through them. But you can control the figure by the way you orient the bowl. In drawing **(3)**, the graining will be very strong with the annual rings cut at a great angle. If the bowl is oriented in the opposite direction **(4)**, the rings will be cut at about 90°, making the graining of the bowl straight.

(5) This log has a quartersawn section removed. Cutting perpendicular to the annual rings gives a straight grain. If used right, straight grain can be quite effective visually. Quartersawn lumber is best suited to lamination and steam-bending.

(6) This log is cut right through the heartwood. The center of the log can't be used but the pieces to either side of the center are usable. There the graining is straight as in quartersawn lumber.

3

4

5

6

7

8

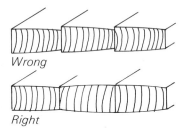

9

(7) The pith, or center of the log, can't be used, because it will crack when it is dry.

Drying As soon as wood is sawn, drying becomes a problem. Whether it will be air-dried or kiln-dried, wood should be kept out of the sun and properly stacked. If planks of wet lumber are piled on top of each other, with no space between them, the lumber will soon discolor and begin to rot.

For air-drying, the boards must be kept off the ground, and sometimes it's advisable to coat the ends with hot paraffin or paint to prevent too rapid drying. The sticks they rest on to keep them off the ground have to be leveled off. Between each layer of wood, sticks of even thickness (about ¾ in. square) should be placed directly over each other for even air circulation. The top of the pile should be covered. If kept inside, they should be stored in an open shed to allow air circulation. To check for dryness, keep some pieces 3 ft. to 4 ft. long on the outside of the pile, about halfway up. Weigh them every month and put a date on them each time. When the weight stabilizes, all the wood should be fairly dry.

Exactly how wood moves depends on how the board was cut and from what part of the tree it came.

We know that the center of the tree is the oldest and the outside the youngest **(8)**, which means the pores or cells on the outside are more open than the center ones, so the outside will shrink more than the inside. This tells how the wood moves after it is cut and dried.

The reason that this is important is that after the wood is dried and made into a piece of furniture, the wood will continue to expand and shrink across both the grain and the thickness every year with the seasons. How much it moves depends on how dry our houses get in winter, and how damp in summer, and on the type of wood.

Just as the new, outside wood shrinks more when it dries, so it expands more when the humidity rises. This means that when joining boards together—say, for a tabletop, or whatever—the boards should be chosen and placed such that new wood should be joined to new wood, old wood to old wood **(9)**. Otherwise, no matter how well you plane and sand the boards after joining them, the different rates of expansion and contraction will guarantee an uneven joint as soon as the humidity changes.

Storing and buying lumber Storing lumber is often a problem, because it occupies too much space in the shop, even if it is stored in a rack. Many times the lumber has to be stored someplace else, in my case in my barn. Usually the barn is more humid than the shop, so I bring the lumber I am going to use for a specific job into the shop a couple of weeks ahead of time. I buy my lumber in the rough from different lumberyards, and prefer to select it myself. It is more expensive, but I can select the pieces for color, width, etc., so there is less waste. I would never buy lumber that is jointed and thickness-planed, because it would warp badly before I got it made into furniture. If I didn't have a jointer and thickness-planer (and didn't want to mill it by hand) I would still buy it rough and get it jointed and planed locally just before I was ready to use it. When using solid wood it is important to work as fast as possible, from the time the wood is cut, jointed and planed until all the joints are made. Storing the wood while the joints are being made is very important. Either leave it so the air can circulate around it or stack it so no air can get to it. Never leave a piece of wood overnight with one side covered and the other side exposed to the air, because it will definitely cup or warp in some direction.

I don't feel it is necessary to use exotic wood to make good furniture. The wood I like and work most with is what grows in my own back yard, such as maple, cherry and walnut. I feel I would be a bad designer if I could not make and design furniture out of that material. □

Designing with Wood

Before designing and/or making a piece of furniture, one must know the characteristics of the material that is going to be worked. With wood, one has to understand how it moves, twists, shrinks and warps, and how it can and cannot be joined together. **(1)** Wood can be glued together long grain to long grain.

(2,3,4) The direction of the grain is not that important as long as the joint is long grain to long grain.

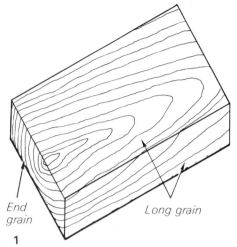

End grain

Long grain

1

2

3

4

5

6

7

8

9

10

11

(5) We cannot glue end grain to end grain. Nor can we glue end grain to long grain (6,7) as is necessary in carcase construction, say, in making a chest, drawers or a box. So when joining two pieces end grain to long grain, we have to choose a joint that will give as much long-grain to long-grain contact as possible. End grain does not count as a glue surface in any joint. My advice is that if you are learning carcase construction and you begin by making, say, a hope chest, make it for small hopes. You will learn as much making a small piece as you will a larger piece, and you will save time and expense, especially if you make a mistake.

In frame construction, we join the width of the wood to the edge of the board (8). This type of construction is used for doors, windows, chairs, tables and the like. Again, unless there is a good joint, one cannot glue long grain to end grain. When choosing a joint for the piece you are going to make, there is usually no doubt which type of construction you are going to use, it is either carcase or frame.

If a piece of wood is cut across the grain, so that there is barely any length of long grain (9,10,11), the piece will break easily. These short sections of long grain are referred to as "short grain" and should never be used.   □

Saws
Chapter 3

1

2

3

Choosing Handsaws

Regardless of how many power saws you have in your shop, there are a number of handsaws you should also have. Of course a handsaw is one of the most difficult tools to learn to use correctly, but it is also an extremely important tool for woodworking, because it can replace a machine-powered saw for every cutting operation. After you have learned to control a saw, it will become easy to cut square and rip accurately, and to make joints that fit the first time.

There are many handsaws on the market, and each one is designed for a special purpose. The **(1)** bowsaw, **(2)** scroll bowsaw, **(3)** offset dovetail saw (top), straight dovetail saw (bottom) and **(4)** rip panel saw are the saws I have found most useful in my many years of cabinetmaking. I would never buy a backsaw; they are clumsy and heavy. Maybe they are all right in miter boxes, but a bowsaw will do the job faster.

On these bowsaws, the tensioning system is twisted wire attached on one end to a threaded eyebolt with a wing nut. The more common tensioning system uses a string instead of wire (see p. 17).

For general sawing, I would recommend buying a 26-in., 6-point and an 18-in., 8-point bowsaw. (Handsaws are sold by length and by points, or teeth per inch—a 6-point saw has six teeth per inch. Lengths might vary slightly, because most bowsaws are made in Europe and so are measured in metrics.) I would also buy a 26-in. scroll bowsaw, preferably with interchangeable blades, and a 10-in. or longer 15-point offset dovetail saw. A 24-in. 6 to 7-point rip panel saw (the standard carpenter's saw) is useful for cutting big pieces such as plywood, where the bridge of the bowsaw would be in the way.

Japanese saws **(5)** are good for special work. I have some but hardly ever use them, except in cramped spaces where I can't get in with a regular saw. The Japanese ripsaw cuts on the pull stroke—not the normal push stroke—which makes the line fuzzy and hard to see when cutting joints the Western way. The Japanese crosscut saw **(6)** has long teeth that might bend when hitting a knot. It's also difficult to resharpen, even with special files.   □

4

5

6

Crosscut saw teeth

Sections

Crosscut   Rip

Ripsaw teeth

1

2

3

4

5

7

8

6

Sharpening Handsaws

Woodworkers should know how to sharpen their tools, because most tools don't arrive from the factory sharpened right. Most new handsaws are filed for crosscutting, especially panel saws, which are used mostly by carpenters who do very little ripping and usually work in wet softwood. I generally use only dry hardwoods in my work.

The first time I sharpen a crosscut saw I change it to a ripsaw by changing the teeth from a point to a chisel edge **(1)**. This makes ripping faster and easier because there are more teeth per inch than would normally be available on a ripsaw, and I find the saw works better even for crosscutting. I usually demonstrate this to my new students because the difference in cutting speed is dramatic. I also use the same kind of demonstration to show that frame saws are much faster than panel saws for both ripping and crosscutting.

What's fastest? In both crosscutting **(2)** and ripping **(3)**, the ripsaw-sharpened bowsaw (cut 1) performs best. The ripsaw-sharpened panel saw (cut 2) is an improvement over the same saw with a crosscut sharpening (cut 3). The wood shown here is poplar.

All handsaws have an alternating tooth setting **(4)**, that is, the upper part of each tooth is bent out to one side or the other to create a kerf (the width of the sawcut) that is wider than the thickness of the sawblade. If the saw is not set enough, it will bind as it cuts. If it is set too much, the cut will be wide and rough and the saw will cut more slowly. If the teeth are set more to one side, the saw will favor that side. To correct this, both sides must be reset. A properly set saw that is started correctly without too much pressure will easily follow the cutting line. There are many good saw sets **(5)** on the market and you should follow their directions for use. I prefer the Sandvik, because it is light, easy to adjust and simple to use. It allows you to see what you are doing. Each tooth should be set approximately $\frac{1}{64}$ in. to each side.

If the teeth are too small to use a saw set (as on dovetail saws), use a small screwdriver instead to push the teeth out.

(6) Press the screwdriver down between every second tooth and twist it to set the teeth. Be sure to twist an equal amount each time. This takes practice.

Once the teeth are set they are ready to be filed. Use a new triangular file or an unused edge each time you file a saw. I never use an old, worn-out file. Using a file more than once will not do the job as well, and you may get uneven results. Use only one edge for each filing. By using the same number of strokes, the same length of each stroke (using your fingers or tape as a guide) and the same amount of pressure, all the teeth will be sharpened identically. The file gradually gets dull, but so gradually that all the teeth are the same length. Don't turn the file to a new edge in the middle of a sharpening—the new side will cut deeper than the worn one. This way the teeth stay the same length and you shouldn't have to level them off for many years.

When filing **(7,8)**, press straight down on the file, just enough so the file works and doesn't skip over the metal. File both the front and the back of the teeth at the same time, working from the front of the blade toward the handle of the saw. The final file stroke on each tooth will then be on the back **(9)**, and the burr that appears when the tooth just comes to a point will be aimed in the cutting direction. Be sure to keep the file strokes at a 90° angle to the blade. Don't file the teeth of a ripsaw from alternate sides, as many books recommend. It is not necessary. Never file or stone the face of the blade, because this will change the set of the teeth.

The saw can be refiled four or five times before it needs resetting. Of course this depends on how dull you let the saw get before you refile it. I always file my saws as soon as the ends of the teeth get shiny white **(10)**. This means the saw has started to get dull. If the saw isn't too dull, two file strokes on each tooth should be enough to resharpen it.

If the wood tears up at the back when crosscutting or ripping, one or more of the teeth are too long. In this case I joint the teeth by filing across their tops **(11)** with a flat mill file to even the length of the teeth. Push the file along the length of the blade.

When all the teeth are the same height **(12)**, refile the teeth with the triangular file until they all come to a point **(13)**. Then reset, and refile as usual.

If the teeth still tear after resharpening, as is likely to happen in softwoods and especially in plywood **(14)**, scribe a line where the cut will be and **(15)** make a V-cut with a chisel on the underside of the piece **(16)**. This will prevent tearing. ☐

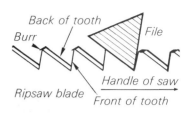

Back of tooth · File · Burr · Handle of saw · Ripsaw blade · Front of tooth

9

10

11

12

13

Kerf · Waste · Good side · V-cut with chisel

14

15   16

8"

3"

1/4"

5/8"

1"

1 1/4"

10"

Plywood

Butt hinge

3/4"

1

Making a Sharpening Vise

Vises to hold saws for sharpening are commercially available, but I prefer to make my own. The one shown here **(1)** requires two pieces of ¾-in. plywood, four strips of hardwood (such as maple), four screws and two butt hinges (with accompanying screws).

Glue the two pieces of hardwood on the ends of the plywood. These will be the jaws for the jig. Once the glue sets, attach the two halves at the other end (which will be the bottom) with the butt hinges. Glue and screw on the other two strips of wood on the outside. These prevent the jig from falling through the bench vise.

Make the jaws parallel using a table saw **(2)** or plane **(3)**. If you use a table saw, insert a thin strip of wood between the two plywood pieces to prevent the jaws from binding on the sawblade at the end of the cut.

To make it possible to use the full length of the file, bevel both jaw ends 45° **(4)**, using either a table saw **(5)** or a hand plane.

(6) The sharpening jig sits in the bench vise and **(7)** holds the sawblade securely. You can change the dimensions of the jig to suit your particular needs. ☐

2

3

4

5

6

7

Using Handsaws

(1) The bowsaw is my all-purpose saw. It takes longer to learn to use than other handsaws, but once you get the hang of it, you will use it for most cutting. All my advanced students use a bowsaw, and I don't brainwash my students. It has several advantages. Because the blade is narrower and thinner than other saws, there is less friction in the kerf. The blade does not whip because it is kept in tension. Because the steel is thinner than in a panel saw, the bowsaw advances more quickly, and it is easier to cut a straight line.

1

When you buy a bowsaw that uses string as a tensioning system (which I prefer), you usually get the saw in pieces. Even if it comes assembled, you must know how to string it in case the string breaks. I use common chalk line. Clamp the saw in the bench so that there is just a slight amount of tension in the blade. After wrapping the string lengthwise, wind it around six times **(2)**. Then finish stringing by weaving the end in and out of the strings about four times. Then place the pin, the short piece of wood that controls the blade tension, between the strings. Release the tension when the saw is not in use.

2

3

When the bowsaw is assembled and tightened, look down the blade **(3)** to be sure it isn't twisted.

The blade need not be parallel to the frame. It can also be angled **(4)** to make cuts beyond the depth of the bridge.

4

5

The correct use and maintenance of handsaws should be practiced until they are second nature. To saw properly **(5)**, coordination of the joints in the hand, elbow and shoulder must be achieved. The biggest mistake most people make when using a handsaw is to hang onto it as if their lives depended on it, bearing down much too hard. This makes it hard to start the cut, and once the cut is started, it is hard to follow the line. A handsaw should lie loosely in your hands. No pressure should be applied after the cut is started.

(6) Use your thumb as a guide to start the saw.

6

7

8

9

10

11

When I rip with a bowsaw I clamp the board down on the bench and cut vertically **(7,8)**. I can cut faster this way because I am sawing up and down and can put more force into the downstroke. I use both hands so I don't tire easily. Also, by clamping the board with the portion to be ripped extended over the edge of the bench, I have to clamp the board only once. If I stood the board up in the vise, I would have to keep clamping and unclamping to reposition it as I cut. I am also able to rip long boards (say, 8 ft.) this way without a ladder and without the board vibrating. When I rip with a bowsaw, I hold it so the blade is 90° to the board. All the force is from the right hand, with the left hand acting as a guide. I saw away from myself so that I can see the line, and so that I can move along with the cut, with my arms in a comfortable position.

For crosscutting I use a rip bowsaw. I lay the board flat on the bench **(9)**, with the piece I am cutting extending to my right off the bench. I start by holding the wood down with my left hand. Then, when the wood is almost cut through, I plant my left elbow on the board to hold it and reach between the blade and the bridge of the saw to catch the cutoff so it doesn't splinter.

For scroll work, I would of course use a band saw if I could. Or I might use a sabre saw. But a scroll bowsaw **(10)** will cut just as fast or faster than a sabre saw, and no electricity is needed. The blade on the scroll bowsaw is considerably longer than that of any other scroll saw or coping saw. The ⅜-in. blade is the easiest to get in this country. In Europe, you could get as small as ⅛ in. and as large as ½ in.

For very small work I use an offset dovetail saw **(11)**. With the offset, I can see the line I am sawing more easily and can use the saw for cutting anything that protrudes above a flat surface flush with that surface. I also change the dovetail saw from a crosscut to a rip the first time it needs filing. I don't like the reversible offset dovetail saw — it is very bulky, and because I change it to a ripsaw, I can use it only one way anyway. □

Circular Saws

Three types of circular saws are generally used in a small woodworking shop: the table saw **(1)**, the radial arm saw **(2)** and the portable circular saw **(3)**. In the table saw, the blade is stationary in a table and the wood is moved through the blade. In the radial arm saw the wood is stationary, and the blade is moved on an extended arm through the wood. In the portable circular saw, or contractor's saw, the saw is moved over a stationary piece of wood. This saw is more useful to the carpenter than to the cabinetmaker. It is less accurate and less flexible than the non-portable saws, but may be useful to the cabinetmaker for making inital cuts in plywood sheets that are too large for stationary saws. A 6-in. saw is adequate for a cabinetmaker, but a carpenter might want a larger blade.

Of the other two types of saws, my advice is to buy a table saw, not the radial arm. The latter is limited in function, much more difficult to use, less accurate for fine joinery or cutting, and cannot perform all the operations a table saw can. The radial arm saw was designed to cut rough lumber to length, but even there it is limited to a certain width. Many of the joints described in this book would be impractical, and even dangerous, to make on a radial arm saw.

Buy at least a 10-in. table saw, which costs only a little more than an 8-in. saw. Get at least a 1-hp motor — 2 hp is even better. Make sure the arbor tilts for making angled cuts. Tilting the top is awkward. I find extension rails on the side helpful for large pieces of wood. You'll find the table saw the most used piece of equipment in your shop, so don't stint on quality.

I use a split knife behind the blade to prevent the piece of wood that is being cut from binding on the blade. Most saw guards that come with circular saws are clumsy, heavy, and, I feel, often dangerous. The split knife pictured here **(4)** is considerably safer and more compact. The block of wood on the top prevents sawdust and chips of wood from being thrown at my face. Before using this safety guard in a school, check first with your safety inspector. Always wear safety glasses or (even better) a face mask when using a circular saw or any power machine. □

1

2

3

4

Miter Gauge

A miter gauge **(1)** fits into the grooves in the top of the saw table. Quite often the same miter gauge will fit into other machines such as band saws or disc sanders. It is used mostly in cutting the ends of boards either square or at angles. The smallest angle it can cut is 30°. A board screwed to the miter gauge gives it more stability.

(2) Three setscrews set (or calibrate) the gauge so it cuts accurately at 90° or 45° in both directions — the most used settings. When the gauge is set exactly, tighten the nuts **(3)** so the screws can't move. ☐

1

2

3

Circular-Saw Blades

There are many kinds of sawblades for special purposes. The craftsman who faces a production job may find that a special blade or cutter shortens the labor considerably, making it worthwhile to consult a saw manufacturer to find how much a custom-made blade would cost. Here I will discuss only those blades necessary for general shop work.

Circular-saw blades are available with or without carbide-tipped teeth. Blades without carbide tips must be sharpened and set quite often. I now use only carbide-tipped blades, except for very fine cutting, for which I use a hollow-ground blade, also called a planer blade.

(1) The three carbide-tipped blades I find most useful, in the order of their usefulness, are: a 40-tooth raker combination for roughing out; a 40-tooth blade for more precise work; and a 12-tooth rip for ripping. I also have a hollow-ground-planer that I use for very precise joinery. This is not carbide-tipped. Other non-carbide blades I have date back to earlier days, but I would not buy them new today. All my blades are 10 in., and in general, the more teeth, the finer the cut.

I have found that a carbide-tipped raker-tooth combination blade **(2)** is very useful for all-around work, including plywood, but not accurate enough for fine joinery. The teeth have a set because the carbide tips are not put all in a line **(3)**, as you can see from the photographs.

Of the carbide-tipped blades I have, I have found the 40-tooth blade with an 80° pitch **(4)** to be most accurate and cleanest cutting for my use, but it does have a tendency to tear a little in the back when crosscutting in soft woods. I also use it for precise cuts in plywood. If you are into mass production you should invest in a blade with more teeth.

The ripsaw blade **(5)** is used for cutting with the grain of the wood. It has teeth similar to those of a hand ripsaw — chisel sharpened and filed or ground to a right angle to the surface of the blade. The one I use is carbide-tipped, but if the blade is not, it should always be set, if necessary, before filing.

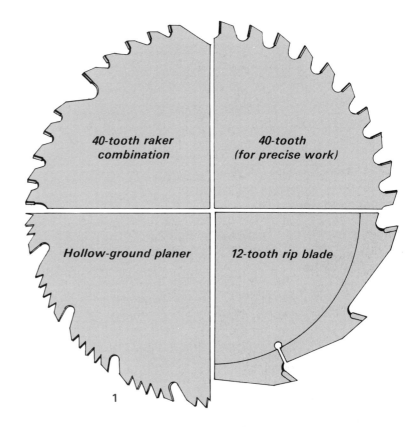

40-tooth raker combination

40-tooth (for precise work)

Hollow-ground planer

12-tooth rip blade

1

2

3

4

5

Hollow-ground blade section

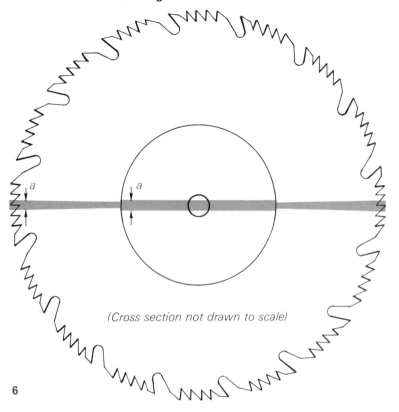

a

a

(Cross section not drawn to scale)

6

7

Carbide tips are brazed to the steel teeth of the blade and given clearance by a bevel from front to back. These tips are exceedingly hard and brittle and must be handled with great care to prevent chipping or breaking. Never allow them to strike any hard or metallic surface.

Carbide-tipped blades are expensive and cannot be sharpened by the usual methods of saw sharpening. They should never be touched with a file or any ordinary grinding stone. Diamond honing stones may be used, but these are very expensive. Diamond grinding wheels suitable for machine grinding are much more so. It is usually better for the owner of a small shop to send carbide-tipped tools out to be sharpened.

The cutting teeth of all flat-ground blades must have some set in order not to bind in the wood. Blades that will be used to cut soft, wet lumber require more set than those to be used for hard, dry lumber. Only the outer third of the teeth should be bent out to the side, or set. In all cases, adjacent teeth should be set toward alternate sides of the blade.

A hollow-ground blade **(6)** is ground concave on both sides of the blade. This hollowing takes the place of the set necessary in flat-ground blades to prevent binding. Hollow-ground blades are never set. They are distinguished by the heavy hub around the arbor hole. On a new blade, this hub is the same thickness (or gauge) as the outer rim of the blade. The hollow grinding extends from near the hub to the circumference of the blade.

Hollow-ground blades give a very smooth cut and should be used for fine joinery rather than rough cutting. They are also good for ripping thin stock (less than ½ in.). Hollow-ground blades, more than any other type of blade, must be kept true and sharp at all times. Otherwise, because of the slight amount of clearance, they will heat up and burn. Photo **7** shows a hollow-ground blade; there is no setting.

The hollow-ground blade is a raker-tooth blade consisting of a group of cutting teeth accompanied by a chisel rip tooth, known as the raker or cleaner tooth. The cutting teeth are similar to crosscutting teeth and have similar bevels. The face of the cutting teeth are usually in line with the center of the blade. The raker teeth, however, have a different pitch. This pitch is best determined by making an outline drawing of the blade when it is new, so that when you file the blade you can check the pitch of the raker teeth with the drawing.

The raker teeth are filed exactly like the teeth of a ripsaw — square across the face and the back of the chisel edge. On crosscut and ripsaws of non-raker-tooth types, all the teeth should be the same length, and all should reach the outer diameter of the blade. But on the raker-tooth type, each of the raker teeth should be $\frac{1}{64}$ in. shorter than the cutting teeth. The cutting teeth, as the name indicates, do the cutting. The raker or cleaner teeth follow behind and chisel out the severed fibers in the saw kerf. If the wood tears up in the back when you cut with a raker-tooth blade, one or more of the raker teeth are too long. This happens only when the saw is not a carbide-tipped blade, and you can then file it yourself.

To find the tooth or teeth that are too long, turn the saw off and hold a piece of wood up to, but just barely clearing, the blade. Rotate the blade manually, checking which teeth hit the block of wood **(8)**. File any long teeth to the right length.

If after several filings, all the teeth have different lengths, the saw must be jointed, or in other words, the cutting circle of the teeth must be trued. This can be done with a stone held over the blade while the saw is running. For safety, the blade should be put on backwards, so that it runs in reverse. Otherwise, the teeth might pick up the stone and throw it back at you. Wear proper eye and face protection. Lower or raise the blade so that the points of the teeth barely touch a block of wood that is held down tightly over the throat of the table insert and passed over the blade with the machine off. Rotate the blade to make certain that the longer teeth barely touch the block.

Now take a grinding stone — an old one if

you have it — and with the saw running, move the stone along the table insert and across the points of the teeth **(9)**. Sparks will fly as the teeth touch the stone. It is better and safer to start with the teeth too low rather than too high, as the only purpose of this jointing operation is to grind off the points of the teeth that are too long and bring them down to the true circle. Move the stone over the revolving blade until no more sparks fly. Stop the saw and examine each of the teeth. Some may be considerably flatter than others; some may show a bright glitter only on the point. These shiny markings show where the stone has touched and whether all the teeth have been reduced to the cutting circle. If some have not been touched, raise the blade slightly and repeat the process. If there is a severe difference in the length of the teeth, I suggest sending the blade to a professional saw-sharpener.

If one or more cutting teeth in a raker blade are longer on one side of the blade than the other, the blade will wander toward that side. The blade will start binding, heating up and smoking. Here you can see that the teeth are longer on the right side **(10)**. To correct this, repeat exactly as when the raker teeth are too long.

Blades gum up if they are dull, if the wood is fed too slowly or when cutting pine or fir. Slow feeding heats up the blade and the heat causes gumming. If you continue to use the blade in this gummed condition, more heat will be generated and you will burn the wood. Even worse, the sawblade will get very hot and eventually blue, and the steel will lose its temper. The blade is no good after that. When my students continue to use a dull or gummed-up blade so that you can hardly see them for the smoke, I lose my temper, too.

A gummed-up sawblade is easy to clean. Pour some ammonia on the blade. Leave it for a few minutes, then scrub off the gum with steel wool. It comes off easily. Or you can brush on commercial oven-cleaner, let it sit for a few minutes, then rinse the blade. Or you can run it under hot water for several minutes, then use steel wool.   □

8

9

10

1

2

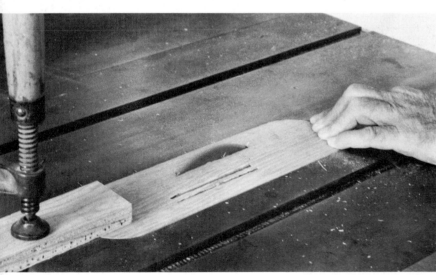

3

Dado Cutters

A dado head consists of two identical saw-blades with chisel-like spacer cutters in between, all of exactly the same diameter. Each blade and spacer makes a ⅛-in. kerf (except one spacer that is only ¹⁄₁₆ in. thick). By using various combinations of blades and spacers, cuts of different widths can be made. If a small adjustment is needed, paper or metal shims can be inserted between spacers. The chisel-like teeth of the spacers are swaged, so they overlap a bit and allow for these small adjustments. A dado can cut across or with the grain. It is useful for making straight grooves, as in drawers to hold the bottom. By tilting the blades you can make V-shaped grooves. **(1)** Always use a sawblade on both sides of the spacers.

(2) Never use one blade and one spacer unless you want to kill yourself. It doesn't matter how the spacers are spaced as long as the swaged tips don't interfere with each other or with the blades. Other dado heads on the market work in different ways, but I don't like them. I prefer the spacer type, which is much safer, easier to adjust, and does a better job of cutting if it is sharpened right, that is, with all the spacer cutters the same diameter as the sawblades. I wouldn't buy an adjustable dado (a one-piece unit) because it tends to kick back if forward pressure isn't maintained.

Dado blades are available with and without carbide tips. As with other blades, the carbide-tipped ones cost more but cut well for a long time before they need sharpening. Blades sharpened as hollow-ground but not hollow-ground are cheaper, but need frequent sharpening. I feel they make a better cut. The main disadvantage is that they gum up easily.

When you use a dado blade, you usually need to make a wooden insert that fits flush with the table top. Make a piece the right thickness, size and shape, put on the dado head the width you will be cutting, and lower the dado blades below the table. **(3)** Put in the insert and clamp it in under a piece of wood in the back. Hold or clamp the front down. Slowly crank up the blade until it cuts a slot the size you need. (The double slots show that I use the wooden insert flipped over for other blades.) □

Circular-Saw Sharpening Jig

Most of my sawblades are carbide-tipped, and I send those out to be sharpened. I do sharpen the hollow-ground blades myself, and, being cheap, I still have a few very old blades that I also sharpen myself. It doesn't take very long. Several different jigs are commercially made to hold the saw while you file it. Most are quite expensive. I made my own and it works quite well. You need a piece of 2x4 hardwood about 18 in. long and two discs of ¾-in. thick plywood about 2 in. smaller in diameter than the blade to be sharpened **(1)**. Dish out the centers of the discs on a lathe or using a router **(2)**. This dishing out helps the outer edges hold the blade securely, especially when filing a hollow-ground blade **(3)**.

To use, clamp the blade in the jig **(4)** and proceed exactly as when filing a handsaw — (see p. 15) **(5,6,7)**. Loosen the wing nut and rotate the blade in the jig to get at all the teeth. For crosscut and hollow-ground blades, I file every other tooth and then reverse the blade and get the rest.

The same jig can be used to file a chain saw **(8)**. I prefer using it to filing the chain on the saw bar. If it is filed when still on the bar, some of the filings will fall into the grooves and act there as a grinding material.   □

1

Disc scooped out on a lathe

Disc routed out

2

3

6

4

7

5

8

1

2

The Band Saw

Band saws are available in different sizes, such as 14 in., 16 in., 20 in., etc., which refers to the distance from the blade to the column. The length and maximum width of the blade and the horsepower of the motor will correspond to the size of the throat. What size to buy depends on what kind of work you will do. If you are making instruments, a 14-in. band saw might be large enough, but for furniture buy at least a 20-in. band saw with a 2-hp motor—that's what I have.

The band saw (1) cuts curves and irregular shapes; it also resaws lumber. It has a continuous blade that is welded together and runs over two wheels (2). Usually the bottom wheel is powered and the top one is free. A guide above the table and one below help keep the blade tracking correctly. Blades of different widths can be used for different purposes. I prefer to use skip-tooth blades. They cut faster, and the steel is harder so they last longer. They should be thrown out when they get dull. The maximum width of blade my band saw can take is 1 in., and the narrowest I use is ⅜ in. For most general work, I use a ½-in. or ¾-in. blade.

A movable guard (3) covers the section of blade that is not needed to cut a particular thickness of wood. The greatest mistake most people make when cutting on the band saw is to cut a thick piece and then cut a thinner one without sliding down the guard (4). A large portion of the blade is thus exposed. If the blade breaks (as it sometimes does), dangerous pieces of the blade could fly all over. With the upper guard close to the wood (5), there is much more control over the blade, so the blade won't wander as easily.

3

4

5

There are different-style guides for the blade, depending on the manufacturer. The best guide is ball-bearing wheels on each side of the blade, but they are very expensive. I am satisfied with the guide that came with my band saw **(6)**, which does not have ball bearings. **(7)** Most band saws have a scale on them that will show the proper tension on the blade.

The upper guide should be not more than ½ in. above the piece being cut. This guides the blade better and lessens the risk of an exposed blade. If a blade does break, it usually makes a lot of noise. Don't open the door to see what happened. Wait until the machine has stopped running completely and is totally quiet. Then open the door, untangle the blade and replace it.

(8,9,10) Always keep your hands to the side of the blade or behind the blade, never in front of the blade.

6

7

8

9

10

11

12

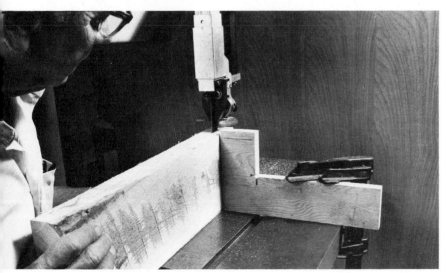

For resawing there is usually no fence available for smaller band saws. Because the blade always has a tendency to wander and favor one side or the other, a long fence won't work. Instead, I use a piece of ¾-in. plywood with the end square to the table as a guide **(11)**. Chamfer the edges nearest the sawblade. Rough-plane one side of the board to be resawn and square one edge. The square edge should be down toward the table. Draw a pencil line on top, follow the line free-hand and use the widest blade your band saw can handle **(12,13)**. ☐

13

Handling a Band-Saw Blade

If you don't know how to unfold and fold a band-saw blade correctly, learn now because it is very easy to cut yourself.

(1) Start with the teeth facing in. Hold the blade in two places at about the width of your body. Step on the base of the blade to secure it.

(2) Pull your hands together so that the blade crimps outward in a circle.

(3) Cross the blade over itself **(4)** while turning the circle under and **(5)** the blade will fold easily.

Another method requires only one hand. **(6)** Step on the blade and hold it at the top.

1

2

3

4

5

6

7

8

9

10

(7) Continue to turn the blade outward, **(8)** around and **(9)** under itself until it folds neatly **(10)**.

To unfold the blade, stand where you have plenty of room **(11)**.

(12) Fling the blade out very firmly away from yourself and **(13)** the blade will spring open. ☐

11

12

13

Preparing Stock
Chapter 4

1

2

5

3

4

6

Planes

There are four different lengths of plane used for dressing wood. They are used in sequence to take the wood from rough lumber to clean boards ready to be shaped, glued and so on. Each plane is designed for a different job. But they are all sharpened and set the same way. The four planes are, in order of their use, the scrub plane (or roughing-out plane), the jack plane, the jointer plane and the smoothing plane.

The scrub plane **(1)** is designed to remove large amounts of wood, for example, a high spot if the wood is warped. It can be used going across the grain at an angle, or with the grain. It usually doesn't have a chip-breaker, and the plane iron is ground convex **(2)**. My wooden scrub plane is 9½ in. long, 1⅞ in. wide, and the blade is 1¼ in. wide.

The jack plane **(3)** continues the job of roughing out, but with a little more accuracy than the scrub plane. It is approximately 14 in. long. Its length carries it over the high spots left by the scrub plane, and this ensures a flat surface. A shorter plane would be more apt to travel up and down.

The jointer plane **(4)** is used for jointing and the final flattening out of boards. It is the longest plane—from 22 in. to 24 in. long. The long sole of the plane enables it to flatten out boards efficiently because the sole rides from high spot to high spot until the surface is level. Here again, plane across the grain and at an angle, but finish by planing with the grain.

The smoothing plane **(5)** is the shortest, and is used to begin preparing the surface for finishing. It is about 9 in. to 10 in. long.

When I learned woodworking we used only wooden planes, but now I prefer steel planes. Today all planes are made in either wood or steel, except the scrub plane, which is available only in wood. Steel planes are easier to adjust and they plane well, but they don't slide as easily as wooden planes. More expensive steel planes have corrugated bottoms to make them slide better **(6)**. □

Adjusting Planes

When you buy a new plane, you will have to spend some time to get it to work correctly. Usually the chipbreaker has to be refitted so that the shavings will not clog. Put the chipbreaker on the blade and screw it down tight. Hold them up against the light **(1)** and check for light between the chipbreaker and the plane blade. If you can see light between them, remove the chipbreaker and file off the high spots, holding the file at a slight angle **(2)** so that it will take more off in the back of the chipbreaker. This makes for a perfectly tight fit in the front, when the blade and the chipbreaker are together. Keep filing and checking until you no longer see light between the chipbreaker and blade, when they are screwed tight together **(3)**.

Then use a buffer or fine sandpaper to polish the top of the chipbreaker. This surface should be perfectly smooth **(4)** so that the shavings will slide over easily.

The function of the chipbreaker is to prevent the blade from tearing up the surface of the wood. If the chipbreaker is set too far away from the cutting edge of the blade, you might as well use the plane without the chipbreaker. For normal use, the chipbreaker should sit back about 1/32 in. For rough work move it back slightly; for fine work, such as planing curly woods, move it closer to the edge.

The setting of the throat depends on the function of the plane. The throat opening on a smooth plane should be smaller than on a jack plane, and the jointer plane is usually set in between. The setting all depends on the kind of work you are doing.

Wooden planes and iron planes are adjusted differently **(5)**. On some wooden planes **(6)**, the piece of wood in front of the blade on the bottom can be moved back and forth. An iron plane **(7)** is adjusted by moving the whole sophisticated adjusting mechanism, sometimes called the frog.

To adjust the plane iron in the scrub plane (or in any wooden plane) for a deeper cut,

1

2

Chipbreaker

Blade

Good   *Bad*   *Bad*

3

4

6

5

7

8

9

10

11

12

13

14

15

tap the back of the blade **(8)** until enough blade is exposed to give you the depth of the cut you want to make. Notice how the blade is convex, to give a faster cut.

To move the blade back for less of a cut **(9)**, hit the back of the plane with a hammer. Then hit down the wooden wedge to secure the blade. If you want to remove the blade, bang the back of the plane down against the bench and the wedge will loosen, freeing the blade.

Steel planes have more sophisticated adjusting systems. The blade is held in position with a steel wedge **(10)** that is clipped down over a screw **(11)**.

Tension on the blade from the wedge will prevent the blade from coming loose. The screw is tightened **(12)** to create more tension. The screw should be tight but not so tight that you can't push down the clip with your thumb. If the blade loosens, you can tighten the screw again. But once it has been set, it shouldn't need to be adjusted for a long time.

The large screw in the back **(13)** adjusts the depth of the cut. The lower the blade is, the deeper the cut it will take.

The lever in the back **(14)** levels the blade. If you move the lever to the right, the left side of the blade will be raised, and vice versa. The blade must be extended evenly for an even cut.

When you set the blade, check by eye **(15)** that it is parallel with the bottom of the plane, and that it is set to the right depth.

On many planes, especially cheap ones, the sole is not flat. If the sole isn't flat, straighten it out on a belt sander. If a belt sander is not available, glue coarse emery paper on a flat surface and move the plane back and forth until it is flat. The latter is a painstaking job. When I'm first truing up a plane sole on a belt sander, I make the sole of the jointer plane a fraction of an inch convex ($1/64$ in. or less) from front to back, so that when I join boards together they will have edges slightly concave along their length. This is what I want for a good glue joint (see p. 54). ☐

Sharpening Planes and Chisels

A plane blade must be sharp to perform correctly. Sharpening requires practice and must be learned. The same techniques used to sharpen plane blades are also used to sharpen chisels.

The blade must be sharpened perfectly straight across the cutting edge. Don't make the edge concave or the corners will dig into the wood. In fact, when I sharpen a blade for rough cutting I usually make the blade just slightly convex so the corners won't dig in.

(1) For both plane blades and chisel blades, the cutting edge should be beveled at approximately 30°, which makes the bevel twice as long as the blade is thick. For example, if the blade is ³⁄₁₆ in. thick, the bevel should be about ³⁄₈ in. long. The initial sharpening can be done **(2)** on a power sander, **(3)** a portable belt sander mounted upside-down in the bench vise, or **(4)** on a stone. I usually use a power sander because it works considerably faster. If you use a sander, be sure to keep moving the blade without changing the angle. Don't use belts coarser than 120 grit, or bad pits will develop that you'll never get out. Old belts are fine. Don't let the blade get too hot or you will ruin the temper and destroy the blade. Either stop to allow the blade to cool, or dip the blade in water before continuing.

If I use stones, I prefer a wet/dry carborundum medium and coarse combination stone, which I use without water. If the blade isn't nicked or too uneven I start with the medium side. If the blade is in rough shape, I start with the coarse side and then go to the medium side. Again, use the entire surface. Make sure the stone is not hollowed. If it is, the blade will not have the correct bevel angle.

In any case, sharpen the blade until any nicks or uneven areas in the bevel are removed. The first step is completed when there is an even burr across the back of the blade. The blade is then ready for honing.

(5,6) I generally use a buffer with a polishing compound for steel. I made this buffer for my own use only. For anyone

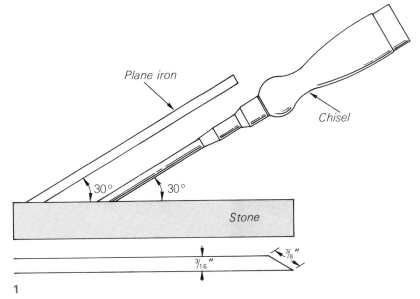

Plane iron

Chisel

30° 30°

Stone

³⁄₁₆″   ³⁄₈″

1

2

3

5

4

6

7   8

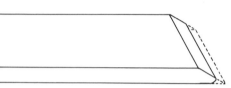

*Blade back becomes beveled
if ground on hollowed stone*

9

else, guards should be put on, in which case it would be cheaper to buy a commercial buffer or grinder already equipped with guards.

If I use a stone for honing I prefer a Belgian clay stone with water, not oil. I don't like oilstones because the oil gets on your hands, the bench and many times on the work, too. Keep your fingers in the same position on the blade so that the blade doesn't rock. Stone or buff the bevel side first **(7)**, and then **(8)** stone any burr off the back, keeping the blade perfectly flat against the stone. Continue to buff the bevel side and the back of the blade until the burr is gone and the blade is sharp. In the honing stage, it is especially important that the stone is not hollowed, or the flat side of the blade would get a bevel on the back **(9)**. Either hold the stone in your hand, keeping the angle constant, or mount the stone in the bench vise.

(10) A sharp plane blade should cut clean, crisp shavings.

10

Preparing Boards by Hand

To prepare a board using hand tools, first **(1)** cut it to rough length and width. Then check with a straightedge **(2)** to see if the board is straight. It may be either concave, convex or twisted. Use a scrub plane **(3)** to remove the high parts.

I always use the scrub plane first at an angle to the grain **(4)**, and then diagonally across in the other direction. The grain won't tear out as easily as if the plane were used with the grain. Continue with the scrub plane until the board is just about flat. Use a straight board **(5)** to check flatness. With the jack plane **(6)**, remove the planer marks left by the scrub plane. Use the same diagonal pattern as before, until you are nearly finished. I finish off the board by planing with the grain.

1

2

3

4

5

6

7

8

9

To check if the board is twisted, take two pieces of straight wood the same width. Place one at each end of the board **(7)**. **(8)** Sight along the sticks to see if the two pieces are parallel. If not, correct by continuing to plane off the high points.

When the piece is finally flat, smooth the board **(9)** with the jointer plane. Pushing down in the front of the plane when starting at the beginning of the board and pushing down at the back of the plane at the end of the board will prevent rounding the edges.

The board is now flat on one side only. If you had been using power tools, the jointer would have gotten you to this stage. Now you are ready to get the other side flat, parallel to the first side and the right thickness. With power tools, you would use a thickness planer to accomplish this, but with hand tools you must use a marking gauge and hand planes. **(10)** Scribe the thickness you want on all the edges of the board. Then go through the same planing procedure as before, using the planes in the same order. I don't square the edges after the first face is leveled because the edges could be torn while thickness-planing with the scrub plane.   □

10

The Marking Gauge

On a new marking gauge **(1)**, the steel pin that scribes the line into the wood is rounded down to a point. When scribing across the grain, the rounded point scratches the fibers and makes a fuzzy line. Therefore the pin of every new marking gauge must be refiled.

First, file half the thickness of the pin flat **(2)**, at right angles to the wooden surface of the tool.

Then bevel the other side of the pin toward the inside **(3)**.

If you are right-handed, the edge that will face you when you pull the tool should be filed as sharp as a knife **(4)**. If you are left-handed, you can reverse the filing to make the gauge easier for you to use.

With the bevel filed in toward the movable guide piece, the guide will be pushed up against the edge of the board to be scribed.

The difference that refiling makes is easy to see **(5)**. The round point makes a fuzzy line (top), while the refiled point makes a crisp, clear line (bottom) with no tendency to wander with the grain.   □

1

2

3

4

5

1

2

3

Rough-Ripping

To get maximum thickness out of a board, I always rip it to approximate width when it is rough lumber. This way, if one side of the board is slightly thinner or is twisted or warped, you won't have to plane the whole board to the thickness of the thinnest section. Remember to allow for jointing the edges and subsequently ripping the board to exact size when you make the first rip cut. A safe estimate is to add about ⅜ in. or more to the width of the board. Be sure the edge that will ride against the fence is straight, or your measurement will be thrown off.

When rough-ripping boards on the circular saw, I always screw a short piece of wood to the front of the fence **(1)**. This piece, which should stop at the center of the blade, is necessary because a board tends to open or close up at the saw kerf as it is ripped. Without the half-length fence **(2)**, a board that is opening up would be forced into the blade. This creates heat and gums up the blade. If forced through, the board may bind or the blade might be ruined permanently.

If a board is twisted so much that planing it would leave you with a very thin piece, rip the board in half, joint each half, then glue the pieces back together. This way you can use more of the thickness of the board.

For ripping the edges on rough boards, I use a jig **(3,4)** that helps me cut a straight edge on a piece of lumber with rough edges or an irregular shape. First fit a strip of wood into the groove of the table saw flush with the top of the groove. Then screw and glue that onto a piece of either solid wood or plywood that is approximately 8 in. wide by 8 ft. long. I locate the piece so that one edge is close to, but doesn't touch, the side of the sawblade.

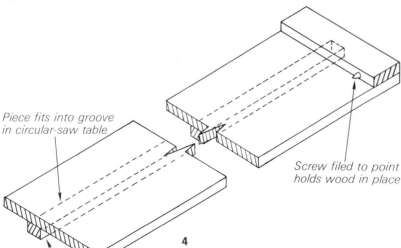

Piece fits into groove in circular-saw table

Screw filed to point holds wood in place

4

Slightly less than distance from sawblade to groove

Next make a piece of wood several inches wide and as long as the width of the jig, in this case, 8 in., and insert a screw into the piece. Saw off the head of the screw with the end sticking out slightly. After filing the end to a sharp point, screw and glue this piece across the front edge of the jig **(5)**. The screw end combined with the fence it sits in will secure one end of the piece to be sawn. **(6)** Some sheets of #50 or coarser sandpaper glued to the top surface of the jig will prevent the piece from sliding.

Lay the wood on top of the jig and push one end firmly into the point of the screw **(7)**. This holds the piece in place. Press the wood down into the sandpaper and cut one edge **(8)**. Slide the jig through the blade **(9)** with the holding block in front.

Once the wood has one straight edge cut, use that edge against the fence and rip a parallel cut on the other edge. □

5

6

7

8

9

1

2

3

4

5

Jig for Cutting Wood to Length

When I have a quantity of wood to square and cut to the same length, I have found this jig **(1)** to be a great timesaver. It is simply a piece of scrap wood with 1 in. cut off one end. **(2)** The cut-off piece is fastened back again with a loose hinge. Slice off ⅛ in. from the underside of the 1-in. piece so that it opens and closes more easily. I clamp the jig to a board attached to my miter gauge. **(3)** To use, lift the hinged end up, square one end of the board (I'm using scrap here) flip the piece end for end, so the same edge is against the miter gauge **(4)**. Drop the hinged piece and cut the other end of the wood to length **(5)**. This is a very inexpensive way to have a well-functioning stopping mechanism. There are some much fancier, more complicated and expensive devices on the market, but I have been using this one satisfactorily for close to 50 years. □

Jig for Sawing Square Cutoffs

This jig replaces the miter gauge for square crosscutting on the table saw. It is much easier to use than the miter gauge when working with large pieces. The jig is simple to make and should last a long time.

(1) Cut two hardwood strips to fit into the grooves in the saw table. The strips should fit well but slide easily.

Place the slides in the grooves and **(2)** glue and **(3)** screw a piece of plywood to them. used ½-in. veneer-core plywood. Don't use a rough piece—the surfaces should be relatively smooth.

Whenever you insert a screw into a hard piece of wood, it is advisable to coat the screw threads lightly with **(4)** paraffin to help the screw go in easier and prevent it from breaking. This is especially important to do with big screws, which are usually harder to screw in.

Once the plywood is fastened to the slides, raise the sawblade to make a kerf in the plywood **(5)**. I prefer to stop the sawcut before the back, which makes the piece more stable. If you run the cut all the way through you will have to put a heavy piece of solid wood in the back as well as in the front.

(6) Glue and screw on the front piece, made of hardwood about 2 in. thick. **(7)** Be sure that the piece is square to the sawcut and square to the plywood table. This "fence" has to be higher in the center than the height of the blade when it is fully raised. (I make it about 3 in. higher than the full height of the blade.) To lighten the jig, I leave the full height only in the center section.

1

2

3

4

5

6

7

8

9

10

Before the glue sets, make a test cut **(8)** to check the squareness of the jig. If the jig is out of square in either direction you can still correct it. **(9)** I was lucky the first time, and was very proud.

The jig can be used for many years. **(10)** Rub the slides and the bottom with paraffin to help the jig slide more easily. ☐

The Jointer

After the circular table saw, I feel that the jointer and the thickness planer are the most important big machines in a wood-shop, especially for a person who wants to make a living from woodworking. These two machines are a big investment but will pay for themselves over the years. An old out dated jointer and thickness planer can sometimes be bought quite inexpensively and will usually do as good a job as a new machine. Don't buy an old jointer with a square head — it's too dangerous. The smallest jointer I would buy would be a 6-in. model, (an 8-in. one is preferable) with a 1-hp motor. The smallest thickness planer I'd buy is a 12-in. one with a 2-hp motor.

Jointing by machine   A jointer is a machine that planes, joints or surfaces a board, ending up with one side perfectly flat **(1)**. The table in the front of the rotating knives is called the infeed table, and the one in the back is the outfeed table. The difference in height between the infeed and outfeed is the thickness of wood planed off with each pass. When setting the knives, be sure they are level or parallel with the top of the outfeed table.

On a jointer with a round cutterhead, I would never run a piece shorter than 10 in. Jointers with square cutterheads have a larger opening. These aren't made anymore, but if you buy a used one it might be of this type. I would never run anything shorter than 15 in. on such a jointer. Never run end grain over the jointer — it is too dangerous. End grain is very hard and often shatters rather than cutting. Don't pass the edges of plywood over a jointer either — the glue will put nicks in the blade.

Setting jointer knives   Knives on a jointer should be parallel to the outfeed table and all at the same height. Use a straight stick to set the jointer knives. *First, unplug the machine.* Then make a pencil mark on the stick at the beginning of the outfeed table **(2)**, while the cutterhead is below the table.

(3) Then move the cutterhead forward (carrying the stick with it) and **(4)** make a second mark, again at the beginning of the outfeed table **(5)**.

Now move the stick to the opposite end of the knife and repeat the procedure. If the stick moves the same amount, the knife is parallel to the outfeed table. If it does not, loosen the nuts that hold the knife in place and correct before retightening. When that knife is parallel, be sure to tighten all the nuts. Move to the next knife and set it in the same way, using the same stick and the same two markings (so the height of the second blade is the same as the first). Continue until all the knives are aligned. Be sure all the knives are secured before you start the machine. Raise the outfeed table so it is level with the knives.

Sharpening the knives   An easy way to sharpen the knives without removing them is to use a router. Remove the plastic plate from the base of the router and **(6)** screw on a piece of ¾-in plywood. Place a medium-grit grindstone in the router. The two grooves in the bottom of the plywood have nothing to do with the sharpening process — I used a scrap piece of plywood.

1

2

3

4

5

6

7   8

9

10

11   *With the grain →*   *← Against the grain*

You must be able to control the position of the knives so they will all be ground the same amount. To do this, drill two holes in the center of the infeed table **(7)**. The first hole, closer to the knives, is about 1½ in. from the opening for the cutterhead. The second hole is directly behind the first, about 3 in. from the edge of the opening. Thread the first hole to receive a ³⁄₁₆-in. or ¼-in. screw. Then cut a thin but stiff piece of sheet aluminum or steel about 7 in. long. Drill a hole in the center of the metal strip about 2½ in. from the end of the piece on the side closer to the cutterhead. Be sure the screw fits snugly into the hole. Then drill a second hole in the strip corresponding to the second hole in the table. The exact measurements may vary with different jointers. The important thing is that the metal strip keep all the knives in the same position.

Fasten the metal strip to the table and **(8)** insert a steel pin into the second hole (I used the end of a nail set). Push the cutterhead tight up against the metal strip. Lower the infeed table until the bevel of the knives is parallel with the outfeed table **(9)**. Secure the cutterhead by inserting wooden wedges at both outside ends of the knife head.

Set the router on the outfeed table with the piece of plywood resting on the table. Set the depth of the grindstone so that it just touches the bevel of the blade. Be sure you are wearing proper face and eye protection. Start the router and **(10)** carefully move it back and forth over the blade until the stone stops cutting. Be sure to keep the plywood piece flat on the table.

When the first knife is ground, remove the wooden wedges and the tapered steel pin. Swing the metal strip out of the way and move the cutterhead so that the next knife is on top. Reposition the metal strip, insert the steel pin and wedge the cutterhead again. Continue sharpening until all the knives are ground. Do not change the height of either the infeed or outfeed tables, or of the grindstone in the router.

The knives are sharp when a small burr appears on the back of each knife along its whole length. It is not necessary to remove this burr. If you want to make the knives a little sharper, you can hone each one by hand with a honing stone. I usually don't bother.

If the knives still are not sharp after one grinding, repeat the process. They can be sharpened this way about five times before you will have to reposition them farther out. After each sharpening you have to raise the outfeed table to the same height as the knives.

Operating the jointer   The infeed table controls how much of a cut is to be taken off the boards. In a soft wood, I would never take off more than 1/16 in. in one pass. In extremely hard wood or a wood with unusual grain pattern (like curly maple), I would take much less at each pass.

Before you pass wood over the jointer, look at the edge of the board to see which way the grain runs. Running the board so that the cutting action goes with the grain produces the smoothest edge **(11)**. However, the grain sometimes reverses direction in the middle of the piece and you cannot avoid roughing up some of the wood. Either handplane the board or take the roughness out later by scraping and sanding after milling is complete.

When using the jointer for a board that is slightly bowed, either take the same amount off of each end first or start jointing in the middle to correct the bowing on one face. Here **(12)** I took it off each end. When one face is roughly straightened out, feed the wood in again with the straight face down. When approximately five to six inches have passed over the knives, push the wood down on the outfeed table and ease up the pressure over the infeed table **(13)**. Because the board is perfectly flat when passing over the knives, putting pressure only on the outfeed table keeps the board flat and straight. Otherwise, if the board is twisted and all the pressure is only on the infeed table, the board will continue to be twisted and the twist will get jointed into the piece so that very shortly you will have a piece of uneven thickness that follows the twist.

Once one face is flat, joint the edge. First put a square at the end of the infeed table **(14)** and check that the fence is square. Then **(15)** joint the edge, keeping the face of the board tight against the fence. When matching edges are jointed, check to see how they fit. If they do not fit tightly for their entire length, joint the boards again. Note: The safeguard has been removed for clarity of the photograph.

(16) Here you can see the joint is convex. The boards have to be jointed again. To correct a convex edge, flatten the curve by running the center of the board over the jointer. Then take one full pass. Whenever you joint an edge for a glue joint, pass the board over the jointer slowly so that the surface gets very smooth. If this burnishes the surface, the knives need resharpening.

When you are jointing boards to be edge-glued, joint each board with the opposite face against the fence. If the fence is slightly off square, the next board will be off square the opposite way and the two will fit together, gluing up straight. But the two faces of the board must be parallel, to use this technique. That is, the board should have been put through a thickness planer.

To demonstrate this point, the fence was set well off square. **(17)** Note how the edge of the board slopes down under the square. Even if the two edges are not square, but the opposite faces of the board are run against the fence, the two boards will still glue up straight **(18)**.   ☐

12

13

14

15

16

17

18

1

2

3

4

Push-Stick

Always use a push-stick when running wood over the jointer. It is much safer, since your hands are sitting on the push-stick and not on the wood, where they could possibly slip off into the knives.

(1) I use a push-stick with a handle long enough that I can keep both hands on it when I run short pieces over the jointer. The sides of the handle are grooved so that my hands fit comfortably and joined to the base with dowels **(2)**.

(3) The push-stick on the right is made out of one piece of wood, so there is end grain pushing against the back of the board when you use it. The push-stick on the left is a piece of plywood with another piece of wood screwed and glued to the bottom of the back. I feel this type of push-stick is too dangerous. The edge that backs up the board is long grain, which will eventually get banged up and start to break.

(4) Even with a long board, always use a push-stick on the end so your hands or fingers won't slip into the knives.   □

Resawing by Hand

Resawing is a way of getting thinner boards out of thicker boards or of producing beautiful bookmatched wood (panels with mirror-image grain patterns).

When you resaw a board by hand, begin by marking the cutting line on both sides and on the end. Clamp the board in the bench vise at an angle and **(1)** start sawing from the back corner of the end down the side. The sawcut will be at an angle.

(2) Follow the line on both surfaces. Once you have a cut that reaches partway from the back corner down one side, turn the board around in the vise. The angle cut will then be in the back.

With the board clamped straight in the vise, insert the saw in the cut in the back **(3)** and start sawing following the top line to the front. The first sawcut will guide the saw, and the board will be started with a very even cut.

(4) A correctly set saw will follow the lines easily in both the front and back.   □

1

2

3

4

Resawing on the Table Saw

It is considerably easier and faster to resaw a board by machine. A band saw is fastest (see p. 28). If the board is not too wide, it can be resawn on the circular saw **(1)**. Set the fence to the right width, and **(2)** cut from both edges. The board has to be square and milled cleanly for the process to work accurately. Don't take more than one inch with each pass or the sawblade will heat up. Continue flipping the board. If the board is too wide to finish off on the table saw, finish the cutting of the center section on the band saw **(3,4)** or with a handsaw.

Start with a board as thick as possible, because wood usually warps after it has been resawn. **(5)** After this board was resawn, it opened up from the center lengthwise. If the board was not thick enough, there would not be enough left to thickness-plane and straighten out the board.

(6) The boards will have to be jointed and thickness planed or hand planed to make the faces clean.

(7) Here are the resawn pieces, planed clean. Note the bookmatched, mirror-image grain pattern. **(8)** If the wood is dried evenly **(a)**, the resawn pieces will look like this. If the wood is drier on the outside than on the inside **(b)**, the two resawn pieces will curve toward the outside. If the board is drier on the inside **(c)**, the board will curve toward the inside.

Remember that if a board has to be resawn, there is a 75% chance that it will warp after it is cut. You must allow for that. It is a good idea to resaw the boards a few days before jointing and thickness-planing them. This way you allow the wood to stablilize a little more before you mill them to final size.

The same thing usually happens when you joint and thickness-plane a board and more is taken off one side than the other. For example, if a board is 1½ in. thick and the wood has to be planed down to 1 in., if the full ½-in. excess is removed from one side there is a great chance the board will warp **(d)**. The same thing is true if you turn or rout out a large mass of wood on only one side of something such as you might for a tabletop or a tray. □

6

7

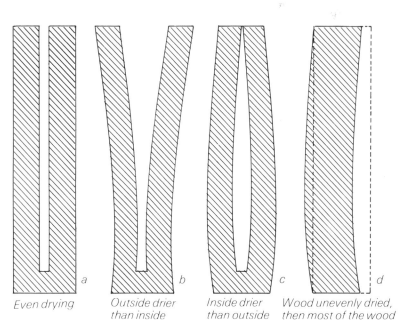

a Even drying
b Outside drier than inside
c Inside drier than outside
d Wood unevenly dried, then most of the wood is removed from one side as might be done with the thickness planer, router or lathe. This piece might move one way or the other, and usually does after a day or two.

Movement of resawn wood

8

1

2

The Thickness Planer

A thickness planer **(1)** makes the top surface of a board parallel to the surface that runs against the bed of the machine, so it is used to make boards an even thickness. Usually, one surface of the board has already been made flat with a jointer or hand planes before putting it through the thicknesser. The cutterhead is usually above the table and the knives have to be set parallel to the table surface below. The table can be moved up and down in fine increments to provide varying thicknesses. There are also two rollers in the table that can be moved up and down independently from the table **(2)**.

There are two spring-loaded rollers above the table, one located in front of the cutterhead and one behind it. These simultaneously press the board down against the table and feed the board through the machine. The front roller is corrugated and does the most pushing. Often this roller will leave marks in the wood, which the cutterhead usually planes out. The back roller is smooth, so that the wood isn't marked up after it is planed.

A handle controls the power feed, so that the wood can be fed forward, stopped or pushed backwards. These directions are usually marked forward, neutral and reverse. The location of the power feed varies among different makes. Always place yourself so that you can reach the handles easily. If something goes wrong, you have to be able to stop or reverse the feed immediately. Never bend down in front of the thickness planer to look between the table and the cutterhead while the machine is running. The cutting action is toward the front, so if a piece should break off, it will fly back right at you. Always stay to the side of the machine. If it is necessary to glance into the machine, at least position yourself to the side.

3

If there are 12 in. between the two power-feed rollers, never run a board through that is less than 15 in. long or the piece will be completely chewed up. The minimum length of board will vary with the size of the machine. Remember to account for the board catching at the front roller, traveling the distance between the rollers, and then catching again at the back roller. Check the manufacturer's instructions for your machine.

Don't always run the wood through the center of the planer. Use the whole bed so the blades wear evenly. If you have to remove a lot of wood from a board, take half off each side, so the board won't warp.

Plane with the grain. **(3)** Here the wood is being passed through the thickness planer. **(4)** The upper corrugated roller is clearly seen. You can see that the wood is sitting off from the table in the corner. The rollers will push down the wood so that the top surface won't be planed off more where the wood is sitting higher off the table.

(5) The wood emerges from the machine with the top surface planed clean and parallel to the bottom surface.

If you want to plane a piece that is ¼ in. or less in thickness, always clamp a board to the table **(6)**. The board must run all the way through the machine and be clamped at both ends. (The board is clamped to the table because the two rollers in the table bottom stick up a fraction of an inch above the surface. Thin wood would begin to vibrate over these rollers as it was passed through, and the piece would be chewed up.) Position the clamps so that they don't interfere with the travel of the board, and keep the board wide enough so that if the piece feeds in at an angle or somehow gets cocked, it will not slide off the board.   □

4

5

6

Edge-Joining Boards

When the boards are thickness-planed, rip them (if necessary) to the desired width. Then match them and **(1)** mark the top side with numbers so you know how they should go together when you glue them up. You can joint them on a jointer, or, even better, by hand. Hand planes leave a perfectly smooth glue surface.

Use hardwood when making the jig **(2)** for jointing boards together. Maple or cherry or any other hardwood will be strong, and the plane will slide more easily against the wood. It is a good idea to put paraffin or wax where the plane slides. When you use the jointing jig, put the first board with its number up and the matching edge on board two with the number two down. **(3)** Then joint the other edge of number two board with its number up and finally **(4,5)** number three down. This ensures that even if the plane or its blade is not square, the boards will still join together perfectly for gluing.

The right way to glue boards long grain to long grain is without using dowels. Run the edges over the jointer slowly, or even better, use a hand jointer plane, and get a slightly concave surface. Then glue the boards together. This puts a slight pressure on the ends. When the wood dries and gives off moisture at the ends first, the pressure is released and the ends will not split **(6)**. At the same time, fewer clamps are used.

If the wood is glued together using this method and we try to break it apart, generally it will break somewhere other than at the joints. If it did break at the joints, it would take wood from both pieces, which proves we have a joint as strong as the material itself. There is no reason for putting a spline or tongue and groove in the joint to get more glue surface. Furniture factories like to use tongue-and-groove joinery because it allows machines to line up boards. But for individual craftsmen, it's a waste of time.

Concave surfaces (exaggerated for clarity)

To check if the joint is correct before gluing, put the two boards together **(7)** so that when twisting one board back and forth the other one follows. If this doesn't happen, the board is convex, not concave.

(8) Put glue on both edges. I usually use Titebond glue and put it on with a squeeze bottle. I then use the cheapest brush I can find — my finger. Spread the glue thinly but evenly.

(9) Put the clamp in the center first and get all the boards flush in the center.

(10) Use a block and hammer the boards down until the joints meet flush.

If you can't get the joints flush, stop hammering. **(11)** Put paper and blocks on both sides of the board over the joint and put on another clamp. Tighten the clamp until the joint is flush. Then remove the blocks. The paper prevents the block from being glued to the board.

Now put two more clamps on **(12)**. I put them on the underside so that if the pressure of the clamps bows the wood, the alternated clamps will counteract each other. When gluing wood together, just squeeze the clamp tight enough with your hand. You should see a slight squeeze-out of glue along both sides of a properly glued joint. Don't use wrenches, pipes or the like to force the joint tight. If forcing is necessary, there is definitely something wrong. One other thing most books advise (but I hardly ever do) is to clamp a 2x4 across the boards to keep them straight. This shouldn't be necessary if clamps are alternated on each side and the wood is planed correctly.

7

8

9

10

11

12

13

15

14

Using a stick and paper **(13)**, clean the glue off both sides while the glue is still wet. Try not to let the clamp touch the glue. If it does, the clamp might stain the wood black because of the tannic acid in the wood.

The line of the joint should not be visible. If it is, the joint is not going to hold. Any gap between the pieces will be filled with glue, and glue is not strong on its own. If you pour glue out and make a sheet of it, you can see that the glue breaks easily. But if you have a good glue joint and you try and split the joint along the glue line the piece will split, taking wood from both pieces being joined.

When you set the boards aside to dry, make sure that just one corner isn't resting against the wall. The weight of the clamps will twist the unsupported wood. **(14)** Be sure both clamps rest against the wall.

When the glue is dry, plane the board level again. Start out using the plane at an angle **(15)**, but this time use only the jointer plane. After one side is done, mark the thickness around the edges with a marking gauge and plane the other side, being careful to follow the thickness lines. You now have one wide board.

If the piece is glued together right, the wood has not warped and the thickness is not critical, just plane and sand the board. □

Clamps

There are many different clamps available, some designed for specific jobs. But for regular clamping, I prefer quick-action clamps **(1)**. They work fast, are very flexible and do an excellent job. In my shop, the smallest clamp is 2 in. deep, with an opening capacity of 6½ in. I have several clamps 4 in. deep (opening capacity is 8½, 12½, 18½ and 32½ in.). I also have a few 7-in. deep clamps with an opening capacity of 18½ in., which I use when the clamp has to reach in deeper.

If you are buying your first clamps, I'd advise getting some 2 in. deep with an opening capacity of 6½ in. Then buy some 4 in. deep, opening capacity 18 in. The difference between, for example, a 12-in. and an 18-in. clamp, is only a few dollars, but the wider clamp can do more work. Later you can add different sizes — it is easier to work with the right-sized clamp for the job.

For bar clamps, I use pipe clamps. They are less expensive, and the same fixtures can be used with ¾-in. black pipes of various lengths. ☐

1

Straightening Warped Wood

If a board warps before the joint is cut, and the joints are cut while the board is still warped, the joints will never fit correctly. **(1)** In this picture, the convex side is up to show how warped the board is. To straighten out the board so the joints can be cut, wet a cloth and place it on the concave side of the board.

Using a hot iron **(2)**, steam the board until it is straight. **(3)** The board will straighten out very fast. Then hurry up and cut your joints while the board is straight. Even if the board warps again, the pieces will go back together straight because the joints were cut when the boards were straight. □

1

2

3

Dovetails
Chapter 5

1

2

3

4

5

Carcase Joinery

Furniture construction is broken down into two main categories: frame and carcase. In frame construction, relatively narrow boards are joined—usually with a mortise and tenon joint—as in a chair or table base, or in a frame and panel door. In carcase construction, boards are joined end to end using dovetails, tongue-and-groove and the like, as in a drawer or hutch. When designing a carcase, as in a box, drawer, bureau or the like, a beginner may find it difficult to know which joint to choose. Some joints are excellent in plywood but weak in solid wood, and vice-versa. Many beginners are so concerned with the "craft" aspect that they design in the most complicated techniques. They use a complex joint where a joint easier to make would work just as well. I always choose the strongest but easiest joint to construct. I cannot see spending time over-constructing a piece. And I expect my furniture to last long after I do.

Except as noted, most carcase joints described in this book are strong enough for all carcase applications. So the choice is really yours—more a question of esthetics and construction time than of utility.

Most joints can be made by hand, but they are usually more easily and precisely made by machine. A table saw is the most widely used and best-suited machine for making joints.

Dovetailing is one of the strongest and most attractive methods of joining the ends of boards together. This is true if you are going to make joints by hand. But most carcase joints lend themselves to machine fabrication. The closest machine joint to a dovetail is a finger or box joint **(1)**. Because of the greater number of pins and the resulting total glue surface, it is stronger than a dovetail, far easier to make and just as attractive.

The lock miter **(2)** is used for either solid wood or plywood. Its advantages are that it is hidden to the outside, and that it requires clamping in only one direction, because of the built-in locking action.

The double-tongued lock miter **(3)** is the best and fastest production joint for plywood but it requires a shaper with special knives. Only one shaper setting is required — the first piece is run through vertically, the second horizontally. The same clamping benefit holds true here. I use this joint only in plywood. In production work, the time saved pays for the relatively high cost of the cutter.

The spline miter **(4)** really lends itself to plywood, but can be used in solid wood on smaller pieces such as boxes. The grain direction of the spline must follow that of the pieces being joined. The spline should be placed $\frac{1}{5}$ to $\frac{1}{6}$ of the way in from the inside corner so as not to weaken the corner. Because of the 45° angle, all pieces must be glued up simultaneously, a real disadvantage in a piece with many parts. Also, a lot of clamps (in all directions) are required to ensure tight glue lines.

A lesser-used spline miter with a parallel spline **(5)** has several advantages but can be used only in plywood. This spline is not as strong as the diagonal one. The spline slots are minutely offset (about $\frac{1}{32}$ in.). Clamps are needed only parallel to the spline, and the offset pulls the pieces tightly together. The ease of clamping this joint is a real advantage. You can glue the inside members and sides first, and when they dry, glue on the top and bottom.

(6) A corner tongue and groove, rounded or square, is good for either plywood or solid wood. In plywood the grain of the corner piece must run lengthwise along the edging. However, in solid woods, the grain must run in the same direction as the grain of the sides so that expansion is constant. The grain should run diagonally from tongue to tongue. Any shaped corner molding can be used. The inside is shaped first, the pieces are glued together, and then the outside is shaped.

The doweled miter **(7)** is used where structure is not crucial — in small boxes, knickknack cabinets, spice racks, etc. It is easy to make and aligns itself correctly for gluing because of the dowels. A dowel center or a brad is useful for transferring the position of one hole to its corresponding hole. This joint works in solid wood or plywood.

I generally do not use a butt joint with dowels **(8)** but when I do, I find it advan-

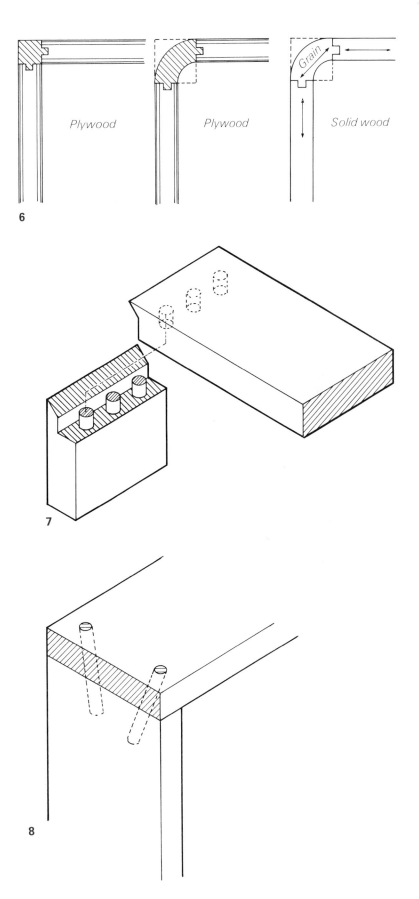

Plywood   *Plywood*   *Solid wood*

6

7

8

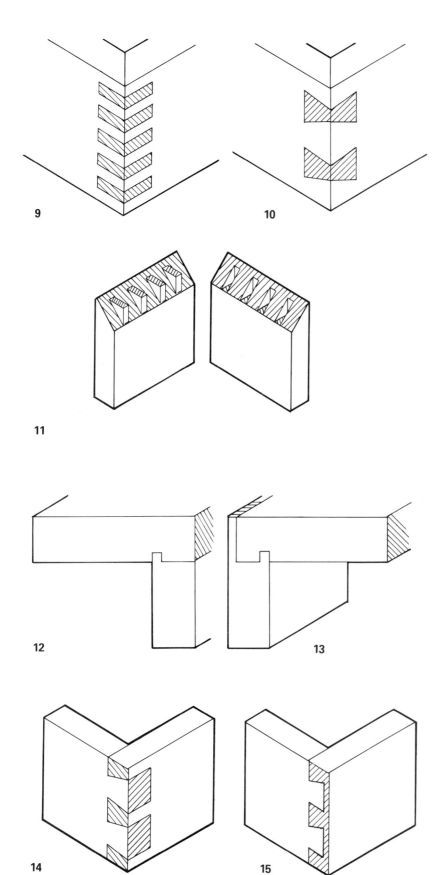

9

10

11

12

13

14

15

tageous to angle the dowels. This adds needed strength to the joint.

Several joints are made by cutting a miter, gluing the corners together, and then cutting slots to receive splines. These joints have great strength and pleasing decorative qualities. With jigs, they can be made extremely quickly. The mock finger joint **(9)** resembles a finger joint without the alternating fingers.

A mock dovetail **(10)** is made similarly, but using a router mounted in a table. If desired, a contrasting wood can be used for splines as a decorative detail.

For hidden splines **(11)**, the slots can be cut using a router with a machine (or your own) dovetail jig. This joint is considerably stronger than a full-blind dovetail because of the greater glue surface.

The tongue and rabbet **(12)** is not the strongest joint but is good enough for the back of a drawer (although not as strong as a dovetail). It is very easy to make. The proportions must be strictly adhered to, as they are determined by factors of strength. The groove should be no deeper than ¼ to ⅛ of the board's thickness, and the same goes for the thickness of the tongue.

The half-blind tongue and rabbet **(13)** is like a lock miter without the miter. It is particularly good for drawer fronts, but in that case be sure to put the drawer stop somewhere other than in the front because of the joint's limited strength. This joint can also be made with a router.

Machine-cut dovetails made with a router and dovetail jig are useful where great quantities must be cut, or where the extra strength of a hand-cut dovetail is not needed. I use them when I have stacks of drawers to do, for example, for kitchens. Otherwise, I prefer hand-cut dovetails for their strength and looks. Besides, if only a few have to be made, when you've made them for many years you'll find them easier to do than setting up the router.

The through **(14)** and half-blind **(15)** hand dovetails are attractive carcase joints. The full-blind dovetail **(16)** is not used to be "crafty," but is used where strength is important, as in a freestanding cabinet without a back, or in a cabinet with glass doors on both sides, like a showcase.

For joints not at corners, a simple tongue and groove **(17)** can be used for any type of wood except composition board. At the ends of the boards the tongue is set off center so that the outside shoulder isn't too weak.

(18) Fiberboard and particle board are made of waste materials, and so there is no grain strength. Since a tongue would break, a spline must be used with these materials. The spline should go into the carcase side about ⅓ of the side's thickness, and twice that amount into the perpendicular piece. Setting the spline further into the side will weaken it, and keeping it shorter in the perpendicular piece will not add enough strength.

I would never use a fully-housed dado joint **(19)**. There are no shoulders to lock the wood and help resist sideway stresses. Also, if the wood is sanded after the joint is cut, the piece becomes too loose. If there are imperfections in the wood, the piece will not fit tightly.

Another strong joint is a series of small mortises and tenons **(20)**. For extra strength, the tenons should run through the sides and be wedged from the outside at assembly.

The sliding dovetail **(21)** is an excellent joint for perpendiculars. The double-shoulder version is machine-cut with a router and a dovetail bit. The single-shoulder joint is cut by hand with a dovetail plane and its corresponding saw, and with a router plane. The machine version is excellent for production. If only a few sliding dovetails are required, the hand method is preferred. It is extremely simple and much faster than one would expect. In the hand version the track is tapered so that the dovetail slides in easily at first and locks at the end as it is hammered into place. Consequently, as the dovetail is forced in tight, a small shoulder is pressed into the straight side and increases at the narrow end. In the machine version, the pieces should mate exactly and thus require a lot of force to assemble, especially if a long dovetail is glued, because the glue swells the grain, making the piece increasingly difficult to slide in.

With both types of sliding dovetails, glue is not necessary, but a spot of glue should be put at the front to fix it in position, or the whole length can be glued. If two different materials are used (e.g., plywood shelves into solid sides), only the front should be glued so that as movement occurs, the front will remain flush.

In a chest of drawers or similar carcase higher or wider than 2 ft., some sort of strengthening brace will be required. I use a sliding dovetail in the center brace, and if additional bracing is needed, a tongue and groove out to the sides. The sliding dovetail holds the center in tight.

If you wish to keep joints from showing through in front, you can stop the joints before the front or else cover them. In solid wood I sometimes cut a ½-in. strip off the cabinet, run the joints through and reglue the strip. In plywood I run the joints through and add a facing for the same result. □

16

17

18   **19**

20   **21**

Tail

Half-pin

Pin

1

2

3

Dovetails

The dovetail has been and still is the mark of fine cabinetmaking. Correctly made, a dovetail is a strong and durable joint. It has a decorative effect and adds a sense of strength to a piece.

There are several types of dovetails. In through dovetails **(1)**, both pieces go completely through each other and the joint is visible on the outside surfaces of both pieces. In half-blind dovetails **(2)**, one piece is joined to about two-thirds the thickness of the corresponding piece, and so is visible on only one outside surface. In full-blind dovetails **(3)**, the pieces are mitered at the edges and the pins and tails stop before the miters so the joint is not visible from the outside of either piece.

Specific tools are required to make hand-cut dovetails. The ease of making the joint and the quality of the finished result depend on the correct use of these tools. Each tool must be sharpened to function correctly.

Once the wood has been milled, the pieces cut to size and the edges squared, marking for the joint begins. The first step in making any dovetail is to scribe the depth of the joint with a marking gauge. ☐

Through Dovetails

For the through dovetail, the full thickness of the wood plus a hair more (about ⅟₆₄ in.) has to be set into the marking gauge **(1)**. The extra bit will ensure that the pieces will go all the way through each other **(2)**, and that any excess will come off the pins and tails. It is much easier to sand off this excess. If the gauge were set too low, the whole side would have to be planed or sanded down.

The angle of the dovetail was arrived at a long time ago through experimentation. The angle is about 80°. If the angle were less the tail might slip out; if the angle were greater the wood on the tail would break. Here **(3)** the angle has been exaggerated to show how the wood breaks off. At the extreme points of both parts of the joint the corners are short grain, which breaks easily.

The easiest way to find the angle is to draw a square line across a piece of wood. Divide the line into six equal parts using a ruler or divider. Mark a point to either side of the line the same distance as one part **(4)**. Connect this base point with the top end of the line **(5)** and you should have a triangle, the hypotenuse of which slopes at the correct angle for any kind of dovetail. This is a one-to-six ratio. The angle can be transferred with a sliding bevel to the end of the piece that is to be joined. A sliding bevel is like a square, but the tongue is movable and can angle and slide.

(6) Two types of sliding bevel are shown here. They're both good.

1

2

3   4

5

6

Tail

Half-pin

Pin

7

8

9

10

11

When making a dovetail, start with the pins. The distance between the pins will vary with the width of the wood, but I would never make their centers more than 3 in. apart. When laying out the pins, start with a half pin on each end **(7)** because tails get their strength from being glued to pins, not vice versa. A tail at the end would not be properly anchored because that part is an end-grain joint. A half-pin is called a half-pin because it is angled on only one side, not because of its smaller size.

Divide the space between the pins evenly. The way you lay out the spacing depends a lot on personal taste. If you wish, you can achieve some highly decorative effects.

When you first learn to make dovetails, it is a good idea to lay the pins out using a sliding bevel on the ends **(8)** and a square on the face **(9)**. When you get more proficient, this might not be necessary.

Now the pins are laid out **(10)**. There are different saws to choose from for cutting the dovetails. The only two that I use are the bowsaw and the offset dovetail saw. I use the bowsaw for wood ½ in. or thicker, and the dovetail saw for anything smaller. The bowsaw cuts much faster than any other saw and makes a narrower cut. With any saw, let the saw lie loosely in your hands, and don't apply any pressure. This is especially true when starting the cut. Use your thumb as a guide, keeping the saw to the *waste* side of the line, following or splitting the line **(11)**. Make sure you don't saw below the scribed line depths.

When the pins are cut, the excess is chiseled out with a chisel and mallet. The chisel has to be sharp. Some chisels are manufactured with handles that have rounded ends. I always flatten these out so the mallet won't slide off the end of the handle. The only exception to this is when I am using the chisel as a carving tool, where I would rest the end in the palm of my hand and push with my hand instead of a mallet.

Use a mallet when striking a chisel. If you use a steel hammer, you will flare out the end of a wooden handle. I like lathe-turned mallets **(12)**. They rest in your hand easily and because they are round, they don't have to be used in a specific position.

Once the chisel is sharp, the wood can be removed between the pins. Clean the area of the bench where you will clamp the board to prevent marring the piece. Use a scrap piece of wood between the clamp and the dovetailed piece so that the clamp doesn't leave an impression in the wood. Clamp the wood to the bench, always over a leg so that as you strike the chisel into the piece, the piece will stay firmly seated. If you clamp the piece over the vise, you run the risk of breaking the vise from the force. And the piece will be harder to chisel out, since the vise doesn't provide as much support as a leg.

Use a chisel to cut the marking-gauge line deeper **(13)**, so that when you chisel out the waste, the grain won't break behind the line. Then make a *V*-cut at the back of the dovetail for the chisel to rest up against **(14)**. If you didn't do this and you didn't set the chisel in just the right spot on the line, the line would be uneven and gaps would show between the two pieces when they were joined.

The back of the joint is undercut slightly **(15,16)**. The end grain does not provide any glue surface. The object is to get a straight line that will be tight when the joint is together. By undercutting, you ensure that the joint will pull in tight and the line between the boards will be closed.

The flat side of the chisel should be away from you **(17)** when you use the chisel vertically to cut at the back, and should be facing up **(18)** when you cut in from the ends to remove the waste.

Chisel only about halfway down from each side. Don't try and take too much wood with one cut. Be careful not to tear the edges of the pins when their wide side is up. Go partway down and remove the excess before chiseling down again. When you have chiseled about halfway down, turn the piece over and continue the same way **(19,20)**. This helps eliminate the problem of tearing wood out from beyond the joint. Remember to undercut on each side.

Sometimes there are still small pieces of wood in the corners that will have to be cleaned out **(21,22)** for the joint to go together tightly.

12

13

14

15

16

Undercut

17

18

19

20

21

22

23

24

25

26

27

28

29

30

31

32

(23) Here is the cleaned-out corner. Note the undercut **(24)** at the back, or bottom, of the joint.

The reason the pins are made first is that it is easier to follow the tail saw line. If the tails were made first and the pins were scribed onto the end of the wood from the tail, the first sawcut on the end grain would destroy the pin line since end-grain fibers become fuzzy so easily. And we all know how difficult it is to follow a line started on end grain. By making the pins first and scribing the tails from them, we can begin sawing on the face side of the wood, and we have more strokes to try to saw the line accurately.

Instead of buying a scriber, I use a scratch awl **(25)** to scribe with. I like the long, slim awl better, and I don't have to buy another tool. If the end of the awl doesn't come to a smooth, sharp point, the line will move away from the pin. Never use a pencil to transfer lines. It is not accurate enough. (In this book I sometimes use a pencil so the lines will show up in the photographs.) The sharp point of the awl breaks the fibers along the line, making a crisp, clean mark.

Always scribe from the inside of the pieces. If you scribe from the outside, as in the picture **(26)**, the point of the scriber will tend to move away from the pin and follow a grain line instead. Scribing from the inside helps force the scriber up against the pin.

The scribed lines should show clearly. On the second pin from the right in the photograph **(27)** you can see where the scriber followed the grain instead of the pin (when scribed from the outside).

(28) The correct way to scribe is to hold the piece with the pins, putting enough pressure on it so it will not slip. Later, when making half-blind and full-blind dovetails, you'll have to scribe from the inside — you'll have no choice. This picture also shows you what to do if the piece warps. By clamping a board across the width you will straighten it out enough to mark it accurately to the other piece.. Once the joint is cut and glued together, the board will stay straight. To prevent marring the surface with clamps, you should always use blocks of wood. I didn't, for clarity.

If the scribed lines are hard to see **(29)** place a piece of white cardboard, or even better, a mirror, in front of the piece **(30)**. The light will be reflected back up and the scribed lines will appear as shadows. This can be a great aid when you begin to saw the tails.

You can also mark the square lines across the end grain using a square **(31)**. This isn't necessary, but will serve as an added guide when you saw the lines.

One common mistake people make when first cutting dovetails is that they try to cut the tails a little oversized so they can fit them later by paring them to size with a chisel. This is a bad practice. It is very time-consuming to fit the tails by chiseling and filing them, and it is much easier and faster to learn to saw them correctly in the first place. When you do learn to cut them right and everything fits correctly the first time, you might be surprised. It does take practice. But through this practice, you will gain both self-confidence and experience with the tools, both of which will help making any joint that much easier. The secret to making joints that fit, whether you are making them by hand or machine, is to learn to split the scribed line in half, and always to keep the sawcut to the waste side of the line. The tails can even be cut on a band saw. The principle is the same: Stay to the waste side of the line and both pieces will go together perfectly.

(32) This cut was stopped partway down to show that the thickness of the sawblade is on the waste side (marked with *x*'s) of the line. The cut just splits the line in half.

(33) Here, the sawcut on the right has gone below the scribed line. This cut will show when the joint is together. The cut on the left is on the wrong side of the line.

(34,35) The tails are cleaned out exactly like the pins, but with the opposite sections chiseled out and using a smaller chisel. Undercut except at the ends.

(36) It is advisable to mark the square lines for the cuts that will saw off the end spaces for the half-pins. Then saw out the two pieces **(37)**. Don't undercut here as this edge will be visible. Again, be sure the corners are clean **(38)**.

33

34

35

36

37

38

39

40

Be sure to sand the inside of the boards before gluing up. Once the pieces are assembled it will be difficult to sand to the inside corners.

Before gluing, you'll want to dry-test your joints, but it is not a good idea to put the joints fully together. Doing so may make the joint sloppy and may even break it. Just check to see if everything fits. Then glue it together and hope. When you glue the pieces, squeeze just a little bit of glue on the top of the pins **(39)** and on the inside edges of the tails **(40)**. As the joint slides together, the glue will be pushed ahead of it. (Of course I would glue up all four sides of a cabinet together at once, not one corner only as in this demonstration.) Use a clamp on the side of the piece with the pins **(41)** to prevent splitting if the joint is too tight.

41

42

(42) Use a block of wood to hammer on when joining the pieces. This will prevent splitting and marking up the piece. If the joint fits right, it should not be necessary to use clamps. As you are gluing it up, check to see that the pieces are square.

Whenever I make a dovetail there is no doubt in my mind that it is going to go together. This is because I make the pins first, scribe them carefully to the tails, and make sure to split the line when cutting the tails. If I can split the line, and I usually can, the joint has to go together. It is that simple.

If one of the pins or tails is slightly loose, the end grain can be hit with a steel hammer, just enough to flare out the fibers **(43)**. This should be done when you are gluing up the pieces.

43

44   45

If for some reason a part of the dovetail does not fit at all, saw a cut a little thinner than the thickness of veneer down the line between the pin and the tails **(44,45)**.

46

(46) Cut and **(47)** hammer a piece of veneer (preferably against a piece of steel) to compress the grain, or squeeze it in a steel vise to flatten it out. Cut the piece of veneer at 45° so that the grain will run in the same direction as the pins.

When applying the glue, rub it into the sawcut using your finger to force it in deep. Don't put glue on the veneer or it will swell up before it is inserted. When inserted **(48)**, the veneer will pick up some moisture from the glue and will expand to fit the slot perfectly. Be sure to choose a piece of veneer—or if you make your own, a piece of wood—that has the same color as the pin.

When the glue is dry, the veneers sawn off **(49)**, and the piece is sanded, no one will see the patch. The marked areas **(50)** show where the veneer was inserted and sanded off. You notice it only if it is brought to your attention. Sometimes, with a perfect color match, it is impossible to see.

If I am making several sets of dovetails, I stack up all the pieces for the pins and chisel them all out at once **(51,52)**, scribe each joint to its corresponding piece and then stack up all the tails and chisel them all at once. This saves considerable time. ☐

47

a

b

c

d

e

f

g

48

49

50

51

52

1

2

3

4

5

Half-Blind Dovetails

A half-blind dovetail **(1)** is used primarily where you want only one side of the joint to show. It is often used to join drawer fronts to sides. In that case, you usually don't want to see the joint on the front of the drawer, but a nicely made dovetail would look fine on the drawer side. With drawers, the sides are usually thinner than the front. Half-blind dovetails can be used for pieces of different thicknesses or for pieces of the same thickness.

Here, pieces of different thickness are being joined. If this were a drawer the pins would be in the thicker piece (the drawer front), and the tails in the thinner piece (the side). The side must be flush with the end of the front. Using an awl, mark the full thickness of the side onto the front piece **(2)**, then scribe with a marking gauge. The depth of the pin should be about two-thirds the thickness of the front So set the marking gauge to that depth and mark the ends of the front, and with the same setting, mark the sides. Then lay out the pins exactly as when making through dovetails **(3)**.

To saw out the pins, hold the saw at an angle **(4)** so that it cuts only between the two scribed lines on the edge and front.

An old scraper blade or sawblade completes the cut. Make sure the scraper isn't sharp so it doesn't split the wood. Hammer the blade down **(5)** until it reaches the bottom corner of the cut. Pop it out **(6)** by hitting the underside upwards with the hammer.

(7) Chisel out the excess the same way as in a through dovetail (see p. 67), but of course, you can work from only one side. Chisel down to the marked line on the end of the front piece.

(8) Clean the rest of the wood out, and again, undercut.

(9) Be sure the corners are cleaned out.

6

7

8

9

(10) To lay out the tails, scribe them from the pins, making sure the board with the pins is offset to make the inside edge flush with the marking-gauge line since these are not through dovetails. Cut and chisel the tails the same way as in through dovetails.

(11) When the joint is completed, tap it together lightly to check the fit. Use a block of wood for better protection.

(12) Don't work it all the way down until you are gluing it up.   □

10   11

12

Full-Blind Dovetails

Most people think it is difficult to make a full-blind dovetail **(1)**. It looks complicated, but it is not. If you can make the through and half-blind versions, you should have no trouble making the full-blind dovetail. The only difference is that when you lay it out, you have to set the marking gauge to the exact thickness of the wood so that the ends will meet in a clean miter. In laying out through dovetails, we set the marking gauge slightly bigger than the thickness of the wood to make sure the ends of the joint protrude so they could be sanded off. Here, the depth must be set exactly right. Otherwise, the joint will not be tight on the inside or outside.

To begin the joint, you must first rabbet the ends of both boards **(2)**. This is most easily done on a table saw. If you do it by hand, you can use a rabbet plane **(3,4)**. There are some very fancy rabbet planes available,

5

6

7

8

9

10

11

12

13

14

15

16

but I prefer a simple one. Or you can saw off the excess with a handsaw. I prefer to use a bowsaw **(5)** if the piece is not too wide. If it is very wide I use a saw designed for making sliding dovetails **(6)**. In either case I make a half *V*-groove for the saw to rest in and get it started accurately. Refer to the section on sliding dovetails (p. 140) for more on the dovetail saw and plane.

After making the cut, use a sharp marking gauge to scribe the end of the rabbet on the end grain. The piece should come out easily with just a light tap with a hammer **(7,8)**.

(9) Be sure the corner is clean. Rabbet out the other piece in exactly the same manner.

To cut the end miters, mark both the front and back and the corners to 45° **(10)**. On a ¾-in. piece, the miter should be about ¼ in. wide — just enough thickness to hide the joint.

(11) Saw, then **(12)** chisel out the angles on both pieces, pins and tails.

When that is done, lay out and saw the pins the same way as in half-blind dovetails (see p. 72). Again, use the scraper blade to complete the cut. Then chisel out the pins **(13)**.

(14) Use the pins to scribe the tails, as in half-blind dovetails. But cutting the tails differs slightly. Here they can only be cut halfway as in making the pins, because the saw is angled. **(15)** The scraper blade again finishes off the cut.

After the waste is chiseled out, the tails are done **(16)**.

17

With both the pins and tails completed, only the miters along the long edge need to be cut. This is most easily done on the table saw. When there are only a few, I cut them by hand with a sharp chisel **(17)** or with a rabbet plane. If you use a rabbet plane **(18)** don't run the plane the whole length in the final cuts. Come in backwards at the end **(19)** so that you don't sliver it off. You could also cut the miter along the edge before cutting the dovetail, as shown in the sequential drawing below.

(20) The pieces are ready to go together. Here I would work them together all the way **(21)** to make sure they fit.

If the corner is slightly open, check that all the corners are cleaned out. If there is still a slight opening, hit the edge lightly with a hammer **(22)** when you are gluing up. This will bend over the fibers and close the imperfection. Here you see the correction almost completed **(23)**.

18

19

20

21

22

23

a
b
c
d
e
f
g
h
i
j

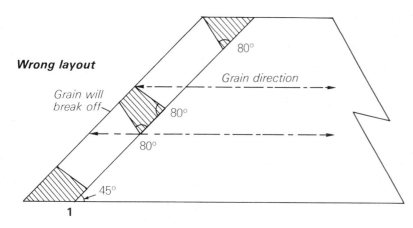

Wrong layout

Grain will break off

80°

80°

80°

Grain direction

45°

1

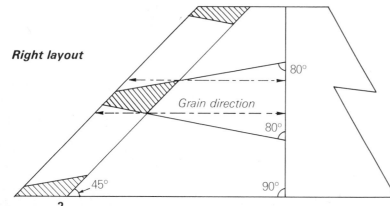

Right layout

80°

Grain direction

80°

45°

90°

2

3

Hand Dovetails with Compound Miter

Through hand dovetails on boards that meet at a compound angle (as in a pyramid) are very difficult to make. It is a good idea to practice on some scrap pieces before cutting the actual joint. Here, I'm making a 45° joint—the steepest angle I would dovetail. But before making this joint, be sure you can make a 90° through dovetail (see pp. 65-71).

The pins are laid out differently from the regular or square dovetail joint. The drawing **(1)** shows the wrong way to lay out the pins. Here the pins are positioned at 80° to the surface, as in a regular dovetail.

This drawing **(2)** shows the right way to lay out the pins. First draw a square line across the board, and mark the pins 80° from that mark.

To make a compound-mitered dovetail, tilt the sawblade 45° (in this case) and cut the top and bottom edges at 45°, the angle the pyramid sides make with the base **(3)**. (For a steeper 60° pyramid, the blade would be set at 60°.) Others may find it less confusing to cut these edges *after* the compound miter is cut.

To cut the ends off, so the pyramid sides meet properly, tilt the sawblade and set the miter gauge to the correct angle using the table provided **(4)**. In this case, the sawblade is set to 30° and the miter gauge at 54¾°. Cut some scrap pieces first and check if the two pieces are square when put together.

Table Saw Settings for Compound Dovetails

Tilt of Sides (from Vertical)	Table-Saw Tilt (from Vertical)	Miter-Gauge Angle (from Sawblade)
5°	½°	85°
10°	1½°	80¼°
15°	3¾°	75½°
20°	6¼°	71¼°
25°	10°	67°
30°	14½°	63½°
35°	19½°	60¼°
40°	24½°	57¼°
45°	30°	54¾°
50°	36°	52½°
55°	42°	50¾°
60°	48°	49°

4

(5) When everything is set correctly, make the first cut with the miter gauge in the groove on the left side of the sawblade.

(6) For the second cut, move the miter gauge to the groove on the right side of the sawblade, but use the miter gauge backwards. Or you could screw a piece of wood to the miter gauge long enough to reach beyond the sawblade when the miter gauge is in the groove on the right side of the blade (in which case the miter gauge is not used backwards). Don't change the angle of the sawblade or the angle of the miter gauge. If the piece is too wide, a plywood jig could be used (see p. 124).

(7) Mark the pins for the depth of the dovetails.

(8) Because the ends are angled, a marking gauge cannot be used.

(9) Set the bevel at the correct angle, and **(10)** scribe the line with a knife.

(11) Transfer the line to the other side of the board by squaring over the line, and use the bevel again.

When you lay out the pins at the end of the board, take the two different angles from the drawing **(12)**, but remember to hold the bevel gauge against the 45° line. When marking the pins on the end of the board, have the bevel square to the surface because the bevel was flat on the drawing when it was set **(13)**.

(14) Set the bevel so it is parallel with the edges when marking down the pins **(15)**.

5

6

7

8

9

10

11

12

13

14

15

16

17

(16) Now the pins are laid out, ready to be cut and chiseled.

After the pins are chiseled out, double-check that the pins are parallel with the outside edges so that when the joint slides together, splitting won't occur **(17)**.

(18) Now scribe the tails from the pins.

On the end of the piece with the tails, set the bevel at the same angle as the edges **(19)** and mark them across **(20)**.

(21) The tails are marked and ready to be cut. Cut the tails a little oversized so final fitting can be done with a sharp chisel. This is one of the few times I fit the tails with a chisel, because I have found it's very difficult to cut accurately.

(22) The joint, glued together and sanded.□

18

19

20

21

22

1

Simple-Angled Dovetails

(1) These dovetails are cut at an angle of 45°, but one side is square. This joint is a little easier to make than the compound dovetail, especially if the pins are in the piece with the angle on the end, as shown here. The pins are cut 80° from the surface, as in straight dovetailing, and parallel to the outside edges, as for compound-angled dovetails (see pp. 78-81).   □

Routing Dovetails

A router is one of the most important electric hand tools in the shop, so when buying one, don't try to save a few dollars, but get a good one with at least a 1-hp motor. Make sure the mechanics that move the router up and down in the base are easy to work and accurate. Check where the switch is located, and if it is easy to turn on and off while routing. And get a router that can take both ¼-in. and ½-in. bits. Don't try to make a router do double duty as a planer using special attachments. The few times you need it it's easier to plane by hand.

The router can be used to make half-blind dovetails, a very strong joint that is easy to make once the jig is set up. I don't think machine dovetails look as good as handcut dovetails, but because of the strength of the joint and the short time required to make them, I always use machine dovetails for a drawer or for anything where strength is needed and the joint won't be exposed.

(1) A special jig has to be used with the router, and it can be used to make only half-blind dovetails. Of the several types of jigs on the market, all seem to work well. When you consider the time that will be saved, these jigs are a good investment. They are especially useful if you plan to make a quantity of drawers, small boxes or the like, where a router-made dovetail would be a good choice for a joint. Buy the widest jig you can find. The price won't be much higher and you will have the added flexibility of being able to work with wider pieces.

I am not going to describe all the adjustments and parts of the jig you will have to set up. When you buy a jig (sometimes called a machine dovetail template) it will come with a full description with all the particulars for that jig.

Different-sized finger templates **(2)** will be available for most jigs. I would buy a ½-in. for larger work, and a ¼-in. one for smaller work. You will also need template guides that attach to the router base and fit into the finger templates, and the correct-size dovetail router bits **(3)**. Be sure the template guide and accessories will work

1

2

3

4   5   6

7   8

9   10

with your particular router — they are usually not interchangeable.

(4) The two boards are placed at right angles to each other, offset by the width of a pin. The whole operation is very simple. Just let the template guide follow the fingers on the template **(5)**. The pins and the tails are both made at the same time.

This picture **(6)** shows the pins and tails after they are cut.

(7) Here the finger template is removed. Notice the offset between the two boards, which is equal to half the distance between the fingers or pins. To put the boards together, the top board is aligned and flipped 180° towards the camera.

(8) By moving the finger template back and forth, the depth of the dovetail can be adjusted to make the dovetails flush, or to make the pins sit deeper, as in a lipped drawer.

In this example **(9)** the finger template was moved back ⅛ in. from the flush position to make a ¼-in. lip. Moving the template ⅛ in. back makes the pins ⅛ in. deeper and the tails ⅛ in. thinner, so do it only where the side is at least ½ in. thick. The dovetails are cut first, and the lip is cut out after they are completed **(10)**.

A disadvantage of using machine dovetails is that you may not always finish with a half-pin if you are limited to a particular dimension. This has nothing to do with the strength, only the looks. If the depth of the drawer or piece is not critical, the pieces could be dimensioned to finish off with a half-pin. In photo **(9)**, the pin at the end is very small. Here, I planned to cut the pieces to size later, finishing with a half-pin. The dimensions were not critical. □

Making Dovetails on a Table Saw

Dovetails can be made on the circular saw with a variation of the miter-gauge jig used for making finger joints (see p. 90). Because small errors tend to accumulate, you have to be sure the spacing is precise when you make dovetails by machine. Lay the pins out the same way you would for hand-cut dovetails (see pp.65-66).

(1) Put in a dado blade about ⅜ in. thick and raise the blade to a little more than the thickness of the wood the tails will be made from.

The first cut to be made will be the half-pin. Fasten a ¾-in. piece of plywood to the miter gauge and set the gauge at 80° — the angle for dovetails — and pass it over the dado blade **(2)**.

Clamp a wood stop **(3)** to this plywood jig so that you can make the same cut in all the pieces that will have pins.

Unscrew the jig from the miter gauge. Make a guide pin insert that fits snugly into the slot and glue it in **(4)**. It should be a couple of inches long.

Return the jig to the miter gauge. Clamp, but don't screw it on yet because you have to adjust now for the distance between pins. Put the slot from the first cut over the guide pin in the jig.

(5) Set the next cut according to your layout for the dovetail pins, being sure to skip one line, which will have the opposite angle. When the blade is in the correct position, clamp the jig to the miter gauge and then screw it on. It is advisable to check all cuts on a test joint (made with scrap wood the same size as the finished stock) to see that everything is set up correctly. Make all the cuts across the piece using the cut for the first pin as a starting point and moving to the right for each cut. Remember to skip every other line, since these will be cut at the opposite angle.

1

2

3

4

5

6

7

8

9

10

11

(6) When these cuts are made, change the miter gauge to 80° in the opposite direction and repeat the procedures so you can cut the other side of the pins. The jig will have to be reset according to your layout. Again, test on scrap first.

(7) Make the rest of the cuts, this time moving to the left. This will complete the sawing of the pins **(8)**. All the pins are the same size and the same distance apart. All the pieces are thus interchangeable.

(9,10) Now set the miter gauge to 90° and remove the excess wood between the pins. If the dado blades are not sharpened perfectly, it may be necessary to clean along the end grain with a chisel. **(11)** This completes the pins.

To cut the tails, use a sawblade instead of the dado head. Great care has to be taken when cutting the tails to be sure they will fit the pins. Tilt the arbor 10° and set the miter gauge at 90°. Check the angle of the pins with a bevel **(12)** to see that they correspond to the setting of the blade **(13)**.

(14) Make the first cut in all the pieces that will have tails. Use a stop so that all cuts are accurate. The first cut must fit the first cut of the half-pin.

12

13

14

15

16

17

18

19

20

Pins

Waste

Marking-gauge line

Waste

Tails

Saw table

Sawblade

21

a

b

c

d

e

f

g

h

With the first cut made, insert a guide pin. The pin should fit snugly into the cut. Move the fence on the miter gauge so the guide pin is to the left of the blade. Align the piece for the second cut, and when correct, screw the jig on **(15)**. Using a scrap piece, make the first few cuts **(16)** and check the piece against the pins to see if your setting is right before cutting your final piece.

When all first cuts for the tails have been made, the jig on the miter gauge has to be moved for the second cut on the tails. Move it and flip it so the guide pin is on the right side of the blade and tilted in the opposite direction **(17)**.

(18) At the same time, the piece to be cut has to be turned 180° because the table saw tilts only one way.

(19) With the guide pin inserted in what was the last cut and is now the first cut (since the piece was turned around) set the jig for the next cut. When correctly set, screw the jig on and make the cut. Again, it is a good idea to check the setting on your scrap piece before making the cut on the final piece.

(20) Continue this way to cut the tails.

(21) Because the circular-saw blade makes a square cut at the top of the tooth, and because the blade is tilted, the corners can not be cleaned by machine. To remove the wood between the tails, use a chisel the same way as you would by hand (see p. 66-67). This ensures that the corners will be clean.

Cutting dovetails on a circular saw is very useful when you have a lot of dovetails to cut. It is considerably faster once you have made the setup. And you can be sure that all the pieces will be exactly the same. The pieces are interchangeable so you don't have to keep track. If you are working on a very wide piece, I suggest you make just the pins by machine and then continue the tails by hand. On a wide piece, if you are off just a little, the mistake will compound itself by the end.   □

Other Multiple Joints
Chapter 6

1

Finger Joints

The finger joint, or box joint **(1)**, is the closest machine-made joint to a through dovetail. The great number of pins and the resulting total glue surface make it stronger than a through dovetail. It is easier to make, and just as attractive. The only drawback with this joint is that clamps usually have to be used when gluing it up.

Setting up to make a finger joint is a simple job, and cutting the joint requires no special skills. How well the joint fits depends solely on how accurate the jig is. Trying to make one the first time may be a very frustrating experience, but after a few times it will become very easy.

Once you have the setup, you can make as many joints as you want. To make finger joints you will need a dado head. The size of the cut depends on the width of the board. When deciding, make sure that you will have a full cut at the last slot. Appearance is another important consideration: There should be a harmonious relationship between the pins and the thickness of the wood.

To make the joint, put in the table saw a dado-blade assembly as thick as you want each finger to be. Set the height of the blades a little higher than the thickness of the wood you'll be joining. For a jig, you'll be using a piece of plywood (at least ¾ in.) attached to your miter gauge. If you've used the jig before, make sure the slot in the plywood jig is not higher than the slot to be cut in the pieces or the cuts will tear in the back of the pieces you are joining. Variations on this type of jig will be used for making many other joints on the table saw.

(2) Starting with a fresh jig, make the first cut in the piece of ¾-in. plywood using the dado blades. The dimensions of the board are not critical; neither is the position of the slot. The miter gauge is set at 90°. Plywood is used instead of solid wood for the jig so that the piece between the two sawcuts will be stronger.

Make a guide pin out of a piece of wood the size of the slot and a few inches longer. It should fit snugly into the slot. Choose a hard wood such as maple so that the guide pin will withstand a lot of use.

2

3

4

5

With the saw turned off, place the guide pin up against the dado head. Move the plywood on the miter gauge so that the next cut will be precisely one thickness of the guide pin over from the first cut **(3)**.

Clamp the plywood to the miter gauge so that it won't slip while you are screwing it on. Try the jig on two scrap pieces to check the fit. If the joint is too tight, move the plywood so that the first cut is closer to the dado blade. If too loose, move the first cut away from the blade to make the pins bigger. If the fit is correct the joint will slide together easily when tapped with a hammer. If the joint is too tight, each pin will swell a little as glue is applied and the pieces will never go together.

(4) Once the jig is positioned, screw it to the miter gauge and glue in the guide pin.

(5) For the first cut, place the wood tight up against the guide pin. This piece will start out with a pin.

After the first cut is made, move the piece over the guide pin to make the second cut. Proceed in this way until all the slots have been cut **(6)**.

(7) On the matching piece, make the first cut by just covering up the cut for the first slot in the plywood. This piece will then begin with a slot to match the pin in the first cut of the other piece. Hold the piece tightly, because dado blades tend to push the wood to one side. Continue the cuts across the board.

(8,9) The joint is now ready to assemble.

6

7

8

9

10

With a little imagination, a finger joint can be used for other applications than carcase construction. It can be used as a hinge joining pieces together lengthwise **(10)**. Finger joints can also be used to join pieces lengthwise at an angle, as for the back of a chair. If you raise the blade to make the slots twice the thickness of the wood, you can make a very interesting and strong joint where four pieces have to meet **(11,12,13, 14,15)**. □

11

12

13

14

15

a   *b*   *c*   *d*

Angled Finger Joints

To make finger joints at an angle **(1)**, the setup is the same as for making them square, except that the jig screwed to the miter gauge is cut at an angle **(2)**, and so the ends of the boards to be joined are cut at the same angle.

(3) The joint, finished and sanded.   □

1

2

3

1

2

3

4

Hot Glue

Hot glue is good if you need quick setting time. It is made from hides, bones, blood, etc. It can be bought in dry sheets, crust, or as pearls. In whatever form, it has to be soaked in water to soften it. When the glue is soft, pour off any excess water. Put the glue into a double boiler or a glue pot. A glue pot is a double boiler with a thermostat, which keeps the glue from boiling. Never put the pot directly on the heat — it should always be over a pot of water. If hot glue boils it loses its strength. Plus, when it boils it doesn't smell like roses!

When starting a new batch of glue, the best thing after it has softened in water is to melt it. Let it cool, and reheat it again and it will be ready to use. Getting the right consistency is something you have to learn through experimenting. If the glue is hot all day, it will thicken and you'll have to thin it by adding more water. If the consistency is just right, the glue should drop from the brush like heavy maple syrup **(1)**.

The best way to check if the glue is made correctly and ready to use is to put a drop between your fingers **(2)**. Rub your fingers together, applying some pressure. You should be able to squeeze out all the excess easily. After about a minute, depending on the room temperature (if it is 60° F, one minute should be about right), your fingers should start sticking together, because when hot glue gets cold it starts binding. But the glue will never reach its full strength until it dries completely — about 24 hours. Under normal conditions you should be able with care to work with the piece after about two hours.

We all know how hard it is to glue two 45°-cut pieces together if there is no spline or no other part to the joint. Since hot glue sticks when cold, we can glue the two pieces together quickly without clamping. **(3)** Spread the hot glue on both pieces. **(4)** Have paper under the joint so it won't stick to the table. Rub the pieces together hard enough to squeeze out excess glue. The pieces will slide easily at first until the excess is squeezed out. Then it will be hard to move them. Force them together making sure the corners line up, and check for squareness. Leave the pieces about five minutes, then set them aside to dry.   □

Mock Finger Joints, Cut by Machine

To make the mock finger joint **(1)**, first miter the ends at 45° as if you were making full-blind multiple splines (see p. 110). Then glue the corners together using hot glue (see preceding page). Because the carcase has to be glued up before cutting the mock fingers, this joint is better suited to fairly small carcases that can be easily maneuvered on top of a table saw.

To make the jig for cutting the slots for the splines, use a piece of wood (any kind will do) about 2 in. thick by at least 8 in. wide by 12 in. long. Make sure the two sides are parallel. Tilt the saw to 45° and make the first sawcut **(2)**, running the edge of the piece against the fence. (The fence is on the left side of the saw.)

(3) For the second cut, turn the piece around and reset the fence so the two cuts meet exactly in the bottom of a *V*-cut **(4)**.

Turn the sawblade back to 90°. Put in the dado blade. In this case I wanted the splines to be ¼ in. thick, so two ⅛-in. dado blades were used. Raise the dado blade so that it will cut as high as possible without coming through on the other corner of the joint or the top of the jig **(5)**.

(6) Make a first cut, holding the jig against the miter gauge. Then cut a spline that fits tightly into the cut.

Decide what distance you want between the splines, and make your second cut with the jig screwed to the miter gauge **(7,8)**. If you make the thickness of the spline and the space between the splines equal, the joint will get its maximum strength and look most like a true finger joint.

1

2

3

4

5

6

7

8

9

10

11

12

13

14

15

16

a

b

c

d

e

(9) Hold the carcase piece to be joined against the guide spline or pin in the first cut in the jig, and make the first cut in the piece.

(10) After the first cut is made, move the piece so the cut fits over the guide pin. Make the second cut.

(11) Continue down the pieces until all the cuts are made **(12)**.

Make the splines exactly the same way as described in multiple spline joints (see pp. 105-107). Insert the splines and mark them for size **(13)**. Make them about ⅛ in. wider than needed.

(14) Set the miter gauge at 45°, and cut the splines as described in half and full-blind multiple splines. Make sure the splines are slightly longer, say ³⁄₃₂ in., than they need to be. Then they can be sanded down to create a smooth joint.

(15) When gluing in the splines, be sure to put the glue in the slots and not on the splines. Check that the spline is seated tight against the bottom of the slot. As a safety precaution, it might be a good idea to clamp the pieces if the splines are loose.

(16) The joint is sanded and finished, and the result is a strong and attractive joint. Using contrasting wood for the splines emphasizes the joint. ☐

Mock Finger Joints, Cut by Hand

If the carcase you are working on is small and delicate, as in a small box, use splines made of veneer in kerfs made by a hand-saw.

(1,2) Mark the 45° on the edge as a guide-line to make sure the splines won't come through on the inside when you make the slots.

(3) Square the line across each side to mark off the depth of the sawcuts.

(4) Locate and mark the positions you want for the splines.

(5) Saw the spline slots with a handsaw. Choose a saw that will make a cut slightly thinner than the veneer to be inserted.

(6) Mark and **(7)** cut the spline pieces, leaving them a little oversized. The grain should run parallel to the bottom of the cut.

(8) Place the veneer on a piece of metal and hammer it so that it is thinner. Now the pieces will slide easily into the slots.

(9) Put glue in the sawcuts and **(10)** force it down inside the slots using your finger. Don't put the glue on the veneer splines. They will swell and you won't be able to get them in the slots.

1

2

3

4

5

6

7

8

9

10

11

12

(11) Slide the hammered veneer pieces into the sawcuts. Be sure you push the pieces all the way down. The veneer will absorb the moisture from the glue and will swell.

(12) Put a clamp across the joint to make sure that the joint will be tight. Clean off as much glue as possible before it hardens.

(13) When the glue dries, cut off the excess veneer and sand the surfaces.   ☐

13

a

b

c

d

Router Table

It is very easy to make yourself a simple router table **(1)**. You will find it an indispensable tool for making joints, moldings and the like. Unless very heavy work is involved, it does just as good a job as a shaper. Also, you can feed the work from the top as well as the side. With a shaper, you can generally feed only from the side. The simplest table is made from a piece of ¼-in. Masonite or plywood. Drill a 1⅛-in. hole in the center. Remove the base from the router. Mark the position of the screws from the router base and drill holes into the plywood or Masonite. Fasten the router to the piece. You now have a very simple but very well-functioning router table.

A more stable router table is made in ¾-in. plywood. The best plywood for this is veneer-core. Mark the holes and drill them the same way as described for the simpler table. Here, though, you will have to rout out a circle **(2)** for the router to fit into on the underside of the plywood. This recess should be ½ in. deep, to leave only ¼ in. for the bit to go through.   □

1

2

1

3

2

4

5

Mock Dovetails

(1) The jig for making a mock dovetail is exactly the same as the one for the mock finger joint (see p. 95), but the slots are cut in a router table using a dovetail bit, and the splines are made dovetail-shaped.

Set up a fence on the router table. The fence board has to be thinner than the bottom of the *V* in the jig. It is a good idea to rub the jig, fence and table top with paraffin or a candle so the jig will slide more easily.

Make a cut with the dado blade for the guide pin so it will fit snugly into subsequent dovetail cuts. Then locate where you want the dovetail cut in the piece. Mark the jig and set the fence for the cut. Because the dovetail cutter sits up high above the table so that it is able to come through the bottom of the *V* in the jig, you will have to make a cut in the bottom of the jig for the shaft of the cutter to pass through **(2)**.

(3) Make the dovetail cuts in the jig.

For the first cut in your final pieces, make a mark on the jig halfway between the dovetail cut and the guide pin. **(4)** Put the piece against the mark and make the first dovetail slot.

(5) Place the first slot over the guide pin, and continue down the piece until all the cuts are made **(6)**.

6

Tilt the table-saw blade to 80° and rip the splines. Then cut them to length **(7)**.

(8,9) Put glue in the slots and insert all the splines. When the glue dries, cut the tails flush with the surface using an offset dovetail saw, and plane and sand the pieces.

(10) Again, we have a very strong and decorative joint. The joint can be emphasized more by using a contrasting wood for the tails. □

7

8

9

10

a

b

c

d

e

f

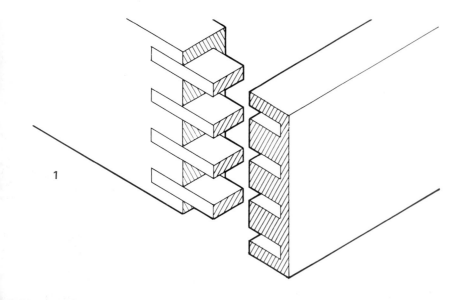

1

Half-Blind Multiple Splines

Multiple spline joints **(1)**, an outgrowth of router-made dovetail joints, are considerably easier to make than full-blind or half-blind dovetails. They are stronger than dovetails because of the greater amount of long-grain to long-grain glue surface. And, because they are cut by machine, they are made more accurately. The only machines required are a table saw and a router—the two most commonly used machines for making carcase joints. The router (with a straight bit) makes the slots the splines fit in, and the table saw (with a dado blade) makes the finger-like jig to guide the router.

The setup for making multiple spline joints takes very little time. The jigs can be used over and over again. The same jig is used for both the full-blind and half-blind versions of the joint.

Making the jig To make the finger-like jig, you need to choose the collar you will use in the router. And the collar is determined by the size of the straight bit you will use. I use a ⁵⁄₁₆-in. bit, because ⁵⁄₁₆-in. thick splines are a good size. Once the collar is chosen, measure its outer diameter, in this case, ⁷⁄₁₆ in. **(2)**.

Then set the dado thickness so that it fits the diameter of the collar exactly. **(3)** Use thin pieces of metal or paper as shims for fine adjusting of the width of the dado cut. I use thin sheet aluminum.

When the correct width is set, **(4)** draw two lines extending from each side of the blade on the wooden insert in the table-saw top. These lines **(5)** will serve as guidelines when making the jig.

(6) Lay out the slots on a piece of ¼-in. or ⅜-in. plywood. The spacing isn't critical, but the distance between slots should be not more than twice the width of the slots. The idea is to get enough splines in the joint to get sufficient glue surface. The slot height isn't critical either, but should be at least ⅜ in. higher than the thickness of the wood to be joined. The exact length of the spline slots will be determined later by how the jig is placed on the wood being joined.

2

3

4

5

7

6

The jig has to be the same width as your actual pieces. Raise the dado head to the exact height of the slot, but to prevent the blade from tearing up the wood in the back of the jig, screw a piece of ¾-in. plywood to the miter gauge. Set the miter gauge to 90° and **(7)** make a cut.

(8) Use the two guidelines on the insert to line up the cuts.

(9) Cut all the slots across the piece of plywood, and the jig is finished.

To determine where to place the jig on the board to be joined, you must first measure the space taken up by the router collar. **(10)** Place the base of the finger slot tightly against the collar. Measure the distance between the router bit and the base of the finger slot. In this case, the difference is ¹⁄₁₆ in.

(11) Set the bit to the right depth—approximately ¾ of the thickness of the wood. This determines how deep the mortises for the splines will be.

(12) To determine the length of the mortises, turn the board over and (in this case) draw a line ¹⁄₁₆ in. back from where you want the mortises.

(13) Now place the jig over the board and line up the bottom of the fingers exactly on the line.

(14) Clamp the jig onto the board and to the bench. Cut the mortises with the router, moving the router into each slot. The collar will guide the router into each mortise.

(15) Here the jig is still in place and all the mortises are cut.

8

9

10

11

12

13

14

16

17

18

19

20

(16) The jig is removed to show the mortises.

(17) Using a marking gauge, scribe a line at the back of the mortises so that when you chisel the backs square, the mortises will all be the same length.

(18,19) Square off the bottoms of all the mortises with a chisel. Undercut slightly.

(20) To make the opposite part of the joint, scribe a line on the end of the board 1/16 in. deeper than the desired depth, or whatever the difference is between the collar and the router bit.

(21) Put the piece in the vise and clamp a scrap piece onto the back. Screw the jig onto that piece, making sure that the bottom of the mortise slots on the jig are right on the scribed line of the piece. Make sure that the orientation of the jig (the edge is marked "front") is correct. Now the pieces are ready to be routed, using exactly the same depth setting on the router bit as on the other piece.

21

(22) Allow the collar to guide the router into each finger.

The slots are cut. Here the are viewed both from the outside **(23)** and from above the jig **(24)**.

Again using the marking gauge, scribe the back of the slots so all the mortises will be the same depth when chiseled out **(25)**.

(26) The slots are squared off and **(27)** the backs of the slots are undercut slightly.

(28) Be sure the corners are clean so that the joint will go together all the way.

(29,30) Remember that the jig will have to be flipped over for the right and left sides of the cabinet so the slots will all match.

Making the splines   The splines have to fit snugly into the slots. You can make them by running a piece of wood through the thickness planer until the board is the right thickness, and then ripping the pieces to the right width on the table saw. But I prefer to make the whole spline on the table saw. It is faster and easier, and I can use pieces of scrap wood, as long as they are thicker than the splines will be wide. If a piece of plywood fits into the mortise, it can be used for splines also — especially in the full-blind version where the splines will not be visible.

22

23

24

25

26

27

28

29

30

31

32

33

34

35

36

37

38

39

40

When cutting thin pieces, always use a push-stick at the end of the pass. The push-stick **(31)** should be thinner than the piece being cut. The back of the push-stick should be rounded and the edges softened, so that if the wood kicks back the push-stick won't cut your hand.

(32,33) Set the fence to the right width, (determined by the width of the mortises you have cut with the router bit) and rip all the splines.

(34) To cut the splines to length, use a hollow-ground blade (see pp. 21-23). A hollow-ground (also called a planer) blade makes a clean cut, and, because the teeth have no set, will not pick up the pieces and throw them at you, the way a blade with set to the teeth would. The splines should be about ¼ in. longer than needed. They'll be trimmed later to exact length.

To prevent the pieces from being trapped between the blade and the fence after they are cut (and getting thrown back at you), clamp a block to the fence and set the fence so that the distance from the block to the blade is the right length for the spline **(35)**. The block should be back at the beginning of the fence so that the splines will not get trapped.

(36,37) For each cut, slide the piece over to the block of wood to get the right length and then, using the miter gauge, move the piece up to the blade.

(38) When the splines are cut, glue and clamp them into the mortises of the piece cut first. Keep the splines a little higher than the finished size so that they can be clamped tightly into the mortises. When the glue dries, **(39)** mark and **(40)** cut the splines to the right length so that they fit the opposite part of the joint.

(41) Plane and sand the splines flush with the surface **(42)**, and the joint is ready to assemble **(43)**. To emphasize the joint, you could use wood of a different color for the splines.   □

41

42

43

a

b

c

d

e

f

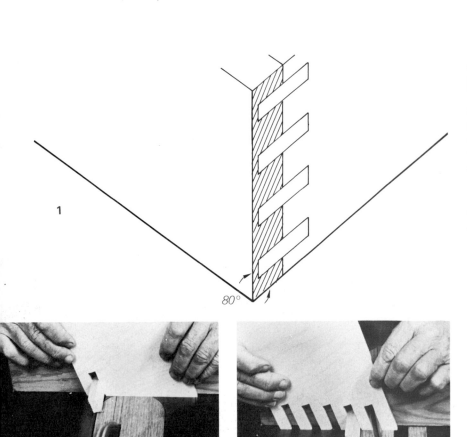

1

Angled Half-Blind Multiple Splines

(1) The jig for routing this joint has to be made very carefully and accurately. The distance between the pins has to be exactly the same, because the jig won't be flipped over as for 90° half-blind splines, but will be turned 180°.

(2,3) To make this jig, the setup is the same as for finger joints, except that the dado blades are tilted to the angle of the multiple spline. So if the angle is 80°, the blade is tilted 80°.

The top and bottom edges of the tilting piece have to be cut to the desired angle, as in making angled dovetails (see pp. 78-79). **(4)** Clamp the jig on the tilting piece and then rout out the grooves.

(5,6,7,8) Now turn the jig 180° to make the opposite cuts. My right hand holds the second board to be routed and the pictures show the sequence of turning the jig in my left hand 180°.

2

3

4

6

5

7

(9) Remove the piece screwed on, **(10)** clamp the jig securely to the second board and use the router.

Chisel the corners clean, then make the spline. **(11)** The joint is ready to be glued after all corners are cleaned.

(12) This joint can be very attractive and decorative with splines of a different color wood.   □

8

9

10

11

12

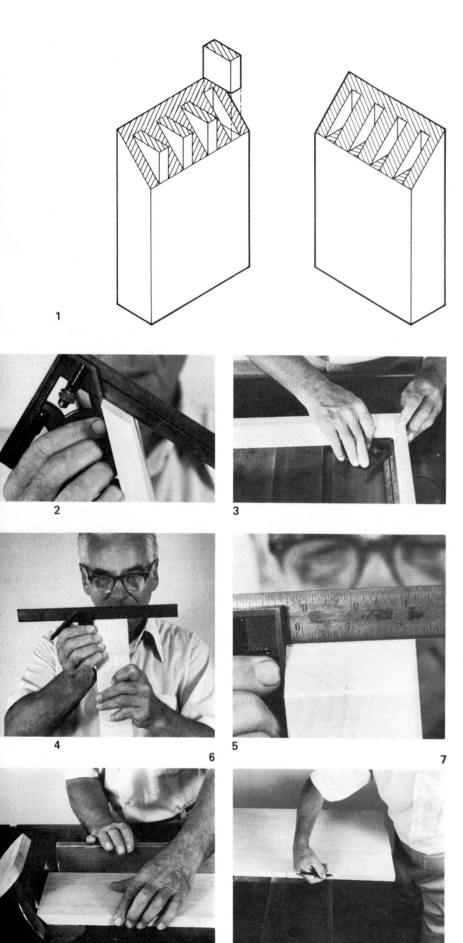

1

2

3

4

5

6

7

Full-Blind Multiple Splines

Making the full-blind multiple-spline joint **(1)** is like making the half-blind version, and the same jig can be used if the boards are the same width. The difference is that in the full-blind joint the edges are mitered so the splines are concealed inside the mitered corner.

When you set the saw to cut the miters, do not rely entirely on the saw's angle scale. Set the blade to 45° and then cut two pieces, each about 12 in. long, at the miter angle. **(2)** Don't bother checking the miter this way, with the 45° angle on an adjustable square. It is not accurate enough.

(3) Instead, put the two 12-in. pieces together, hold them tight and check the whole corner with a square. If the angle is wrong, adjust the tilt of the blade slightly and try again.

(4,5) Also check that the piece is square down the edge of the miter so that the pieces will meet in a clean corner the whole way down. If it isn't square, check your miter-gauge setting.

(6) Once the setting is correct, cut your final pieces.

If the board is too wide for you to use the miter gauge, you can make a fence to guide the board instead. Place the board on the table with the blade exactly in the position where it will cut the angle. Mark the end of the saw table onto the piece **(7)**.

(8) Square the mark across the underside of the board.

(9) Clamp a straight board right on the line.

(10) Then cut the miter.

(11) Mark ¹⁄₁₆ in. from the corner. This distance is determined by the thickness of the router collar and the size of the router bit (see p. 103).

(12) Square the line across. When the jig is clamped on, the bottom of the fingers must be right on the line the whole way across so the mortises will have the same depth. Here again, set the depth of the bit so that the mortise is about ¾ the thickness of the board.

(13,14) Cut the mortises in the mitered pieces.

8

9

10

11

12

13

14

15

16

After the slots are cut, remove the jig, chisel the corners square **(15,16)** and be sure they are all clean **(17)**.

When making this joint, you will have to flip the jig over for the right and left sides so the slots will line up accurately. Place the two boards end to end **(18)**.

(19,20) Flip the finger jig over to ensure that the mortises will match when they are cut in the second board. Then clamp the jig on and repeat as before.

(21,22,23) When cutting the spline to the correct width, you must be very accurate.

17

18

19

20

21

22

(24) The spline should be exactly flush with the inside piece so that it fills up the entire mortise.

When cutting splines to length, follow the same procedure as when cutting them for the half-blind joint (see pp. 105-106). But to be sure you end up with a perfectly square spline that will fill up the whole mortise, adjust the fence so that the stop block is exactly the spline width away from the blade **(25)**. If the splines are too big, the joint won't go together. If they are too small, you will have a problem lining up the corners. Keep the blade high so it doesn't catch the small pieces after they have been cut **(26,27)**.

(28,29,30) The joint is now ready to be glued up. But this time, glue the splines and both pieces together at the same time, because of the 45° angle. This can be a real disadvantage in a piece with many parts. Also, a lot of clamps are necessary in all directions to ensure a tight glue line, and to keep the pieces from sliding. If done carefully, the splines could be glued on one piece first, but be sure all excess glue is cleaned off.   ☐

23

24

25

26

27

28

29

30

a

b

c

d

e

1

Multiple Tenons

Another strong and attractive carcase joint for mid-section structural elements is a series of small mortise and tenon joints **(1)**. This is an excellent joint in solid wood. The joint does not have to run all the way through the other piece, but running the tenons through and wedging them from the outside at assembly will add strength.

Using the marking gauge, mark the full thickness of the piece with the mortises onto the piece with the tenons (if the tenons are through tenons). This gives the depth or length of the tenons. Then lay out their width. If you are making them by hand, cut them out with a handsaw **(2)**.

(3) Remove the outside pieces with a handsaw. Don't undercut here—we want a tight joint, front and back.

(4) With a chisel, score a *V*-cut where you will be chopping out (as done in making dovetails—see p. 67).

(5) Chisel out the waste between the tenons. Here we do want to undercut in the back so the joint will go together all the way.

(6,7) An easier way to make the tenons is to cut them with a dado head. Mark the tenons and make the cuts. In the same saw cut you will make the cheek and remove the waste. One or two passes (depending on the spacing) should complete the tenon. If you are making a lot of joints at once, you can set up a finger-joint jig to make all the cuts the same and complete the joints faster (see p. 90). Remember to mark the width of the dado cut on the saw-table insert as a guideline.

2

3

4

5

6

7

(8) When all the tenons are made, mark the full thickness of the tenoned board on the board the tenons are going into.

(9) Square the lines across.

(10) Mark the mortises from the tenons with a scriber. Be sure that the front side is flush **(11)**.

(12) Square the lines over to the other side. Scribe the tenons on this side the same way as you did on the other side.

(13) Draw diagonals from corner to corner to mark the center for the drill bit. Do this on both sides.

(14) Use either an auger bit or a spur bit to drill the holes. The bit should be slightly smaller than the finished mortise. Drill until the tip of the spur comes through on the other side, then flip the wood over and drill from the other side. This way the wood won't tear out in the back.

The holes are drilled. Now square off with a chisel **(15,16,17)**. Be sure to undercut the end grain in the holes. But the sides must be square to the surface to ensure good glue surface and a good fit.

8

9

10

11

12

13

14   15

16

17

18

19

20

21

22

23

24

a

b

c

d

e

f

(18) Before gluing up make a sawcut from corner to corner in the tenons (for the wedges). This is done so that if for some strange reason the joint doesn't fit you can insert wedges to expand the joint so that it fits perfectly into the hole. When you glue and hammer the wedges in you will have a perfect fit. This is a good idea even if the tenons fit perfectly into the holes because it will add strength to the joint.

(19) The wedges can be made with a hand-saw or band saw.

(20,21,22) The wedges are glued and hammered into the diagonal cuts, then trimmed flush **(23)**.

(24) The joint is finished and sanded. It looks perfect — you will never know if it fit before the wedges were put in, and I am never going to tell you. ☐

Tongue and Groove
Chapter 7

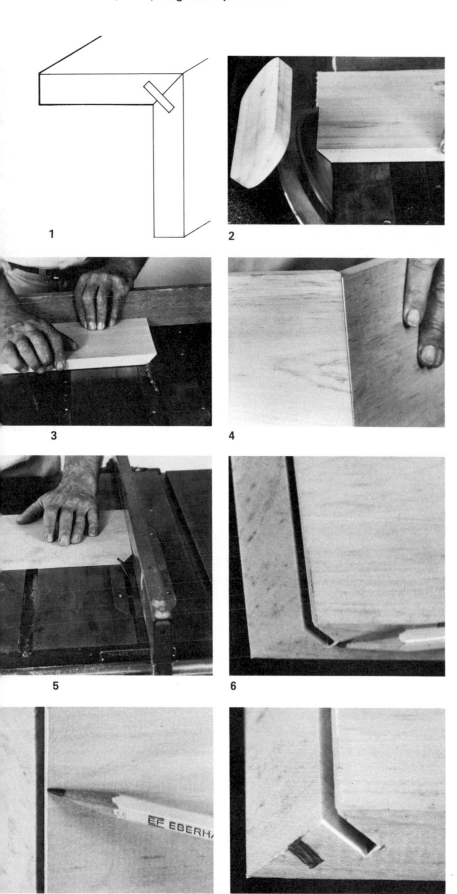

1

2

3

4

5

6

7

8

Diagonal Spline Miter

The spline miter **(1)** is a relatively strong joint, especially when used on veneer-core plywood—you will have 50% long-grain to long-grain glue surface. This is also a good joint for composition board, particle board, Novaply, etc. A spline miter is not a good choice for solid wood if strength is required of the joint. But it is all right for pieces such as small boxes.

Making a spline miter is very easy. First, cut a 45° miter in two scrap pieces to check the saw setting, and once you have the proper angle, **(2)** cut the miter in both pieces to be joined (as for full-blind multiple splines—see p. 110).

(3) Don't use the miter gauge for cutting the groove for the spline, because if the miter gauge is a fraction of an inch off square, the spline groove will not be parallel with the edge. Afterwards, when gluing the pieces together, the corners would not line up **(4)**. If you are using plywood, this could cause a real problem. When you sanded the corners flush you would go through to the veneer, and you would have an awful-looking corner. (But if you do go through the veneer, choose a felt-tipped marker the same color as the veneer and shade in the plywood to hide the mistake.)

However, the right way to cut the groove is to lower the blade and move the fence to the left side of the sawblade **(5)**. Raise the blade to the desired height, and cut the spline groove with the end of the board guiding off the fence. This method will keep the cut parallel with the edge and prevent the pieces from skewing as a result of a misaligned spline.

On a very narrow piece, use the miter gauge in combination with the fence to guide the piece through. To do this, push the end of the board tightly up against the fence. Move the miter gauge up to the side of the board and set it to whatever setting falls against the edge. This will prevent kickbacks in the cut.

Cut the groove for the spline as close as you can to the inside corner **(6)**, so you can get as wide a spline as possible. But do leave a small edge of wood towards the inside **(7)**. If a ¾-in. thick piece is used, I leave about a ¹⁄₁₆-in. edge, and I would make the thickness of the spline about ⅛ in.

(8) Here you can see how the spline gets narrower if it is moved closer to the outside corner.

If the spline miter is made in solid wood, the grain of the spline must follow that of the pieces being joined. **(9)** Here you can see how to cut splines on a table saw. If a lot of splines were needed, I would use a thickness planer first. **(10,11)** For safety, fasten a piece of wood to the fence with its lower edge higher than the piece you are cutting out so the piece doesn't get caught between the fence and the board.

(12) If the grain of the spline ran lengthwise down the spline, which would be across the grain of the pieces to be joined, the spline and the pieces would not move together, and the spline would be weak and could easily split.

If you use this joint in plywood, use a plywood piece for the spline, too. Make sure you have a piece that will fit snugly into the spline groove you make. Check the fit on scrap before you cut the spline groove.

(13) The spline in place.

(14) The joint assembled.   □

9

10

11

12

13

14

1

2

3

4

5

Parallel Spline Miter

The parallel spline miter **(1)** has several advantages over the diagonal spline miter (see p. 118), but it can be used only in plywood, and clamps are needed only in the direction parallel with the spline. The spline slots are minutely offset, about $\frac{1}{32}$ in., from one piece to the other. When clamped together, the spline will give a little, and the offset will pull the joint in tight.

The ease of clamping this joint is a real advantage. In a cabinet with many pieces, you can glue the inside and side members of the cabinet first, and when they dry, glue the top and bottom on. In some situations this might be much easier than trying to glue the whole thing together at once.

The joint is not for solid wood because the wood will chip off **(2)** and because the spline would be glued into only end grain in one of the pieces, which would result in a weak, unstable joint.

To make the parallel spline miter, you can cut the groove in the vertical piece with the wood running against the fence **(3)**. For safety, or with a wide piece, use the jig described in the section on splines for particle board (see p. 131). For very narrow pieces, use a tenoning jig (see p. 174).

(4,5) When you mark for the second cut, be sure to offset the spline slightly so that the pieces will pull in tight with clamps in only one direction.

(6) Cut the slot in the mating piece by running the edge up against the fence. With a narrow piece, use a miter gauge, setting it to the edge of the piece with the piece pressed tight to the fence.

(7) The grooves are finished.   □

6

7

a

b

c

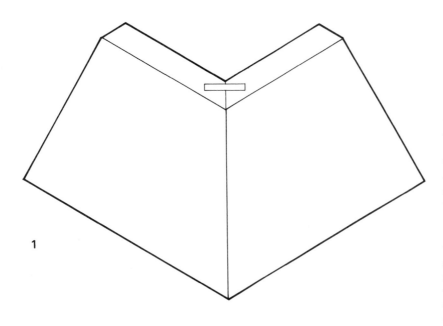

1

Compound Miters

To make a compound miter **(1)**, use the chart **(2)** to find the correct angle settings for the miter gauge and the sawblade. In this case I wanted to make a four-sided compound miter—where the sides are angled at 15° from the vertical and the corners come together in a miter joint. As the chart indicates, set the miter gauge to 75½° and the sawblade to a 43¼° tilt. Check the angles on two scrap pieces to make sure the pieces are square.

Sometimes you will have to adjust one of the angles (or even both angles) if the angle scales on either the saw or miter gauge are not accurate. To be sure of accuracy, check the angles by setting a T-bevel to a protractor and then transferring these angles to the miter gauge or sawblade. I always do a test set of joints **(3)**.

(4) Once the angles are correct, cut off the ends of the first board.

Compound Miters

Tilt	4-Sided Miter		6-Sided Miter		8-Sided Miter	
	Blade Tilt	Miter Gauge	Blade Tilt	Miter Gauge	Blade Tilt	Miter Gauge
5°	44¾°	85°	29¾°	87½°	22¼°	88°
10°	44¼°	80¼°	29½°	84½°	22°	86°
15°	43¼°	75½°	29°	81¾°	21½°	84°
20°	41¾°	71¼°	28¼°	79°	21°	82°
25°	40°	67°	27¼°	76½°	20¼°	80°
30°	37¾°	63½°	26°	74°	19½°	78¼°
35°	35¼°	60¼°	24½°	71¾°	18¼°	76¾°
40°	32½°	57¼°	22¾°	69¾°	17°	75°
45°	30°	54¾°	21°	67¾°	15¾°	73¾°
50°	27°	52½°	19°	66¼°	14¼°	72½°
55°	24°	50¾°	16¾°	64¾°	12½°	71¼°
60°	21°	49°	14½°	63½°	11°	70¼°

2

3

4

(5) For the second board, you will have to twist the miter gauge at the same angle, but measuring in the opposite direction. Another way to do this is to move the miter gauge to the groove on the right side of the sawblade, but use the miter gauge backwards **(6)**.

Raise the piece to 90° to the table and do not change the angle of the sawblade. The groove for the spline will then be at 90° to the compound angle. **(7)** With the piece clamped to the tenoning jig (see p. 174) and the edge of the miter down on the table, make the sawcut. **(8)** Then make a similar cut on the second board.

(9) The grooves are ready for the spline.

5

6

7

8

9

10

11

12

13

14

15

(10,11) Rip the two sides parallel at the same angle as the angle you want the joint to sit at. Since I want a 15° angle, I rip the edges to 15°.

(12) The result is a clean, tight, square joint.

(13,14) If you want the miter to be on the long-grain sides, first square off the boards, cutting the ends to the same bevel as the tilt (in this case 15°).

On tall pyramids, where long compound miters have to be cut, it would be dangerous to use the miter gauge **(15)**. Instead, make a jig out of plywood that will hold the work at the proper angle to the sawblade **(16)**. Use a piece of plywood long enough to give good support against the fence. Mark off the angle on the plywood and then draw a 90° line off the widest end of the angle. Bandsaw out the piece and you will have a jig that will house the piece to be mitered.

16

(17) In this case the board sits in the jig at 75½° — the same angle as the miter-gauge tilt would be. Draw a point on your board where you want the angle to begin (how wide you want the board to be, in effect) and move the fence the correct distance away from the sawblade. Make the cut, holding the piece securely in the jig. Save the cut-off piece.

(18) To make the second cut, reverse the jig and place the cut-off in the jig first, and then place the piece to be cut up tight against the cut-off. You can just hold the two together while you are running them through the saw, but this can be dangerous. I sometimes use masking tape on both sides to hold them together, but the safest way to keep them together is to glue blocks with paper underneath them over the two pieces. Use hot glue or some other quick-drying glue. (Use the same method as when gluing on corner blocks for clamping — see p. 127). If possible, it helps to have two people make the cut if you don't use the glue blocks.

17

18

19

20

(19,20) The pieces should fit tight both in-side and out. Since the glue surface is all long grain to long grain you don't really need a spline. But it is a good idea to use one so that the pieces will align properly when you are gluing them. Otherwise, they might slide all over the place as you try to get the clamps on. ☐

a

b

c

d

e

f

g

h

Gluing Miter Joints

Gluing a 45° miter joint together is always a problem because of the difficulty in clamping the pieces. In a carcase, we have to clamp from all four sides simultaneously. In many cases we can't even see the corner because of the blocks and clamps involved.

I glue blocks cut to 45° with paper underneath them onto the pieces to be joined. This takes a little longer, but I have found that it is worth it. With the paper, the blocks can easily be removed by hitting them with a hammer. The paper will rip, and the blocks will come off easily without tearing up the surface of the wood.

(1) Locate where you want to place the blocks. They should be exactly across from each other on both sides.

Brush hot glue on the block. Use hot glue in a case like this because it sets fast and doesn't require clamps. Remember to glue the long-grain side. Then put the paper onto the block **(2)**. Don't use newspaper — use a heavier paper such as brown paper.

(3) Next put glue on the other side of the paper.

(4) Place the block in its location, and rub the block back and forth until it sticks.

(5) When all the blocks are glued on, let the glue dry before gluing up the joint.

(6) After gluing the joint, clamp the boards together. □

1

2

3

4

5

6

Tongue and Groove

A simple tongue and groove **(1)** can be used in any type of wood except composition board, but is best suited to plywood. If it is used on the end of a board, the tongue should be set off center so the outside shoulder is not too weak.

Fiberboard and particle board are both made out of waste material, so there is no grain strength. Since a tongue would break, a plywood spline **(2)** must instead be used with these materials. The spline should go into the carcase side about ⅓ the thickness of the side, and at least twice that amount into the perpendicular piece to add more strength.

I would never use a fully housed dado joint **(3)**. There is no shoulder to lock the wood and help maintain strength against sideways stresses. Also, if the wood is sanded after the joint is cut, the piece will become too loose. Even if you sand all the pieces before you cut the joint they will never all be exactly the same thickness, so your joint will be sloppy. Even plywood varies in thickness.

The easiest way to make the groove for the tongue-and-groove joint is on the table saw, if you don't mind showing the joint. If you are using plywood you will usually cover the edges with a facing, which would hide the joint. Use the dado blades set to the width of the groove and run the edge of the board against the fence if the piece is wide enough. Use a miter gauge to guide the board if it isn't wide enough.

If you don't want to show the joint, use a router for cutting out the groove. You can use a *T*-square as a guide for the router (see p. 132) and stop the joint before it goes through the front. Clamp the end of the *T*-square to the piece and let the base of the router slide along the extension of the square.

(4) If you start the router the wrong way, the router will tend to pull away from the tongue because of the direction in which the router bit is rotating.

(5) You can see how the cut pulled away from the line. If you want to use the side of the *T*-square as a guide, you must push the router away from you so the rotation of the bit pushes the router against the side of the *T*-square. If you use the other side of the square, you must pull the router toward you.

Once the groove is made, the easiest way to make the tongue is to use two sawblades or dado blades that are exactly the same diameter, and held apart by a spacer of wood or metal **(6)** that is the thickness of the tongue. With the spacer between the two blades, the blades will cut a tongue that will fit into the groove exactly. Once these spacers are made they can be used over and over again. (Of course, the shaper is the best tool for cutting tongues.)

(7) Measure the depth of the groove.

(8) Set the height of the sawblades so they are a fraction lower than the depth of the groove.

(9) Mark exactly where you want the tongue to be.

(10) Set the fence to the right distance, or use the tenoning jig (see p. 174). You could also fasten a high piece of plywood to the fence for stability, or use the jig for particle board in the section on splines (see p. 131).

(11) Make the double cut. Using the fence is quite safe because the cuts are very shallow.

(12) Set the height of the blade for cutting the shoulders. Use a blade that will cut across the grain.

8

9

10

11

12

13

14

(13) Clamp or screw a piece of wood to the fence so the cutoff doesn't get caught.

(14) Mark and cut a section of the tongue in the front so the joint is concealed, and your joint is ready to be glued. Here, the saw-blades were too high when cutting the cheeks of the tongue, so the cuts are visible in the front. □

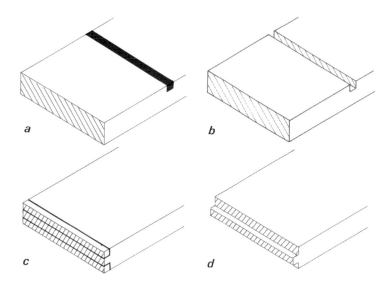

a

b

c

d

Jig for Cutting Grooves in Composition Board

Making a spline joint in composition board is like making a tongue-and-groove joint. Here, though, you make spline slots in both pieces, glue the spline into one piece, and then glue the two together as if they were joined with a tongue and groove. The groove in the perpendicular piece is done on the circular saw with a dado blade. The cut in the corresponding piece is made with the piece standing vertically against the fence. This cut should be twice as high as the first, to give the joint more strength. A special jig makes this cut an easier, safer operation.

The jig **(1)** will run over the fence to guide the pieces that will receive vertical saw cuts. This jig is particularly useful for tall pieces. You can clamp the pieces to the jig and move the jig down the fence to make the cut safely.

The jig is made of two pieces of plywood with a piece of solid wood sandwiched between. Dimensions for this jig are given in the drawing **(2)**, but you can easily change the dimensions to suit your particular needs.

Make and fit all the pieces. Be sure the solid piece between the plywood pieces is exactly the same thickness as the fence so there will be no play. The jig should be able to move freely through, so don't make it too snug. Clamp the jig together and check for fit and squareness before gluing it together.

(3) Be sure the jig is square to the table top of the saw.

(4) Set the dado blade to the depth of the groove you want and move the fence and jig to position the cut on the composition board **(5)**. Using the jig to make a tongue-and-groove or a tenon takes a little longer to set up but is considerably safer and more accurate than running the pieces through freehand.

(6) Here is the piece with the vertical spline slot with the spline inserted.   □

1

2

Plywood ³⁄₄"

24"

9" 3" 6"

(To match fence dimensions)

3

5

4

6

18″

⊘ ⊘

3″

□◄2⅞″► ⊘ ⊘ ◄2⅞″►□

1

32″

Wood is ¾″ thick.

◄3″►

2

3

T-Square for Router

An easy way to guide the router for making straight grooves in a board is with a *T*-square made for the router. To make the square, take some ¾-in. stock about 3 in. wide that is exactly straight with parallel sides. Drill the holes for the screws, then glue and clamp the pieces together, checking to be sure they are exactly square. When dry, put in the screws.

The dimensions given in the drawing **(1)** are those I find most suitable for all-around work. For smaller work, make a smaller *T*-square. The distance to the bit mark depends on your router. Of course the same jig could be used for sliding dovetails (see p. 144).

(2) When the square is complete, use the router with the bit you will normally use for grooves to rout the ends of the square. The most common size I use is ¼ in. This locates the bit for your router in relation to the *T*-square arm.

(3) You can now use it for lining up the square in making cuts. □

Tongue and Rabbet

The tongue-and-rabbet joint **(1)**, really a tongue-and-dado joint, is very easy to make. It is not a very strong joint because end grain is glued to long grain. But it is good for small boxes, knickknack shelves and the backs of drawers. The proportions shown in the drawings should be strictly adhered to, because they are determined by factors of strength. The dado should be no deeper than one-quarter the thickness of the board. The thickness of the tongue should be about the same. If possible, don't make the joint flush. Move the dado in and the joint will have considerably more strength.

Before cutting the joint, sand the inside, especially the piece with the tongue. If you sand after the joint is cut, the fit might be too loose.

Choose a blade or dado setup ¼ to ⅕ the thickness of the wood. If the joint is going to be flush, set the fence to the exact thickness of the wood to be joined, so that the outside of the blade is flush with the outside of the edge **(2)**.

(3) Raise the height of the blade to ¼ the thickness of the wood.

(4) Holding the end of the wood up against the fence, cut the dado. If the board is very narrow, use a miter gauge or there will be kickback, but make sure the board presses snugly against the fence.

(5) Mark the thickness of the tongue on a scrap piece.

(6) Make the cut in the scrap, without changing the height of the blade. For safety, use a tenoning jig (see p. 174). Check to see if the piece fits. If so, make the cut in the good piece.

(7) Mark the piece to be cut.

8

9

(8) Raise the blade to the right height.

(9) Push the end of the tongue against a piece of wood fastened to the fence, but raised above the small piece being cut, and make the final cut.

(10) The joint is ready to be glued up. □

10

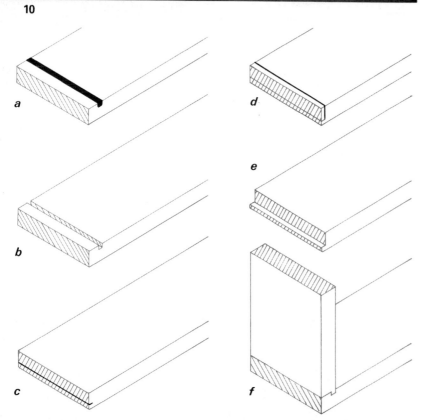

a

b

c

d

e

f

Half-Blind Tongue and Rabbet

(1) A half-blind tongue and rabbet (or dado) is similar to a half-blind dovetail but is not nearly so strong. It is particularly good for a drawer front. If used as such, the drawer stop must be put somewhere other than in the front because of the limited strength of the joint. If a router with a dovetail jig is available, I would definitely use it instead for joining a drawer front and sides.

When used in drawer construction, its most common use, the front is usually thicker than the sides. When making a half-blind tongue and rabbet (or a lock miter), always sand the sides before cutting the joint. Otherwise the joint will not fit as well.

The dado is cut exactly the same as in the through version (see p. 133), but not as far in from the edge because it's half blind. The pencil lines show how the joint should be laid out **(2,3)**.

(4) After the rabbet is cut, mark the tongue.

(5) Then measure the thickness of the sawcut required and **(6)** make your dado blade that thickness.

(7) Raise the dado blade to the exact thickness of the board that has the rabbet in it.

(8) Make the cut with the dado blade. Using a tenoning jig (see p. 174) to hold the wood is the safest way to make the cut. Try a scrap piece first.

1

2   3

4   5

6   7

9

10

11

12

a

b

c

d

e

f

(9) If I am using a soft wood and the blades are sharp, I run the board against the fence. This is much faster, but I would not advise doing so until you are 100% sure of yourself, as it is much more dangerous, especially if you don't know what you're doing.

Then mark **(10)** and **(11)** cut the tongue to length.

(12) The joint is finished, and ready to be glued together. ☐

Lock Miter

The lock miter **(1)** can be used in either solid wood or plywood, but it is stronger in plywood. Its advantages are that it is hidden from the outside and that it requires clamping in only one direction because of its built-in locking action. It is a strong joint, but not as strong as the full-blind multiple spline (see p. 110).

(2) Although the joint looks complicated, if you follow through the steps in the drawing you will find it easier than you think. I would suggest having several scrap pieces the same thickness on hand. Use them to check the accuracy of the fit at each step. This joint will be considerably easier if you have made the tongue-and-rabbet and the half-blind tongue-and-rabbet joints first. In the lock miter, though, you will be working with pieces of the same thickness, and you will have a few more steps to complete.

Great care must be taken when marking the wood and setting the machine cuts. First make sure the fence is set for the exact thickness of the wood, with the outside of the blade flush with the outside edge of the wood **(3)**.

(4) Raise the blade so it makes a rabbet ¼ the thickness of the wood and **(5)** make the first cut, using a push-stick or a miter gauge on the fence side. Check to see that the cut is at the right distance in.

Mark for the second cut. This is taken from the dado width and should be about half the thickness of the wood. After setting the dado blade, raise it up to the full thickness of the piece **(6)**.

(7) Use a tenoning jig (see p. 174) to help make the cut.

(8) Then check it for depth against the other piece.

9

10

11

12

13

14

(9,10) Mark for the third cut.

(11) Attach a board to the fence higher than the cut you are making so the piece you are cutting off won't get trapped between the blade and the fence, and make the cut.

You can use a dado blade, or use a single blade and simply break off the excess **(12)**.

(13) Mark for the fourth cut. Again, fasten a piece of wood to the fence so the cut-off doesn't get trapped.

(14) Make the fourth cut.

(15) Lower the blade, move the fence over to the other side of the blade and tilt the blade 45°. Attach a thick piece of wood to the fence so it is higher than the blade but low enough to slide the tongue against. Make the fifth cut.

(16) Reset the fence and make the sixth cut, the final bevel.

(17) The joint is now finished.   □

15

16

17

a

b

c

d

e

f

g

h

i

Sliding Dovetails, by Hand

A sliding dovetail **(1)** is very important in carcase construction. It can be made by hand or by machine. It works in any type of wood. It is easy to make, especially after you have goofed it up ten or twelve times until you get the hang of it. If I have only one or a few to make, or if the piece is very wide, I prefer to make them by hand. This way it is easier to fit, and the joint slides together more easily because it is tapered.

(2) Locate and mark the full thickness of the piece on the board it is to be joined to.

(3) Square the lines across, and **(4)** mark the end of the groove (to keep the joint hidden in the front).

(5) If ¾-in. lumber is used, mark ⅛ in. in from one of the lines at the back.

1

2

3

4

5

(6) At the front, on the same line, make a mark in ¼ in. Connect the points to form a new line **(7)** that will represent an overall taper of ⅛ in.

(8) Scribe the lines.

(9) Score the lines with a chisel.

(10,11) Make a *V*-cut down both lines. This is important as it will provide a groove for the dovetail saw to slide in.

6

8

7

9

10

11

12

13

14

15

16

17

18

19

20

21

22

(12,13) Chisel out the front for the stop.

Saw the lines with the sliding dovetail saw **(14)**, which is designed for cuts like this (see p. 146).

(15) On the line that is square, keep the sawcut square or undercut just a little. The depth of the cut should be approximately ⅓ the thickness of the board, but should never exceed ½ in., no matter what the thickness is. The same is true of the tapered cut.

(16) For the tapered cut, tilt the saw to approximately 80°.

With both cuts finished **(17)**, rough-clean the groove with a chisel **(18)**.

Use the router plane **(19)** for the final cleaning of the groove so that it will have a consistent depth **(20)**.

(21) The groove is now ready to be fitted for the sliding dovetail.

(22) Mark the length of the tail with the blade in the router plane that cleaned out the groove but move it just a little back so the tail will be a little shy of the depth, to be sure the dovetail will fit tightly.

A dovetail plane **(23)** is like a rabbet plane, but the bottom is tilted about 80°. Because a dovetail is usually made on the end of a board, a knife in the front of the plane blade cuts the fibers so the blade doesn't tear up the board.

(24,25) Set the fence of the dovetail plane at the mark made with the router plane.

(26) Plane the piece to form the angled edge, and keep trying the tail in the groove to see if it fits **(27)**. When you have the piece in the groove, try and move both the back and the front up and down. If one end is looser than the other, plane off the tight end and test again. When the joint fits, you should be able to push it in by hand except for the last two or three inches (depending of course on the width.) Because the joint is tapered, it will fit tightly when the piece is hammered up to the end. So I put glue on only the last two or three inches in the front.

(28,29,30) Before gluing up, remove the piece in the front so the joint will be flush.

The finished joint, seen from the back **(31)**, after it has been glued and hammered home, and from the front **(32)**. □

23

24

25

26

27

28

29

30

31

32

a

b

c

d

e

f

1

2

3

4

5

6

Straight Sliding Dovetails, by Machine

(1) To make a sliding dovetail by machine, use a router with a dovetail bit, the same way as when making a tongue and groove (see p. 128).

Either clamp a board across the plywood router table to serve as a fence, or **(2,3)** use a board or the same *T*-square used in a tongue and groove (see p. 132) to guide the router. With this method, both sides of the groove will of course be angled. In very dense woods, it is easier to run a straight bit first to remove most of the stock.

To locate the right size for the dovetail, measure the width of the groove at the top **(4)**, and then mark the piece to be cut **(5)**.

Using the router table, set the depth of the fence to make the right size sliding dovetail. On a scrap piece of wood the same thickness as your actual pieces, run one side.

(6) For the second cut, reset the fence over the router, keeping the same side of the board up against the fence. This way, if there is a difference in the thickness of the wood to be cut, the dovetail will still be straight. Great care must be taken when setting up to make the dovetail because the groove is not tapered, and therefore it has to be exactly right or it won't work.

(7) Here again, notch out the front of the joint if you want it hidden.

(8) The joint should fit so that you can hit it in with your hands except for the last couple of inches. Then use a mallet.   ☐

7

8

a

b

c

1

Making a Sliding Dovetail Saw

To make a sliding dovetail saw **(1)**, you will need a piece of hardwood (maple, beech or fruitwood) 1 in. by 5½ in. by 13 in., and two flathead ³⁄₁₆ by 1-in. bolts with *T*-nuts. The blade can be an old band-saw or bowsaw blade. It should have ten points to the inch, although eight will do. I use a ripsaw blade, which I find cuts better and faster than a crosscut. The slots allow the blade to be set to the desired depth.   ☐

Jig to Rout Tapered Sliding Dovetails

(1) You can make a jig out of ¼-in. plywood that will enable you to make a tapered sliding dovetail slot with a router instead of by hand.

(2) Mark the full thickness of the board that is to house the tail onto the jig. In this case the board is ⅞ in. thick, and I want the depth to be ⁵⁄₁₆ in.

(3) Square the lines across. The collar in this case is ⅜ in. and the dovetail bit at its widest is ½ in., a difference of ⅛ in., which makes the bottom edge of the bit stick out ¹⁄₁₆ in. beyond the collar.

(4) Mark the line that will stay square ¹⁄₁₆ in. in from the squared lines. Square this line across.

(5) Make a mark ¹⁄₁₆ in. from the back of the other line.

1

2

3

4

5

6

7

8

9

(6) Mark ³⁄₁₆ in. in at the front end of the same line.

(7) Draw a line to connect the two points and shorten the length of the cut if you don't want the joint to show through in the front. Then cut out the center section.

(8) Here is the jig, ready to be used. It can be used over and over again for many, many cuts.

(9) With the jig clamped down to the piece that will be routed, let the router collar follow the edges of the jig.

When you make the corresponding piece, do exactly the same as when making a straight sliding dovetail by machine (see p. 144). But since this piece is tapered, I would make the final passes by hand with a dovetail plane.

Corner Tongue and Groove

The corner tongue and groove **(1)** is a good joint in solid wood or plywood. In plywood, the grain of the corner piece must run lengthwise along the edging. In solid wood, the grain must run in the same direction as the grain of the sides so the corner and sides expand and contract equally.

The grooves in the plywood are cut like a simple tongue and groove (see p. 128). The tongues in the corner pieces are a little more difficult.

(2) When marking the position of the tongue, especially if you are using plywood, place two pieces of veneer under the plywood so the solid wood sticks out a veneer thickness beyond the plywood. If it were not, you might sand through the plywood when sanding the joint.

First cut the cheeks of the two tongues. Then cutting the outside two shoulders is easy. Remember to screw a piece of wood on the fence for safety **(3)**.

(4) The first inside shoulder cut is made exactly like the outside shoulders. Of course, you will need to raise the blade to the correct height.

For the next cut, make a jig as shown **(5)**. This jig screws onto the fence. The center is cut out to clear the blade, and the bottom piece is dimensioned so the shoulder of the tongue will run over it, making an otherwise dangerous cut very safe.

Solid wood   *Plywood*

1

2

3

4

5   *Blade*

6

7

8

9

10

11

(6,7,8) The joints have now been cut. In this case I want to round the inside corner (9). The easiest way to cut the curve on the inside is to make a cove cut on the table saw before gluing up the joint.

A cove cut is made by running the piece against an angled fence made of wood and chiseled out to make room for the blade. Since the front of the blade and the back of the blade will cut the pieces at different positions the result will be a curved cut. This is something that is very hard to visualize, but once you see it done you will believe it. Clamp a piece of wood across the saw table. The angle depends on the size of the cove. I place the piece to be cut up against the angled piece, eye it out from the back, and move the angled piece until the circumference of the blade fits the curve of the cove I want (10).

In picture (11), the fence is at the wrong angle. In (12), the angle is correct. Note also that the fence fits exactly under the tongue so the piece rides securely on the fence.

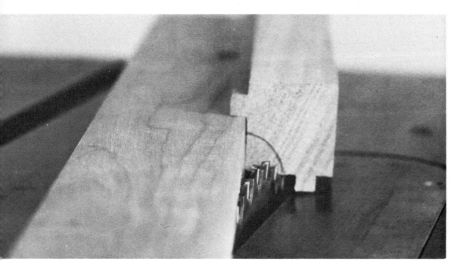

12

(13,14,15) Don't try to take the whole cut in one pass. Start slowly, and keep raising the blade so that it cuts about ⅛ in. with each pass. Leave a tiny bit of wood to allow for sanding.

(16) After sanding, glue the pieces together. Leave the outside corners square so you have something to set the clamp on when you are gluing up.

After the glue has dried, cut the corners off, then hand-plane and sand them round **(17,18)**.

If you want to hide the joint there is a little problem, especially if using plywood. The end of the corner block is end grain, which is not the best thing to glue veneer or a facing to. Before gluing any facing or veneer on, you have to glue-size the end grain. A glue size is a very thin layer of hot glue. Here it is applied to the end grain to seal the pores. If the glue has the right consistency (see p. 94), I would use about 1 part glue to 5 parts water. When the glue size dries, it will prevent the glue used to apply the facing or veneer from soaking in, and you will get a fairly good bond.   □

13

14

15

16

17

18

a

b

c

d

e

1

2

3

4

5

6

Piece 2

Piece 1

Doweled Butt Joint

I generally don't use a butt joint with dowels **(1)** but it is a stronger and more attractive joint than one with "steel dowels" (nails). If I do use the doweled butt joint I angle the dowels to add needed strength to the joint. In piece 1 the dowels are surrounded by long-grain to long-grain glue surface, a good glue joint. But in piece 2, the dowel is in mostly against end grain. So the dowels are set in at opposite angles, to act something like a dovetail. Even if the glue didn't hold, the angled dowels would hold the pieces together.

When you make the joint, first square all the ends that will be joined. Use hot glue to keep the pieces together when drilling the holes for the dowels.

(2) You can drill the holes using a brace and auger bit. Steady the auger using the weight of your body to apply some pressure. Use your head—literally. To control the depth of the hole, put a piece of masking tape on the bit at the depth you want and stop drilling when the tape reaches the surface **(3)**.

(4) You can also use an ordinary electric drill. For depth, use the tape, or even better, make a wooden guide. Drill a hole through a block of wood big enough for the bit to fit through. Cut the block to the right length. It should fit between the chuck of the drill and the depth you want to go into the wood. The bit (not including the point) should stick out the same amount as the depth you want the hole to be. This same method can be used for auger bits or any kind of drill. I prefer the block to other stops that you can buy. These are usually made out of steel and fasten to the bit or drill. When the full depth is reached, the steel stop will usually mark or scratch the surface of the wood. Using a wooden block is much better. When the block hits the surface it will stop rotating, especially if the bit or drill fits loosely into the hole in the wooden stop.

When the holes are drilled, cut off some sections of dowel longer than the finished length. Chamfer or soften the edges of the dowel so they will slide in easily without marring the edges of the holes. You can buy a dowel sharpener **(5)** to chamfer the edges. I prefer to use sandpaper **(6)**.

(7) Put the glue in the hole, not on the dowel. Don't overdo the glue—don't spatter it all over. The dowel will push the glue into the hole as it is hammered down **(8)**. If glue is put on the dowel, all the glue will be scraped off at the edge of the hole. Hardly any will get into the hole. When the glue dries, cut the dowels off flush with an offset dovetail saw.   □

7

8

1

2

3

4

5

Hidden Doweled Miter

The hidden doweled miter **(1)** is used where structure is not critical—in small boxes, cabinets, spice racks and the like—where we don't want the joint to be exposed. This joint is as strong as a half-blind tongue and rabbet (see p. 135). The hidden doweled miter is an easy joint to make. It aligns itself correctly for gluing because of the dowels. This joint works in either solid wood or plywood, but is best suited to plywood.

(2) Make the cuts and the miters first, the same way as for lock miters (see p. 137).

(3) Now drill the holes in piece 1.

You can then use dowel centers **(4)** to transfer the position of the holes in one piece to the corresponding holes in the other piece. I don't use dowel centers. It is an extra thing to buy and you usually need quite a few of each size. I use wire brads instead. They work just as fast and as well, and are considerably cheaper. And you don't need any special sizes for each hole.

(5) Hammer the brads three-quarters down into the center of where the holes will be in piece 1. I use 1-in. wire brads, #16.

(6) Then bite off the heads, leaving about ³⁄₁₆ in. sticking up.

(7) Put piece 2 in place and hit it with your fist or with a mallet to mark the holes in the corresponding piece **(8)**.

The two pieces are marked. Remove the brads and drill the holes **(9)**, using the brad marks as centers for the dowel holes.

(10) Bits come in many shapes and sizes. You can use a brace and auger bit (third from left), or an electric hand drill with a spur or spade bit (three rightmost bits). I prefer the spade bit in an electric drill.

When drilling the holes in piece 2, be sure to mark the depth on the bit **(11)** so the bit doesn't come through the outside. Use masking tape if you want to make the mark more visible.

(12) Chamfer the edges of the dowels and glue the dowels into piece 1.

(13) After the holes are drilled in piece 2, measure their depth.

(14) Mark the dowels that are already glued in piece 1. Make them shorter than the holes in the opposite piece; the amount shorter depends on the thickness of the wood used. In a ¾-in. thick piece, I would make them ¹⁄₁₆ in. shorter.

6

7

8

9

10

11

12

13

14

15

16

17

(15) Cut the dowels to length. I use an off-set dovetail saw. Again, chamfer the edges so the dowels will glide easily into the holes when you glue the joint together.

(16,17) The joint is ready to be assembled with glue on all surfaces. ☐

a

d

b

e

c

f

Doweling for Frame Joints

I would never use a dowel joint to construct a frame that needed to be very strong, but for simple frames, a dowel joint might be enough **(1)**.

Although I usually use brads instead of dowel centers to position dowel holes precisely (see p. 154), here I'll demonstrate the use of dowel centers while making a frame dowel joint. Dowel centers **(2)** are available in different sizes.

Begin making the joint by drilling holes in one of the boards, and insert the dowel center **(3)**.

(4) I usually begin in the end-grain piece. For me it is easier to line up and mark the pieces this way. But you could start with the other piece.

(5) The opposite piece is marked. If you line up the pieces correctly the dowel center will mark the exact location of a hole that will correspond with the first hole. Now drill the other holes and glue the dowels into the first piece. Be sure to hammer the dowels all the way to the bottom. Measure the depth of the hole in the second piece, and cut the dowels to length, leaving them ⅛ in. shorter than the depth of the hole. This way, the excess glue has somewhere to go.

1

2

3

4

5

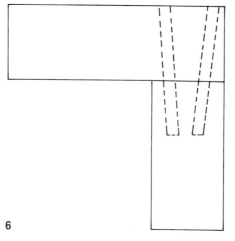

6

If I use a dowel joint, I try to make it as strong as possible, so I usually run the joint through. I don't mind the ends of the dowel showing. **(6)** This is the dowel joint I prefer. I always drill the holes at opposite angles, with the wider portion at the top, to make a "dovetail" effect. In the lower piece the dowel is surrounded by long grain, so there is a lot of strength. But in the upper piece, this is not the case. By angling the dowels, the upper piece is held securely, and a reasonably strong joint results.

(7) Before drilling the holes, glue the frame pieces together using hot glue. Drill the holes after the glue has dried enough so that the pieces won't move. Make the holes at about an 80° angle, using either a hand or machine drill. A wooden dowel jig like the one on p. 170 but made at an angle may help the beginner to drill the holes accurately.

When gluing in the dowels, it is very important to put the glue in the hole. Usually, I also put a spot of glue around the bottom edge of the dowel, which helps the dowel to slide in, and the glue pushes up as the dowel is hammered down **(8)**. □

7

8

Mortise and Tenon
Chapter 8

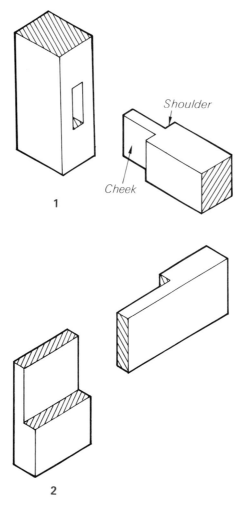

Shoulder

Cheek

1

2

Frame Joinery

The mortise and tenon is one of the oldest and most essential joints in woodworking. An Egyptian sarcophagus now in the British Museum was framed with mortise-and-tenon joints at least 5,000 years ago. During the Middle Ages, the development of the mortise permitted the framing of chests. Elaborate variations of paneling led finally to a distinction between the crafts of carpentry and cabinetmaking. In house construction, the use of the mortise and tenon has just about disappeared. We no longer have the skill or the patience, nor can we afford the time, to use mortise-and-tenon joints to frame houses. But still we find esthetic and practical satisfaction in making a well-constructed piece of furniture.

Many different types of mortise-and-tenon joints and both simple and complicated variations will be described. The joints will be made by different techniques. This is not meant to show that one technique is the best way to make each joint. All of the techniques can be interchanged from joint to joint. For example, a slip joint will be made by hand—sawn with a bowsaw. The same technique could be used for sawing any mortise and tenon. And the slip joint could be made on the circular saw. My intention is to show you as many ways as possible to make all the joints so that you can suit the techniques to your own equipment and personal choice.

A mortise-and-tenon joint should be designed and made so that it has the maximum long-grain to long-grain glue surface. The strength of the mortise-and-tenon joint depends entirely on the interplay between the cheek and shoulder of the tenon, which is the projecting part of the joint **(1)**.

If two crossed boards are glued together, they can be twisted apart relatively easily, because it's only the glue that holds them together and prevents them from twisting. The strength of the joint can be greatly increased by taking a small amount off each of the touching surfaces, thus creating shoulders to prevent twisting. The full use of such a design is called the half-lap joint **(2)**. It is the easiest frame joint to make, and is so called because usually half the amount of wood is removed from each piece. Each piece has one cheek and one shoulder. The strength is greatly increased because of the stopping action of the shoulders. The cheek is the glue surface that holds the joint together, and the shoulder, which should be tight up against the edge of the joining piece, makes it impossible for the piece to wiggle loose.

Now double the surface area of the glue by making a slip joint **(3)** — a form of mortise and tenon — and we have an extremely strong joint that is easy to make and requires minimum tools. The disadvantage of the slip joint is that not only do we have to clamp the tenon shoulder tightly against the mortise, (as in all mortise-and-tenon assembly), but we must use a second clamp to make sure the cheeks are glued to the mortise sides.

We get around these drawbacks by changing the slip to a haunched mortise **(4)** where only part of the joint is exposed, or to a mitered haunched mortise **(5)** where the tenon is completely hidden.

When designing a mortise-and-tenon joint, one should aim for the maximum glue surface. A tenon of about one-third the thickness of the stock is usually the best choice. If the tenon is thicker, the mortise sides become too thin; if the tenon is thinner, it becomes too weak. (But sometimes in table construction, where the leg is much thicker than the aprons, the aprons may have tenons half or more the apron thickness.)

Four shoulders **(6)** should never be used unless absolutely necessary. The joint becomes more difficult to fit because all four shoulders must be precisely located in the same plane. Also, glue surface is lost. On the other hand, if the design calls for carving and material will be removed around the joint, four shoulders ensure that the joint will not be revealed.

(7) If the design calls for round corners, it is advisable to glue a block on, or to have the mortise stock wider. These provisions prevent problems with the end grain, which will break and crumble, especially if carved.

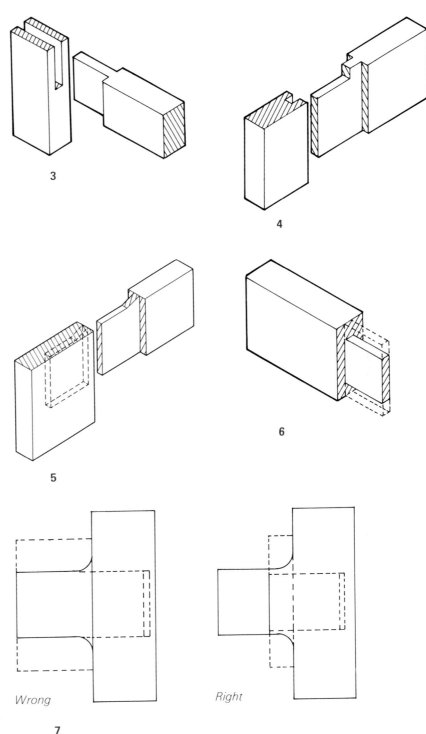

3

4

5

6

Wrong

Right

7

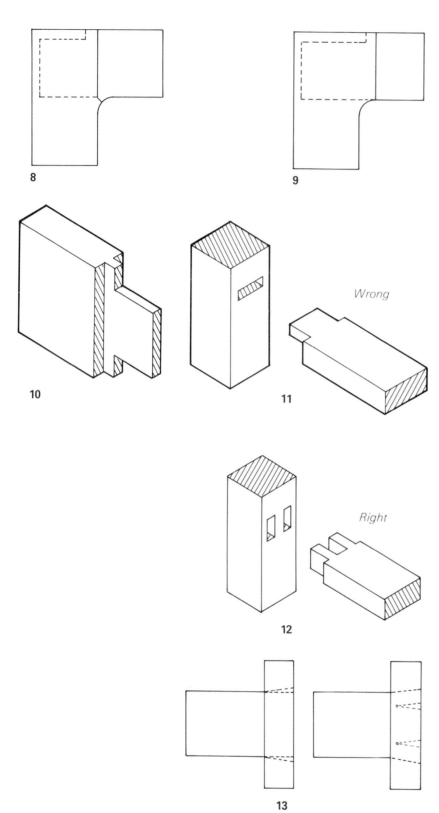

8

9

10

11

Wrong

12

Right

13

There are two different ways to make a round corner in a frame. One **(8)** is used if the inside corner is going to be carved or shaped for a molding, and the other **(9)** is fine if the edge will be left straight, because then you don't have to worry about carving into the joint. (But in fine cabinetmaking, carved or not, I would not use this joint.)

(10) When a tenon is very wide, haunches should be put in at either end. A wide tenon is more difficult to glue because it requires extra clamps for gluing the cheeks. But the haunches are necessary to keep the wood from twisting.

(11) When the stock is very narrow, the temptation is to run the tenon across the grain. But this should never be done because then the cheeks glue into end grain, which is not a glue surface. The way to join the pieces is to use double (or triple) tenons **(12)**, running the mortises in the direction of the long grain to provide good glue surface.

(13) Wedges can be used to strengthen the joint. When the tenon is cut to receive the wedge, be sure to drill a small hole at the base of each sawcut to prevent splitting. When hammering in wedges in a through tenon, be sure to hammer evenly on each wedge so as not to force one half or the other too far, which could result in splitting. If the tenon is to be hidden and wedged, use this method.

(14) If a mortise and tenon is to be disassembled, a loose wedge is used. The wedge could be replaced with a wedged dowel for the same effect. If the piece that receives the wedge is too thin, the two shoulders could be placed on the top and bottom instead of the sides.

In a chair, the back is usually one or two inches narrower than the front. This is done more for appearance than for any other reason. This requires the sides to angle into the back. Usually the angle is made in the tenon **(15)**, because it is easier than angling the mortise. Of course there is a limit to how much the tenon can be angled, but as long as some long grain reaches the full length of the tenon, it is safe. Notice that the tenon in the side apron going into the back leg is longer than the tenon in the back apron. The reason is that the joint in the side apron is more important.

(16) A variation of the slip joint is used where a third or fourth leg is necessary, as in a sofa. This is also used where a table apron is joined to the legs if the table apron is bricklaid round or oval, as in a Hepplewhite table.

14

Back

Front

15

16

(17) There are several ways to make a mitered mortise and tenon. Often a spline is used, as it is easier to cut. Sometimes a spline is used purely for visual effect. The spline can also be hidden.

(18) If a tenon should break, a spline can be inserted. The same method is often substituted for a mortise and tenon. Although it is not as strong, the spline is in most cases sufficient, and is again much easier to make.

For extra strength or for pure decoration, a cross member that joins in a half-lap can be made as a dovetail **(19)**. This joint is used a lot in post-and-beam construction. Joining a piece to a frame this way adds strength to the frame. The same joint could be made at an angle, simply by angling the shoulder cuts.

(20) If glass or a panel has to fit into the frame, the easiest way is to cut the rabbet first and then simply offset the shoulders the same amount as the rabbet. Just be sure the cheeks of the tenon line up with the rabbet.

17

18

19

20

21

The next joints are drawn as slip joints because they are easier to explain this way, but they could be made as haunched joints instead. If both pieces to be joined have a molding and will receive a panel or a piece of glass, the easiest way to get the profiles to meet is to cut them the full length of the pieces first, **(21)** cut the profiles to 45°, and then remove the rest of the profile at the joint. When I was young, we used two cutters that met perfectly, one for each side of the molding profile **(22)**, and called them male and female cutters. But today we can no longer use the sexist terms male and female, so I refer to them as person-to-person cutters. If I have to build many frames of the same pattern, I have a set of person-to-person cutters made and cut the moldings on a shaper — that would be the easiest way. You could use a router, too. With a router, first make the joint on the tenon piece, then rout the profile (in this case the negative profile) in the shoulder.

(23) If a panel is to be inserted into the frame inside a groove, try to make the tenon the same width as the groove, or at least a little bigger. Also remember to deduct the depth of the groove on the inside width of the tenon **(24)**. Be sure to remember one thing — if a solid wood panel has to be inserted into the groove, never glue the panel in. If you do glue it in, it will definitely split.

There are many other variations of the mortise and tenon, but virtually all depend on the cheek and shoulder action for their strength. Similarly, the technique used in making these joints is basically the same. □

22

23

24

1

2

3

4

5

6

7

Chopping Mortises

In making any mortise-and-tenon joint, you should always make the mortise first and the tenon last. In this case we will chop out the mortise for a mitered haunched mortise and tenon **(1)**. The joint is completely hidden. Besides being hidden, this joint has the advantage of not needing a clamp across the cheeks. Because wood is left on the top of the mortise, the cheeks will be pulled in tight on their own. It is a good idea to keep the piece with the haunched mortise longer than you will need, to lessen the chance of it splitting when the pieces are glued up. You can cut off the excess after the pieces are glued together.

To chop out this mortise (or any mortise) with chisels, use a heavy-duty mortising chisel **(2-left)**. The steel is considerably thicker than that of a normal chisel. The chisel for making a ⅜-in. mortise is about ⅜ in. thick. The two sides are parallel, so once the chisel is started correctly it will guide itself to make a straight cut. The chisel can be used after holes have been drilled, to clean out the excess and square up the holes. I find, though, that the chisel works just as well without predrilling.

(2-right) The swan-neck chisel is like the heavy-duty mortise chisel, but the lower part is rounded to clean up the bottom of a mortise. Both chisels are sharpened like regular chisels, with the bevel at 30° (see p. 35).

(3) Locate the position of the mortise. (I'm using lines on the side for clarity). To set the width of the mortise, mark the board by hammering down the mortise chisel.

(4) Set the marking gauge to the width of the chisel mark and scribe.

(5) Mark the depth the mortise will be onto the chisel, using a piece of tape.

(6) Start to chisel out the center of the mortise. Work toward the edges until the chisel is down to the right depth.

(7) At the bottom of the mortise, undercut slightly to help ensure that the tenon will go in easily.

(8) Clean out the hole with the swan-neck chisel.

(9) Never use a chisel with your other hand in front of the tool, as demonstrated in this picture. Sooner or later, you are sure to cut yourself.

(10) After the mortise is cleaned out, the miter can be chiseled out and the mortise is finished.

(11) The tenon is marked with the marking gauge, and then cut with the bowsaw (see pp. 180-181).

I cut the cheeks of the tenon and the bevel before cutting the shoulders **(12)**.

(13) Now the joint is finished and is ready to assemble.   □

8

9

10

11

12

13

1

2

3

4

5

6

Drilling Mortises

Mortises can also be drilled out. I prefer auger bits **(1)** for hand-drilling. The drills come in different sizes. The center of an auger bit is longer than normal, and it is threaded to help pull the bit down. The other end is square to fit into the chuck of a brace. Auger bits will not fit into electric drills. Sometimes auger bits are hard to start in end grain. The end grain is often so hard that even the screwing action of the threaded end and the weight of your body are not enough to force the bit down. If that is the case, put a little water or spit at the start of the hole, and the wood will expand enough to give the thread a chance to grab.

(2) This is a brace. It is designed to hold drill and screwdriver bits. The smooth, round top handle spins easily. In this picture you can also see a piece of wood with a center hole drilled out. This is used as a depth stop (see p. 152). It is easy to make and doesn't mark up the surface of the wood the way steel stops often do.

(3) I use my head and hand to force the bit down. That is one time using my head comes in handy.

(4) When using any bit free-hand, mark the center of the mortise and the diameter of the bit. Drill the outside two holes first, to be sure to get clean, straight holes. If you try to drill the end holes after the center holes are drilled, the bit will tend to slide into the center holes, and you won't get a straight-sided mortise. Then continue drilling the rest of the holes. To control the depth, I use a piece of tape or a wooden stop like the one in picture **2**.

(5) A doweling jig can be used to guide the bit, but for some reason I cannot find a doweling jig and a set of auger bits in this country that fit together. I have tried sets manufactured by the same company, and was very frustrated when the auger would not fit into the corresponding bit guide. I finally gave up and made my own (see p. 170). Of course, an electric drill with a stop will do the job much faster.

(6) After all the holes are drilled to the right depth, mark the outside of the holes with a marking gauge.

(7,8) Use a wide chisel to clean the sides of the mortise.

(9,10) Then, using a chisel the same width as the bit, square the ends and clean the rest of the mortise. A heavy-duty mortise chisel and a swan-neck chisel of the right width could be used instead (see p. 166).

(11) A drill press can also be used for drilling mortises. In that case I would clamp a board to the table to act as a fence for the piece to slide against.

An attachment is available for most drill presses that holds a square hollow chisel. Or you can buy a mortiser **(12,13,14)**, a specialized machine designed solely to cut square holes. It uses a hollow chisel bit. The bed slides from right to left and moves backwards and forwards, and up and down, making positioning and cutting the mortise very simple.

With a square hollow chisel, the drill is inside and drills the hole while the chisel squares the hole. I have found these attachments to be fine for soft wood, and I mean soft wood. In hardwoods, the chisel has a tendency to get stuck in the first two outside holes. But after those are drilled, it is easy to drill the rest of the holes. ☐

7

8

9

10

11

12

13

14

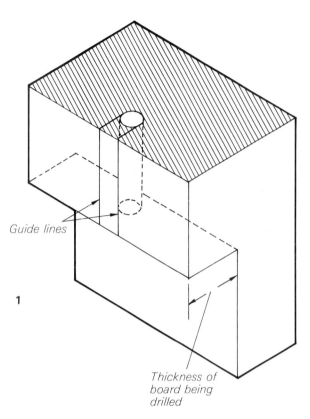

Guide lines

1

Thickness of
board being
drilled

Wooden Doweling Jig

The wooden doweling jig **(1)** is made from a piece of hardwood thicker than the piece you will be drilling into.

(2) Mark off the thickness of the piece that is to be drilled into.

(3) Then mark off a hole in the center and drill that hole through the end grain, using the same bit you plan to use to drill the mortise. If the hole is drilled by hand, it would be advisable to mark the center of the other end of the piece and drill halfway in from both ends.

(4) Then remove the area that is shaded.

(5) The diameter of the bit is marked on the outside of the block to locate the hole easily. The jig gets clamped to the piece **(6)**. I find it works very well. □

2

3

6

4

5

Long-Hole Boring Machine

(1) A long-hole boring machine, or slot mortiser, is like a drill press lying on its side, so the drill is horizontal. Instead of a drill, use a long router bit. In front of the bit is a table that can move up and down, in and out and sideways. The piece that will receive the mortise is clamped down to this table. This machine is one of the fastest ways to mortise—much faster than with a hollow chisel bit. The only thing to watch with the long-hole borer is that if the hole is drilled too fast or forced to take off too much in one pass, the drill will whip, and the mortise sides will not be straight. Here again, drill the two outside holes first.

(2) Then move the table from side to side and in and out, slowly removing the excess between the holes, nearly the way you would if you were using a router. Here, though, the machine stays in place and the work is moved.

(3) The mortise is finished. This one will be used for a haunched mortise and tenon joint.   □

1

2

3

1

2

3

4

5

6

7

8

9

Routing Mortises

Routing is a fast and easy way to make a mortise if it does not have to be very deep. **(1)** Screw a piece of wood to the router fence. The piece has to be at least 1 in. wider than the length of the bit sticking out above the router plate. This way the fence can guide the router as the bit is dropped into the piece.

(2) Start the router and lower it down all the way. **(3)** With the fence tight up against the piece, slide the router until the whole mortise is made.

(4) Stop the router motor before lifting the bit out of the mortise.

(5) The mortise is much smoother than if made with a hollow chisel bit.

Be sure to move the router in the right direction so the bit is cutting in the mortise away from the fence. This will pull the fence tightly up against the piece being cut. If the router is moved in the opposite direction, the cutting action will be toward the fence, which will push the fence away from the piece. If you then try to force the fence against the piece, the router will be fighting you and the inside mortise will be very uneven. This picture **(6)** show what happens if the fence is not tight up against the piece. If you are not sure which direction to move the router in, try the router on a scrap piece. Don't push the fence all the way up against the piece. Move the router in both directions. In only one direction the fence will be pulled in up against the piece. This is the right direction. The router will tell you which way to move.

(7) The corners of the tenon can be rasped round, or the ends of the mortise can be squared with a chisel. I find rounding the tenon faster than squaring the mortise.

(8) If a tenon breaks, a spline can be inserted. The same method is often substituted for a mortise and tenon. It is not as strong, but in most cases is sufficient. It is much easier to make, especially with compound miters.

(9) Make the mortise in both pieces using a long-hole boring machine or router. Then fit the spline. □

Making Tenons
Chapter 9

1

2

3

4

5

6

7

a

b

c

Half-Lap Joint, on a Table Saw

The safest way to make a half-lap joint on a table saw is to use a tenoning jig. The tenoning jig **(1)** is an attachment for the circular saw that fits into a groove in the top of the saw table normally used for the miter gauge. The upper plate that supports the work is 90° to the table, so that the work can run over the blade in a vertical position. On the right side of the jig, a screw or vise holds the piece to the upper plate. The position of the screw can be adjusted using a wrench, so that the screw clamps the wood in the center.

(2) The whole upper plate can be moved in and out from the sawblade to position the piece correctly for the cut. It will always be parallel to the sawblade.

To cut the half-lap joint, raise the sawblade to the width of the opposite piece to be joined. Set the tenoning jig so the blade cuts half the thickness of the piece, with the thickness of the sawblade on the waste side **(3)**. Make the cut for the cheek. Do the same for the second piece.

(4) With the cheeks cut, lower the sawblade to half the thickness of the piece. Remove the waste piece, using the miter gauge to push the work through.

(5) If you use the fence as a stop to guide placement of the cut, clamp a piece to the fence. Guide off this piece **(6)**, and you will control the length of the cut while preventing the cut-off piece from getting trapped between the blade and the fence and shooting back at you.

(7) This cutting method gives you a very clean, quick and accurate half-lap joint. ☐

Half-Lap Joint, with Router

(1) The half-lap joint can also be in the middle of a board.

(2) Set the router bit depth to half the thickness of the board to be joined. A ¼-in. straight bit is fine, although you could use a larger one, too. (You might notice that one side of the plate on my router is flat. I did not buy it that way. Once, I forgot to put some grooves in a cabinet, and I had to make them after the cabinet was glued together. Some of the grooves were close to the joining piece, so close that I had to remove the handle and cut a piece off the base so the router would fit in. Being a cheapskate, I never bought another base. But I have never missed the part I cut off in 20 years of using the router. It works just as well and serves as a good reminder.)

(3) Measure from the cutting edge of the bit to the edge of the router baseplate. In this case the distance is 2⅞ in., although the camera angle makes it appear 2¾ in.

(4) Mark the piece for the shoulder.

(5) From the shoulder, mark in toward the other end 2⅞ in., or whatever the distance you measured on your router, and **(6)** square the line across the piece.

(7) Clamp a piece of wood right on the line.

(8) Run the edge of the router plate against the clamped-on board, and make the first cut.

(9) If you made a router *T*-square for cutting tongue-and-groove joints (see p. 132), use that instead. This way, you have to mark only where the shoulder is, and set the *T*-square to the mark with the router cut in the waste side.

Clamp the square down and make the first cut. Now rout out the rest of the excess wood, starting at the end of the board so you don't cut out all the stock the router is riding on **(10)**. Repeat the process on all the pieces to be joined. When you finish, the pieces are ready to be glued together.

1
2
3
4
5
6
7
8
9
10

11

12

9"

12"

2⅞" 2⅞"

1⅞"

8¼"

(11) If a piece has to join inside the frame for strength, a variation of the half-lap can be made.

(12,13) If you have several joints to make, it is worthwhile to build one of these jigs. The inside cut-out is the size of the joint plus 2⅞ in. more (or the distance from the cutting edge of the router bit to the edge of the base on your router) in each direction. Change these dimensions to fit your router-and-bit combination and the size joint you are working. This jig was made for the joint to go all the way across the width of the piece, but by moving out the piece of wood underneath the plywood, the joint can be made to go only partway in, as shown in drawing 11.

(14) Clamp the jig to the board and use the router, letting the base edges guide against both sides of the jig. Clean out the rest of the wood by moving the router back and forth **(15)**.

(16) One part of the half-lap is finished, and the jig is still on.   □

13

14

15

16

a

b

c

d

e

f

Half-Lap Joint, with Router Plane

If you make half-lap joints by hand, begin by marking two lines where the pieces will intersect. Set the router plane to the depth of half the thickness of the board and draw the blade along both sides of the cut to mark the depth **(1)**.

(2) Saw the two outside cuts down to the halfway line, with the saw kerf on the waste side.

(3) To make it easier to chisel out the excess, I also saw an *X* in the center.

(4,5) Rough-chisel the waste wood out.

(6) For the final cut, use the router plane to even up the depth and make a smooth surface.

(7) The joint is finished.   □

1

2

3

4

5

6

7

1

2

3

4

5

Half-Lap Joint, with Dado Head

A dado head can be used on the circular saw to make the half-lap joint. Set the height of the dado to exactly half the thickness of the wood **(1)**.

Mark the width of the cut. If many pieces are to be cut, use stops so all the widths are the same.

Make the two outside cuts first **(2)**.

(3) Then clean out the remaining wood, and **(4)** one piece is finished.

(5) The opposite part can also be made using a dado head. In this case, the dado head was not sharpened right. One of the spacers was longer than the other, causing ridges in the cut. ☐

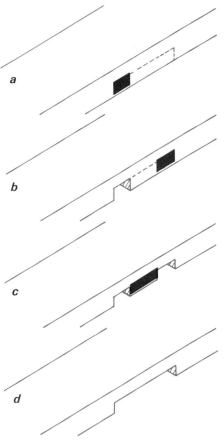

a

b

c

d

Half-Lap Joint, on the Band Saw

Use the widest blade the band saw can take, preferably at least ¾ in. wide.

(1) Clamp a board to the table to use as a fence. Set it for the distance of the cut of the cheek. Be sure the fence is parallel to the groove in the table and that it is square to the table. If the band saw has a fence attachment, you should of course use that.

(2) Clamp a stop for the back of the cut to the fence.

(3,4) Make the cheek cut.

(5) Using a miter gauge and a stop, make the shoulder cut and the joint is finished. This is a fast way to make the joint. The cut should be clean, but may not be as clean as if it were made on a circular saw.   □

1

2

3

4

5

1

Slip Joint, with Bowsaw

The slip joint **(1)** is like a half-lap joint with two cheeks and two shoulders on each tenon piece. This doubles the glue surface and makes a very strong joint. The slip joint is easy to make, but like the half-lap, has the disadvantage of needing a lot of clamps to glue up correctly.

(2) When you glue together pieces that join in a slip joint you will have to clamp the joint in the direction of both the shoulders and the cheeks. So in a frame, you would need four clamps to get the shoulders tight, and four more to make sure the cheeks are clamped together. When you clamp the cheeks, use a block of wood under the clamp so you don't mar the pieces. It is advisable to put paper between the blocks and the frame so that the blocks are easier to remove if the glue should get underneath.

(3,4) Mark the two pieces on all four sides for the depth of the mortise and tenon. In a slip joint, this is the full width of the opposite joining part. Mark the face of the wood with an X, so that in laying out the joint, all pieces are marked from the same face. This ensures that the joints will go together perfectly, even if the two pieces differ slightly in thickness.

(5) Using a marking gauge, lay out the tenons on both edges and the ends of both pieces. Mark down to the line of the shoulders and the bottom of the tenon. You can also use a double marking gauge or two simple marking gauges at different settings. The important thing is to mark everything from the same face. Never mark from one face first and then from the back face. The same rule is good to follow when you use the circular saw. It is much more accurate to make two settings using the same face as reference than to turn the piece around and have only one setting.

Once the pieces are marked, clamp them in the vise at an angle. The trick to cutting accurate cheeks is to cut the back line and part of the top first, then turn the pieces around and use these cuts to guide the saw when making the final cuts **(6)**.

2

3

4

6

5

7

(7) The sawcut is on the waste side, just splitting the line in half. The piece to the right is the tenon, so the cuts are on the outside of the line. The piece to the left is the mortise, so the cuts are on the inside of the line.

(8) Turn the boards around and cut the rest of the top and front lines. Remember, leave the saw lying loosely in your hand and the saw will easily follow the sawcut in the back.

I have found a trick to improve the accuracy of the fit of the shoulders. This trick is especially useful for beginners. Essentially, you are making a small mini-shoulder for the saw to lean against. Scribe the line of the shoulders using a scratch awl **(9)**.

(10) Deepen the shoulder line by drawing the corner of a chisel along the line. The first pass should be very light, and more pressure should be applied successively in two or three more passes.

(11) Turn the chisel around and cut a second line at an angle, making a small half-*V* **(12)**.

(13) This *V* serves as a guide for the saw.

(14) Chisel out the center cut for the mortise from both sides. Undercut slightly, as in making dovetails.

(15) The joint is ready to glue together. I was lucky again—it fit perfectly. □

8

9

10

11

12

13

14

15

Tapered Slip Joint

Wood moves differently, depending on what part of the tree it comes from. In a slip joint **(1)**, pieces a and b will move differently. If veneer is applied to the face of this joint, the differences in expansion and contraction will cause the joint eventually to telegraph through the veneer, showing a sharp line.

(2,3) By using the tapered slip joint shown here, telegraphing will be minimized. The difference in movement is reduced where the thin edge of the mortise meets with the shoulder, and the difference will appear as a slight curve rather than a sharp line on the veneer.

(4) A tapered slip joint that will be veneered over is laid out as in this picture.

(5) Here is the joint glued together. If I had only a few frames to make, I would cut the joints by hand with a bowsaw exactly as when making a regular slip joint (see p. 180).

If you want to make this joint by machine, use a table saw. Tilt the blade to the desired angle for the tenon, and make a jig out of wood to hold the mortise pieces at an angle for the cut **(6,7)**. The jig angle is the same as for the angles of the mortise.

(8) Here the piece is inserted in the jig.

To hold the wood for making the cuts, I find it easiest to use the jig made for cutting tongue-and-groove joints (see p. 131). Or use the tenoning jig. **(9)** Clamp the tapered jig and the piece to be cut to the jig that sits over the fence.

(10,11) With the blade vertical and the tenoning jig in place, cut the tapered mortise first, with the piece clamped to the tapered jig.

Then without the tapered jig, cut the other side of the mortise.

(12) Now cut the tapered cheek of the tenon with the blade at an angle.

Change the blade back to vertical, cut the other cheek of the tenon, and then the two shoulder cuts (as described in the section on half-lap joints — see p. 174). ☐

9

10

11

12

1

2

3

4

5
6

7

Tenons, with Miter Saw and Plane-Iron Jig

A fast and easy way to make small tenons by hand is to use a miter box and saw, and a special jig that consists of a block of wood with a hole in it, a plane iron, a screw, and two small blocks of wood.

(1) A miter saw is a large backsaw that is inserted into a guide in the front and the back. The saw can be set to make cuts at different angles. The table and the back fence are square. To hold the piece of wood firmly, the face of the table is a little bit rough. There is a stop that can be set for any length cut. The depth of the cut is controlled by setting the saw so that it cannot cut below a certain point. Each miter box works a little differently. How to set and operate each type is described thoroughly in the pamphlet that comes with the saw. If you get a used saw and there are no instructions, try out the adjustments and it will become obvious which knob or screw adjusts which setting.

(2,3) Using the depth stops, set the saw to make the right depth cuts for the shoulders.

(4) Set the stop for the correct length.

(5) Cut all the shoulders. Now we are ready to use the plane-iron jig (see p. 186).

(6) Clamp the jig to the bench with the hole to the outside so the waste can fall through. Set the blade to the right position.

(7) Secure the blade by tightening the screw. For fine adjusting, the screw can be tightened a little more and the blade will bend slightly. Don't tighten it too much.

Hold the piece with the tenon down against the jig and hit the back end with a wooden mallet **(8,9)**.

(10) The cheek is cut.

(11) Do the same on the other side, and the tenon is finished.

This is the safest way to make a tenon by hand. However, the grain in the tenon has to be straight or it might not cut cleanly. I use this jig only on small tenons, and usually where a lot of pieces have to be inserted close together, such as in a gate. It is surprising how well the tenons come out. If you use this system, I would advise making a couple of extra pieces in case one or two of the tenons don't work out.   ☐

8

9

10

11

a

b

c

1

Plane-Iron Jig

The plane-iron jig **(1)** is used to cut tenons quickly.

(2) Here the plane-iron jig is disassembled. The large hole allows the waste to fall through. The block that goes across is movable and controls the height of the blade (and therefore the cut). When the screw is tightened, the block with the hole prevents the blade from moving.

(3) A *T*-nut is inserted in the bottom of the jig. A *T*-nut has a threaded hole and sharp metal points that can be hammered into a piece of wood and will stay in place.

(4,5) *T*-nuts come in a variety of screw and thread sizes, and are used frequently in furniture that is meant to disassemble easily.

(6) Here the jig is assembled. □

2

3

4

5

6

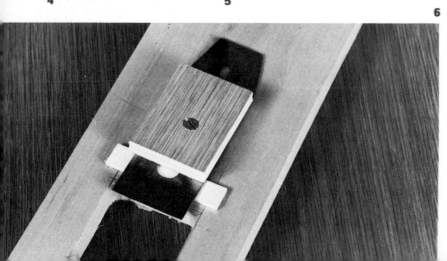

Tenons on a Table Saw, Using Two Blades

The tenon is made exactly like the half-lap joint (see p. 174), but two settings have to be made because there are two cheeks and shoulders. Always make the mortise first.

To cut a tenon on the circular saw with only one blade and a tenoning jig (see p. 174), make the first cut **(1)**, then reset for the second cut **(2)**. Don't flip the wood around, because there might be a difference in the thickness.

(3) An easier way to cut tenons on the circular saw is to use two sawblades of exactly the same diameter. Make washers the same size as the different tenons you need, corresponding with the bit you use to make the mortises. These washers can be made out of steel, aluminum or wood. If you use wood, be sure the two blades clamp up against end grain so humidity will not change the thickness of the washer.

(4) Put both blades on the arbor with the washers in between.

(5) Clamp the wood in the tenoning jig and make both cheek cuts at the same time. Then cut the shoulders as described in half-lap joints.   □

2

3

1

a

b

c

4

5

1

4

5

6

2

3

7

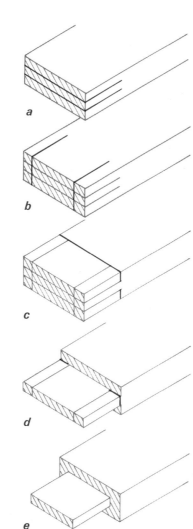

a

b

c

d

e

Tenons on a Table Saw, Using One Blade

A fast way to make tenons, which I have been using for years, is to use the fence instead of the tenoning jig. This technique is not nearly as safe, and I would not recommend it for beginners. Wait until you are familiar with the circular saw. Don't use pieces that are too wide, and use only one sawblade.

(1) Screw a piece of plywood to the fence that is wide enough so your hands will be above the blade. Then cut the cheeks. Here I am making a four-shouldered joint.

(2,3) With two cheeks cut, I make the other two vertical cuts. For safety, I use a miter gauge behind the piece.

(4) Then I cut the four shoulders. Use a stop as for half-lap joints (see p. 174) to ensure that all four shoulders are precisely in the same plane **(5)**.

(6) I have an old Danish machine for cutting tenons. I am sorry to say it isn't available any more. It has two knives, a track that is bolted to the table on which a sleigh slides, and a clamp that holds the wood down.

(7) With the piece of wood secured and the shaper turned on, the sleigh is pushed forward. A spacer between the knives allows both cheeks and both shoulders to be cut in one sweep. With a little engineering, a track and a sleigh could be designed to fit any shaper. For small production, it would be worthwhile to invest the money, because so much time is saved making tenons this way. □

Tenons at an Angle

(1) In a chair, the back is usually 1 in. or 2 in. narrower than the front. This is done more for appearance than for any other reason. This means the sides will angle into the back. Usually the angle is in the tenon—it is easier to make an angled tenon than an angled mortise. There is a limit to how much a tenon can be angled. As long as some long grain reaches the full length of the tenon, it is strong enough. (In critical cases you can angle the mortise, but that is much more difficult. I would make a special jig to hold the stock at an angle for the router or mortising machine.)

Making an angled tenon is just as easy as making a straight tenon. **(2)** Tilt the two blades to the correct angle and make the cut as if it were straight. If you use only one blade, set both cuts from the same side of the board and lower the blade for the lower cut.

To cut the shoulders, if using two sawblades, remove one sawblade and the washer. Leave the blade at the same angle as when cutting the cheeks. Set the blade to the right height, and using the miter gauge, make the shoulder cut **(3)**, which is perpendicular to the cheek.

(4) For the other shoulder, keep the same blade tilt, but lower the blade. Move the miter gauge to the opposite slot in the table. Set the piece so the blade is exactly in line with the other shoulder. Then make the cut. □

Front

Back

1

2

3

4

a

b

c

1

2

3

4

Assembling a Mortise and Tenon

(1) To make the joint easier to assemble, cut the corner in the width of the tenon.

To test the fit of the tenon, push it in the mortise by hand, using only the weight of your body to force it in. If you have to use a hammer, the tenon is too tight and the mortise could split. If the tenon is too loose, glue a piece of veneer or a thin piece of wood to one or both cheeks and saw it again on the table saw. If you make the cut with a bowsaw, you will need a thicker piece of wood so the thickness of the blade is secured on both sides.

(2) Remember always to plane and sand the inside edges of the frame before gluing it together. It'll be much more difficult afterwards.

(3) When gluing, put the glue in the mortise, especially on the top edges. When the tenon slides into the mortise it will push the glue ahead of it.

(4) I also put a little glue on the end of the tenon. The glue will be pushed up as the tenon slides in. Don't put too much glue on either piece or it will be all over the bench, the floor and you. And the excess glue will be forced up to the surface and could split the joint. □

Mitered Frame Joints
Chapter 10

1

Jig for Cutting Miters

A fast and accurate way to cut a 45° corner is on the circular saw. A special jig **(1)** makes the procedure easy and foolproof. The jig is made exactly like the jig for cutting square cut-offs (see p. 43). Fit two pieces into the grooves in the top of the saw table, and screw and glue them underneath a piece of plywood. Then make a cut halfway through, and attach a piece of hardwood at exactly 45° to the cut. Then fasten on another piece of hardwood, mitered square to the first piece. Check the angle with a square.

(2) Make sure that the two pieces are also square to the surface of the plywood.

When you use the jig, always cut one piece on one side of the jig **(3)**, and the mating piece on the other **(4)**. This way, you can be sure the two will come out square. □

2

3

4

Frame Spline Miters

There are several ways to make a mitered frame joint. A strong and easy way is with an exposed spline **(1)**.

(2) Cut the miters and apply hot glue to the edges. Make sure the glue isn't too thin.

(3) Put a piece of paper under the joint. Rub the two surfaces together while the glue is still hot. Work fast and rub hard so that all the excess glue gets squeezed out. Stop rubbing as soon as the excess is squeezed out and the glue is cold. The joint will stay together. You won't need to use any clamps. After an hour or two the joint will be strong enough for cutting the spline.

(4,5) A jig holds the mitered pieces while you cut out the spline slots. This piece should be fairly wide to get a large enough 90° section cut out of it. Use a handsaw or band saw.

(6) Put the jig against the fence. Raise the sawblade as high as it will go without coming through the inside of the joint.

Ideal depth

Spline

1

2

3

4

5

6

7

8

9

10

11

12

(7) Set the fence so the blade will cut through the center of the frame. (Sometimes you may wish to use more than one spline.) Or if you need a thicker spline, use a dado head to cut the slot.

(8) Hold the mitered piece down firmly in the jig, and push the jig through the blade. The spline slot will be cut into the mitered piece.

(9) A safer but more time-consuming way to hold the piece is to clamp the jig to the over-the-fence tenoning jig used for tongue-and-groove joints (see p. 131).

(10) Once the kerf is made, fit a piece for the spline and glue it in, with the grain running across the cut. Make splines on a circular saw or by putting them through a thickness planer (with a board underneath if they are less than ¼ in. thick).

(11) I would advise that you clamp the spline in to get a tight joint.

(12) The joint is finished. Contrasting wood splines make it decorative. In a thick piece, several splines can be used. □

a

b

c

d

e

f

g

Miter Box

A miter box with a saw is costly. You can make an inexpensive box **(1)** out of ¾-in. or 1-in. stock that will work just as well. Make the side pieces about 3 in. wide, and the bottom 5 in. wide. Be sure the bottom is the same width throughout its length (so the sides will sit parallel) and that the sides are the same height throughout, too.

(2) Attach the side pieces a little lower than the bottom, so that the box will be more stable. Once the side pieces are aligned, glue and nail them on.

(3) The side pieces must be square to the bottom.

For the square saw slot in the box, draw a square line across the top and down both side pieces. For the 45° cut, measure the width of the box (in this case, 6½ in.). Mark off a distance that is exactly the same as the width measurement. Square the lines across at each end. **(4)** Draw lines between the two outside points of the square on each diagonal.

(5) Once everything is marked, cut the angled saw slot. Hold the saw so that it matches the point on the back piece and the line down the front side simultaneously. Finish the sawcut the opposite way, and you will have a perfect cut. This is essentially the same method used to make tenons by hand (see pp. 180-181).

(6) If the box is to be used along with the plane-iron jig for slicing tenon shoulders, place a piece of wood in the bottom of the box of the right thickness to control the depth of the cut, and clamp a block of wood at the right distance to make a stop for the correct length. □

1

2

3

4

5

6

1

Block Plane

The block plane (**1**) is designed to plane end grain.

The screw in the front of the plane adjusts the slot in the front (**2**) where the shavings come through.

The plane adjusts and the iron is secured exactly like any other steel plane, but there is no chipbreaker, and the blade is actually inserted upside down with the bevel facing up (**3**). Also, the blade is tilted at a much smaller angle.

If a joint is not perfect (**4**), you can straighten it out with a block plane.

(**5,6**) With the wood secured in a vise, the surface is planed smooth and the angle corrected. The block plane works better if held at an angle.

(**7**) The joint is corrected and ready to be glued. □

2

3

4

5

6

7

Hidden Spline Miter, on a Table Saw

(1) The spline miter can also be hidden from the outside but exposed on the inside.

(2,3) Cut the slot with a dado head or saw-blade and the tenoning jig with a stop (see p. 174).

With the piece clamped to the jig, push the jig to the stop and one cut is made **(4)**. Here the spline must be exactly in the center because the two pieces are clamped to the jig from opposite faces.

(5) Both cuts are made and are ready for the spline. Because the cut does not go all the way through on the outside, the cut will be rounded at the end. The end of the spline will have to be cut round to fit.

(6) The spline is fitted in the joint and **(7)** the joint is ready to be glued. This joint could also be made using a router. ☐

1

2

3

4

5

6

7

a

b

c

d

1

3

Hidden Spline Miter, with a Router

(1) Another quite strong miter can be made that is completely hidden from both sides. It is quick and easy to make using the long-hole boring machine or a router, which I am using here.

(2) When the miters are cut, rout a slot in each mitered piece using the wooden fence as a guide, exactly as if making mortises. The router bit may wander when first inserted into the wood, as in the piece on the left in picture 3. To avoid this, raise the bit up beyond the plate, place the router on the piece to be cut, start it and then lower the bit to the desired depth. Then rout out the slot, stop the router and remove it. The drawback to this method is that it takes two people. Cut from the same face on both pieces.

(3) Make a spline to fit, and **(4)** the joint is ready to go together.   ☐

2

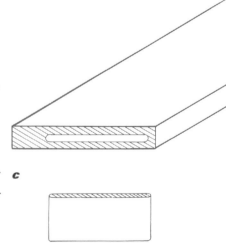

4

a

b

c

d

Hidden Mitered Mortise and Tenon

To make a hidden mitered mortise-and-tenon joint **(1)**, miter the ends of both pieces that will be joined.

Make the mortise by one of the methods described earlier (see pp. 166-172).

(2) Clamp the tenon piece to the jig that rides over the fence, or use the tenoning jig that can be purchased for the saw. Be sure the 45° surface rests tightly on the saw table. After the cheeks are cut, cut the shoulders.

(3) Mark the tenon to the right length so it fits the mortise.

(4) Cut off the excess, and the joint is ready to assemble.

(5) The mortise-and-tenon construction is hidden on the finished miter. □

1

2

Joint Where Two Pieces Cross

If you are making a joint where both pieces meet in the center, as in a cross, a half-lap joint might not look very good. **(1)** Here, for example, the striped lines match, and a half-lap joint **(2)** would ruin the effect.

To make the joint **(3)** cut the four pieces 45° from both sides **(4,5)**.

3

Be sure the point is exactly centered in the width of the wood **(6)**.

(7) Clamp the pieces in the *V*-cut jig that slides along the fence (see p. 193).

(8) Slice the piece for a spline the same way as when adding a spline to a 45° butt-jointed frame (see p. 194).

(9) When all four pieces are cut, insert a plywood spline, and glue and clamp the pieces together. ☐

4

5

6

7

8

a

b

c

9

d (x 4)

Three-Way Miter, at End

A three-way 45° joint where three pieces meet at right angles **(1)** is very difficult to make. But it is useful for making parsons tables and the like. All the pieces have to be exactly square and the same size and thickness. The circular saw blade must be square to the table, and the 45° miter gauge setting or jig must be accurate. I suggest that you make a full-scale drawing of the side and front view of the piece to refer to for your exact measurements. I made a small table here to show how the joint is glued together, and I had one of those days. I goofed up one piece three times and the table got smaller and smaller. So if it doesn't work for you the first time, don't feel bad.

If the pieces are to meet at the end, cut all three pieces alike. **(2)** Cut the ends to 45°.

(3) For the second cut, turn the piece so the first 45° cut faces up.

When you set a stop for the second cut, make sure that the cut is made so that it meets exactly with the corner of the square piece **(4)**.

Cut all the pieces the same way. Then use a router with a jig **(5,6)** like the one for making multiple spline miters (see p. 112) — but here there is only one slot on each angled face. If you have a long-hole boring machine or a mortiser, you can cut the slots more easily and precisely.

(7,8) Chisel the corners square and make the splines.

(9) The joint is finished and ready to glue.

(10) I finally got lucky and made that joint fit. A web clamp covers part of the joint. □

1

2

3

4

5

6

Three-Way Miter, in Middle

When three pieces meet at right angles but not at the end of the pieces, the three-way miter joint is considerably harder to make. A lot more machine setup is involved.

(1) If you are using a three-way joint at both the end and at the center, make sure you position the second joint so the piece will go in the same direction as on the top joint.

Tilt the sawblade to 45° and set it to the right height so the bottom of the V-cut is precisely in the middle of the piece. Be sure the miter gauge is at 90°. Then make the first two cuts **(2,3)**.

Turn the piece around, put a stop on (clamped to the fence), and make the next two cuts **(4,5)**.

Then make the mortises in the cuts for the splines. **(6)** So the two pieces will fit the joint mate, make them as for the joint where two pieces cross (see p. 200).

(7,8) Because the two pieces have to meet in the corner, the insides of the pieces also have to be cut to 45°.

(9,10) The joint is ready to be glued.   ☐

7

8

9

10

a

b

c

d

e

a

b

c

d

e

1

2

3

Gluing Up a Three-Way Miter

If you make a table that uses three-way miter joints, gluing up can be a very difficult task. It's less hectic to do it in two stages.

(1) First glue up the joints that are not on the ends. (In this table, these joints are in the lower apron.) Use a strap or band clamp to pull the pieces in snugly. The other joint (here the upper apron) has to be clamped, too, but should not be glued. Check the table for squareness.

(2) When the glue is dry, the other joint can be glued, using a strap clamp and bar clamps. Again, check for squareness.

(3) If you have help and can work fast, the whole table could be glued in one shot, but I wouldn't recommend trying it. □

Book Designer: Roger Barnes
Photographers: Rosanne Somerson, Roger Birn
Layout and Illustrations: Blackbirch Graphic Arts
Additional Illustrations: Christopher Clapp
Typeface: Compugraphic Univers 9 point

Contents

Acknowledgments

Almost two years after my first book was published, I finally finished this one — a far cry from my original agreement with The Taunton Press to write three woodworking books in 1½ years. Even with practice, it still takes a lot of time to write a book, and a lot of patience from the people who worked with me. I am especially grateful to John Dunnigan for helping to edit the text, to Roger Birn for taking the photographs, and to my wife, Emma, for being the extra pair of hands throughout the work. And a special thanks, too, to Dr. Peder Estrup for translating the chemical stains in the finishing chapter from Danish to English.

Bending
Chapter 1

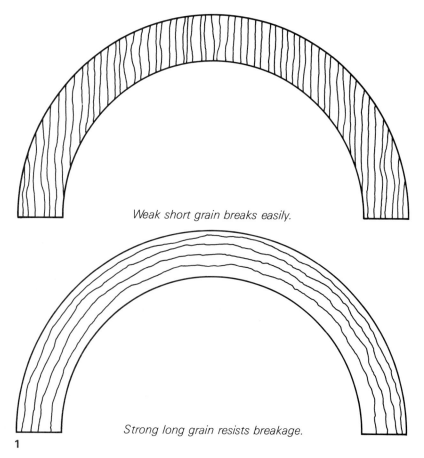

Weak short grain breaks easily.

Strong long grain resists breakage.

1

Steam-Bending

If you need a curved, solid piece of wood, the easiest way to get it is to bandsaw it out of a board. Bandsawing, however, means that the fibers of the wood will not follow the curve and the weak, short grain will break easily **(1)**. Another way to make a curve is bricklaying (p. 98). Sometimes it is even possible to find a piece of wood that has grown to the right shape. In Denmark, a boatbuilder or a woodworker could take a pattern to special lumberyards and order a naturally curved piece of wood to match.

Bending, either by steaming, laminating or kerf-bending, is another way to get a curved piece of wood. I never use kerf-bending because the saw kerf will eventually telegraph through the wood and the bend is not strong. It is just as easy to laminate, and laminated construction is considerably stronger.

Steam-bending is particularly useful in the mass production of furniture and in chair-making. Because it eliminates the need for some joinery and increases the strength of the wood, pieces can usually be made considerably lighter.

The most difficult part of the bending process is figuring out and making the forms — the bending itself is quite easy. In this chapter I will cover what I have found necessary to make basic bends in my own shop, without going into the complicated equipment necessary for bending large pieces of wood. It isn't hard to design and make the special forms necessary for bending more complicated pieces once you've mastered the fundamentals. If you do have to bend many large pieces, it's probably a good idea for you to look into factories that specialize in custom bending.

Recently, bending with ammonia has attracted attention, but in its current state of development, this is impractical and dangerous in the average small shop. □

Wood for Bending

Quartersawn wood, which is cut perpendicular to the annual rings **(1)**, is the best for bending. Quartersawn wood is difficult to find in small lumberyards and usually has to be specially ordered. Plainsawn lumber is not well suited for bending because it is cut tangentially to the annual rings, which makes it break easily if forced too much.

If the piece to be bent is not too wide, you can use a plainsawn board of the right thickness, because the section you rip off will be close to quartersawn **(2)**. Make sure to select a board with good straight grain.

Some larger lumberyards handle what is called veneer backing. This is the center stock that is left over from veneer logs, and it is close to quartersawn. These boards are beautiful and inexpensive. Remember that the centers of these boards contain the pith **(3)**; cut it out, or else the board will crack.

Some woods bend more easily than others. For example, white and red oak, birch and black walnut bend well, but mahogany does not. Of the common woods, beech and ash are best suited to bending. Most exotic woods will bend with work and luck, but the rate of breakage is usually quite high.

Generally, green wood bends much more easily than kiln-dried wood, which, for sharp bends, should be soaked in water for several hours before steaming. Industry uses green wood extensively, kiln-drying it after bending. Most woodworkers don't have the necessary equipment, so they have to air-dry their wood afterward. This takes a long, long time and most people can't wait, so they start by using kiln-dried wood.

If you do use green wood for bending and don't have a moisture meter, weigh the wood continually to determine when it is dry enough for furniture. Record the date and weight every week. When the wood has weighed the same for several weeks, it's dry enough to use. ☐

Quartersawn

Plainsawn

1

2 *Ripped*

3 *Waste*

The Steambox

Once you have your wood, you'll need a steambox and some device for making steam. There are elaborate and expensive steam generators available, but my setup of a 5-gal. can and a campstove works well enough **(1)**. Make sure the can is galvanized because the combination of tannic acid in the wood, moisture and iron will stain the wood black. Never use any iron or steel in a steambox. If you're going into steambending in a serious way, a better steamer would be a worthwhile investment.

I use exterior plywood, good one side, for my steambox (marine plywood is, of course, the best). The box measures 7 in. by 7 in. inside and is 6 ft. long — big enough for my work, with an interior cubic footage just right for the steam generated by my setup.

If you have to steam a longer piece, make a longer box, but try to cut down on the other inside dimensions. For example, if the piece of wood to be steamed is ¾ in. by 4 in. by 8 ft., the box should be 5 in. by 6 in. inside and 9 ft. long. Pieces to be steamed should always be at least ½ in. smaller than the inside dimension of the box. Never put in a piece of wood that fits too tightly, as the wood will expand and either break the steambox or wedge itself in so that you won't be able to get it out.

When you make your steambox, paint the good side of the plywood with two coats of porch or deck enamel and keep it on the inside of the box. Leave the outside unpainted, so that the plywood can shed any moisture caused by steam or water escaping through the paint on the inside. Assemble the box with tongue-and-groove joints, painting the joints with enamel and screwing the box together while the paint is still wet to seal the joints.

1

Paint one end piece and screw it on, but hinge the other end piece for a door and devise a lock to secure it. Make the door bigger than the box — the overhang makes a good handle to keep you from burning yourself while opening the box. Sometimes it's good to have doors on both ends so that if long pieces have to be steamed in the center, they can stick out the box ends. In this case, stuff rags into the openings to seal the ends.

The steam must flow around the wood in the box, so place ½-in. dowels between the box sides to raise the wood, elevating them about 1 in. to 1½ in. from the bottom.

Set the steambox on two sawhorses. The campstove and 5-gal. can should be accessible but not in the way.

When setting up, make sure to tilt the box slightly toward the end with the drain hole. The steam will fill the whole box, and as it condenses, the water will run slowly along the bottom of the box to the front. This will maintain a high moisture level, helping to soften the fibers of the wood.

I use ½-in. copper or aluminum tubing inserted into cork to connect the hose between the bottom of the box and the 5-gal. can **(2)**. Cork seals easily, but it will pop out if too much pressure builds up in the steamer — a good safety valve. Cement the copper tubing in with epoxy glue.

Keep the hose relatively straight so that as the steam condenses, the water won't get trapped **(3)**. With a hose as short as this there is very little heat loss.

Before you fill up the tank, consider that ¾ gal. of water will evaporate each hour with my system. Don't put in 4 gal. if you need only two hours of steaming. Although you should always test for yourself, the rule of thumb for most dry wood is an hour of steaming for each ¼ in. of thickness. Be careful not to overcook the wood, because too much steaming will weaken the fibers and cause them to break easily when bent.

For a quick steambox that will work well, you can use a galvanized, aluminum or ceramic pipe. □

2

3

1

Bending Straps

When wood is bent, the fibers on the convex side of the curve will be stretched while those on the concave side will be compressed. You can see how this works by bending a piece of foam rubber **(1)**.

When a piece of wood is forced to bend too much, the outer fibers will start to run **(2)**. With more force, more fibers will run **(3)**, and eventually the piece will break **(4)**.

A spring-steel strap **(5)** with steel or angle-iron end blocks will prevent the fibers from running. The strap works by keeping the fibers from stretching; if the fibers can't stretch, they can't run. I prefer spring-steel straps because they will always return to their original shape and they give uniform pressure, but when using steel straps, keep wax paper between wood and steel to prevent black tannic-acid stains on the wood.

When you're using straps, the wood to be bent should fit snugly between the ends of the strap. Bolt the angle-iron end blocks to the straps securely. Have straps of three or four different lengths available. Then you'll have a good chance of finding one that is the length you need.

I seldom use bending straps unless it's a very complicated bend. I prefer to laminate because I usually make one-of-a-kind pieces, but even when making ten chairs I feel I have more control of the shape. Straps are most often used in mass production or for bending heavy pieces to be carved, where you don't want gluelines.

Before bending, it's a good idea to remove planer marks by sanding. An uneven surface is often what gets fibers running in the first place. Don't sand when you're going to laminate, because a sanded joint is not a good glue joint. □

2

3

4

5

Forms

Steam-bending usually requires a form, and clamps to fasten the wood to it. Forms are often made out of plywood, but any inexpensive material will do.

1

A simple one-part form like this one **(1)** is made by gluing up several layers of material into a block thicker than the width of the pieces to be bent. Glue a full-scale drawing of the desired curve to the block with rubber cement and bandsaw out the curve, using the widest blade that will take the curve. The cut must be accurate, smooth and square. Fill in low spots on the form with auto-body putty and remove high spots with a rasp. Sometimes it is helpful to cut the form to a sharper curve to allow for springback. When possible, cut the bottom edge of the form to match the top curve, to ease clamping.

For sharper curves, it is often not practical to bandsaw out the bottom of a form because the form would be weakened. In such cases, drill holes in the form to receive the clamps you're going to use **(2)**.

2

If you screw and glue a block onto the back of the form **(3)**, you can securely hold it in a bench vise while bending.

This form, which I acquired from a former student, was bandsawn out of particleboard. Normally I would make this form from the cheapest plywood I could find, because particleboard breaks easily and dulls the bandsaw blade. Here, since the form is a solid block, particleboard is okay. ☐

3

1

2

The Steam-Bending Process

When you have prepared the piece of wood you are going to use and have steamed it long enough to make it pliable, you are ready to bend. Using tongs and wearing gloves, remove the wood from the box and quickly place it on the strap (1), which should have been warming on top of the box.

Both the piece to be bent and the form should have center marks on them, so that the wood can be lined up in the right place quickly. Clamp at the center marks first (2), and bend both ends simultaneously (3,4), clamping as you go (5). Bend the wood to the form smoothly and carefully, but don't waste any time, as wood bends most easily when it is hot and moist. It's always helpful to try a test piece first, to check whether the wood is pliable and to get the feel of how it will bend.

The wood here (6) is kiln-dried ash ¾ in. thick by 2 in. wide. Steamed for three hours, it bent easily on this form. Drilled holes accept the ends of regular quick-action clamps. (More clamps are discussed on p. 14.)

After about 24 hours, I removed the clamps and the strap (7). You can see that there is more springback on the left side than on the right. On purpose, I had clamped up the right side about a minute before the left to show that the faster you bend the wood, the less springback there will be.

Before taking the wood off the form, fit a retainer board with two end blocks to the piece so it will keep its shape while drying (8). This will also help minimize springback.

Finally, remove the piece from the form and allow it to dry (9). Drying time depends on the size of the wood and the amount of moisture in the air. The wood usually will dry in three to four days. □

3

4

5

6

7

8

9

Saw kerfs

1

2

4

3

Laminating

When you are attempting a curve with a small radius, it is usually better to laminate several layers of wood than to steam-bend one thicker piece. Both steam-bending and laminating have advantages and disadvantages, and usually a combination of the two is most effective. In steam-bending, you only have to bend the piece once over a form, and there are no gluelines. A disadvantage is that it's difficult to predict springback. When laminating, you've got to contend with gluelines, but springback is minimal.

The thinner the laminates, the sharper the radius can be, and the less springback. Sometimes, however, in both steam-bending and lamination, when the radius of a bend is very small the curves may creep inward instead of springing back. This happens when the compressed fibers on the concave surface shrink and pull the ends in as they dry.

If you decide on laminating, cut the laminates from the same board and keep them in the order they come off the saw. After you run them over the jointer in preparation for gluing and put them back together, the grain will match and the finished piece will look as though it is made of solid wood. I use a triangular marking system **(1)** to keep the pieces in order.

For curves with a very sharp radius, you will often have to steam-bend the wood before laminating it. When steaming several pieces at a time, put small wood spacers between the laminates and tie them together with string so the steam can flow around each piece **(2)**. Take care to mark each piece and to keep the pieces in the same order during steam-bending, drying and gluing. Mark the center of the laminates.

Set up the wood on the dowel rack inside the box **(3)** and set up your form **(4)**, marking its centerline. When steaming is done, align the centerlines of the laminates and the form.

When you bend several pieces (or a very thin piece), using a steel strap is impractical. A 5/16-in. thick piece of wood, plywood or hardboard **(5)** placed on the convex side of the bend will help prevent breakage.

Clamp at the center first **(6)** and work out toward the ends, adding a clamp at a time to each side **(7)** until you are done **(8)**. Here I am working with laminates that are tapered on both ends (p. 25), which are not the same as the laminates shown in the steambox.

Remove clamps 24 hours after bending and allow laminates to dry. Put scraps of wood between them so that air can circulate freely. Under average weather conditions with kiln-dried wood, drying will take about three days. To minimize springback, keep the pieces in tension with a string. This photo **(9)** gives the idea, but obviously these are not the laminates shown being clamped. □

5

6

7

8

9

1

2

Gluing Up the Laminates

The kind of glue used for laminating depends on the job and individual preferences. If the wood is a light color (such as maple or ash), use Titebond, a light-colored glue. Titebond starts to set in five to ten minutes, so if you need more time, plan to glue up in sections or to get some help. If you are working with dark wood, use Cascamite, a slower-setting brown glue.

Have everything ready before spreading the glue. Cover the form with wax paper or a similar material so that the laminates will not be glued to it **(1)**. The three blocks of wood clamped to the form will serve as a backboard to keep the laminate sides flush.

Now, spread the glue evenly on both sides of the laminates **(2)**. This is essential for a good bond. Work quickly, and when all the laminates are covered with glue, put them on the form. Don't get nervous.

Begin to clamp at the middle first, and then put a clamp at each end **(3,4)**. Do not tighten down these end clamps all the way, as you want the laminates to be able to slide lengthwise against one another.

3

4

Before you continue to clamp, put a piece of wood as shown **(5)** to force the laminates flush against the three blocks already clamped to the form. Then continue to clamp, starting again at the center and working toward both ends of the form **(6)**. Tighten the clamps as you go. Clamp the two end clamps tightly, and you're finished **(7)**. Remove the backboard blocks as soon as the laminates are fastened to the form the way they should be, so that they don't interfere and get glued to the laminates.

Notice that on this form the bottom edge has been cut to the same curve as the top edge so that the clamps will be perpendicular to the laminates. ☐

5

6

7

Clamps and Clamping

Whenever possible, I use regular, quick-action clamps **(1)** because they are fast and easy to use. Many times, however, these clamps can't do the job. Here are some different types of clamps.

The clamp that I find most useful for handling pieces up to 6 in. wide is made of ⅝-in. hexagonal, cold-rolled steel rod that is 7½ in. long **(2)**. Hexagonal stock is better than round because, for example, a ⅝-in. hexagonal rod won't move around when hammered into an 1¹⁄₁₆-in. hole. It will move enough, however, so that when you are tightening up the two threaded rods that go into it, the pull will stay straight.

To make this clamp **(3)**, drill four ⁵⁄₁₆-in. holes in the hex stock to hold the two threaded rods. Two nuts lock the threaded rods in place. Make a 1-in. thick piece of wood with matching holes to clamp down on the piece of wood to be bent.

Use a ⅜-in. reversible electric drill with an extension bar from a socket set to speed up clamping **(4)**. Grind one end of the bar to fit the drill chuck and use a deep socket to drive the nuts onto the rods.

You could use a wood dowel, with holes drilled for the threaded rods, in place of the hex rod **(5)**. The diameter of the dowel depends on the strength required and the pressure needed to bend the wood. Notice again the two nuts that lock the rod in place.

1

3

4

5

Before the form is set up and the rods are in position for clamping (**6**), shellac or wax the form to prevent the laminated pieces from being glued to it, or put wax paper between the form and the laminates.

Place the pieces to be bent on the form so that the center marks of form and laminates line up. Tighten the center clamp first (**7**), being careful when using the electric drill to get the same amount of pressure on both sides. Uneven pressure results in a joint that is tight on one side but open on the other (**8,9**). It can also result in a flattened surface (**10**).

6

7

8

9

10

11

Here **(11)** the same pressure is applied to both sides of the clamp.

After tightening the first clamp, continue putting on the blocks and tightening them down **(12)**. Because it is sometimes difficult to push the piece down and get block, washer and nut on with only one pair of hands **(13)**, you might need someone to help you.

Here everything is clamped — twelve clamps were used **(14)**. It would have been impossible to get that many regular clamps on in such a small space.

12

13

14

When clamping any laminates, especially when they are steamed first, don't clamp directly on the wood, whichever type of clamp you use. This photo **(15)** shows what happens if you do. The outside piece has flat spots where the blocks were clamped, the middle piece has a more even curve, and only the inside piece is perfect.

To get even pressure and to prevent flat spots, place a strip or two of scrap wood to clamp to on the outside. Plywood can be used, but for best results, especially with steamed laminates, use solid wood. If the laminate is ³⁄₈ in. thick, for example, use two ³⁄₁₆-in. outside pieces. Don't steam these pieces and they'll give more even pressure.

I also use clamps made of Unistrut channel iron **(16,17)**, which, although more complicated than hexagonal clamps, are excellent for bending especially sharp corners.

On a corner, three of these clamps can be anchored to the same rod **(18)**, but they can also be used in the same way as hexagonal clamps. Unistrut clamps have a center screw that swivels, so they are able to exert very even pressure. The disadvantage in using these clamps is that it takes two people to operate them.

15

16

17

18

19

20

Make the clamps out of Unistrut #P-3300, 7/8 in. thick by 1⅝ in. wide by 6¾ in. long. A ½-in. Jergens flange nut (#19906) fits right into the Unistrut. For pressure, I use a Jergens clamp shoe assembly (#36307). Unistrut is available from the Unistrut Corp., Elizabeth at Clinton, Wayne, Mich. 48184; Jergens parts are available from distributors for Jergens, Inc., 19520 Nottingham Rd., Cleveland, Ohio 44110. I make the side pieces out of ¼-in. thick by 1⅜-in. wide cold-rolled steel, 8 in. long, with three 9/16-in. holes drilled in it **(19)**. The round piece that fits into the holes is made out of a ½-in. cold-rolled steel rod, 6¾ in. long.

In this photo **(20)**, regular clamps are used on the straight sides, but hexagonal or Unistrut clamps could be used there, too. This clamp is experimental and can certainly be improved, but it works.

In this case, the laminates had to be steamed first because of the sharp bend **(21)**. Notice the springback after the clamps were removed. After the laminates were glued together, however, there was very little springback **(22)**. I checked it a year later and the springback was the same. □

21

22

Complicated Bends

For complicated bends, a piece of steel or aluminum the same width as the laminates, and strips of inner tube make a good form and clamp **(1,2)**. Surgical tubing, which stretches more than the inner tubes manufactured today, is excellent to use. If steel is used for the form and the piece is going to be steamed, be sure to keep wax paper between steel and wood to prevent staining. Make sure the metal is thick enough so that it won't straighten out when you bend the wood on it. If you've ever wrapped a rubber band around your finger, you have an idea of the tremendous pressure an inner tube can exert. Also, the pressure is equally distributed over 360°.

Secure the form and pieces to be laminated, glued up, in a vise **(3)**. For sharper curves than shown, you may have to steam-bend and dry the laminates. Clamps temporarily hold the pieces in shape **(4)**. Don't put too much pressure on the clamps — as the piece is wrapped with inner tube, the laminates should be free to slide. This operation works best with two people. The inner tube here **(5)** was started at the bottom, but, depending on the shape of the form, it might be better to start at another point.

1

2

3   4   5

6

7

8

Wrap the inner tube around the form as tightly as possible **(6)**. Remove the clamp when you reach it, and continue. As you move up the form **(7)**, remember to loosen the clamps just enough so the wood can slide and you will get a tight glue joint.

Put a clamp on the end of the inner tube when you get there **(8)**. If you take the piece out of the vise, replace the pressure there with another clamp.

Here, the glue is dry and the piece has been removed from the form **(9)**. There was no springback at all.

The piece is sanded and finished **(10)**.

9

10

Two-part form Sometimes it is better to use a two-part form when laminating. It will allow more even pressure than a one-part form, but be careful in its construction.

You'll need an accurate full-scale drawing on which are marked all pieces with their exact thicknesses **(11)**. Notice that in this drawing radius *A* is shorter than radius *B*, so the two curves will be different.

When the drawing is complete, glue it on the form material with rubber cement, and then bandsaw it out carefully with the saw kerf on the waste side of the line. (For more about two-part forms, see p. 146.)

If the curves are each a part, but not more than half, of a circle, guide pins are not necessary to align the two halves of the form. The pressure will be even whether or not the two halves line up exactly **(12)**.

11

12

13

If the curves on the form are not part of a circle **(13)**, you will need guide pins. To make them, dado out the ends on both halves of the form first, and then fit pieces of wood snugly in the grooves. Glue and screw the pins to one of the halves **(14)**.

With the guide pins in place, the two halves should fit together perfectly **(15)** and give uniform pressure.

Now cover the laminates with glue, place them on the form and clamp up **(16)**. Before you do, however, make sure to shellac or wax the form so the pieces won't stick to it, or use wax paper.

After gluing up, set the piece back on the form **(17)**. As you can see, there is hardly any springback. ☐

14

15

16

17

Compound Lamination

For certain types of work, you might want to bend a piece in two different directions. One way to do this, if the bends aren't too complicated, is to laminate the piece one way and then the other. When the glue is dry from the first bend, joint one edge of the piece and rip it into thinner pieces for laminating in the other direction. Use a sharp hollow-ground blade and you shouldn't have to joint the pieces again before the next gluing.

Here **(1)** four laminates are glued together and placed back on a form with a simple curve. The dried glue has been scraped off and one edge has been jointed.

The piece is then ripped into four new pieces for the second lamination **(2)**.

Here the pieces are put back on the form just to illustrate what is being done **(3)**.

1

2

3

4

5

7

6

8

The four pieces are then placed together and flipped 90° **(4)**. Now the four pieces are clamped back on the form for the second bend **(5)**. (When they were actually being glued, I used more clamps along with backing strips on which to clamp.) Finally the piece is glued together and sanded **(6)**.

In this case, the same form was used for both bends. For photographic clarity, I have eliminated glue, blocks and straps. Remember, when using a one-part form, always put the screw end of the clamp on top. The flexible head on the end of the screw will even out pressure.

This is the end of the piece after the second gluing **(7)**. Notice it is made up of small, square laminates. More complicated bends can be worked by milling small, square laminates to begin with. You can either bend freehand or use a form of wood or metal, clamped with inner tube strips **(8)**. □

Tapered Lamination

When you cut through a glue joint in a laminated piece, the glueline will show up **(1)**. It can be covered by veneering the piece, but that is inefficient.

If a laminated piece has to be tapered either toward one or both ends and you don't want the glueline to show, you can taper the laminates individually.

These two pieces **(2)** are tapered — one toward one end and the other toward both ends. Ash and walnut laminates are used here just to show the techniques clearly, but they could actually be used quite effectively as part of a design.

For making tapered laminates, you need a special jig to plane the pieces. In this drawing **(3)**, *A* and *B* show a jig for making laminates that taper in one direction; *C* shows a jig for making laminates that taper toward both ends. The jigs are best made out of solid wood. Here is one of the jigs bandsawn **(4)**. Each laminate is placed in the jig and sent through the thickness planer to achieve the desired shape. Here **(5)**, the piece that is tapered toward one end has passed through the thickness planer.

1

2

3

4

5

6

7

Here is a jig for laminates that taper toward both ends **(6)**. Notice that the laminate side toward the jig is jointed flat. The other side is sawed to the approximate shape to speed up the operation.

A piece with a clamp on it in the jig demonstrates what happens when the jig is passed through the thickness planer **(7)**. As the jig and laminates go through the planer, the pressure bar and rollers that push the piece through will force the laminate down into the jig, and the piece will be planed to the appropriate shape.

Gluing procedures and clamping techniques for tapered laminates are the same as those used for other types of lamination. □

Scrapers
Chapter 2

1

2

3

The Scraper Blade

Scrapers are available as a simple, rectangular piece of steel, called a scraper blade, and as a blade mounted in a handle resembling a large spokeshave, called a cabinet scraper. Scraper blades are also available in a curved shape of varying radii **(1)**. These are called gooseneck scrapers (also swan-neck scrapers) and are excellent for smoothing out curved surfaces like the insides of bowls or moldings. Because of the irregular shape, there is usually some place on this type of scraper that will fit the work. Gooseneck scraper blades are sharpened the same way as straight scraper blades.

The scraper blade is an important, versatile tool for cabinetmakers and wood sculptors. It can be used for crude and fine work — to scrape glue, to smooth out a surface before sanding and to produce a high-gloss finish with lacquer or shellac. It's better to use than sandpaper between coats of finish. When an old scraper blade gets too narrow to use, it can become a tool for making half-blind or hidden dovetails. I feel that the name scraper blade is incorrect because, when used properly, a scraper blade cuts the fibers of the wood instead of scraping or pulling them.

The surface of an inexpensive scraper blade is very rough and does not make a clean burr when sharpened **(2)**. I use a Sandvik #475 scraper blade **(3)**, which costs about twice as much as a cheap one but is worth every penny. The polished edges and high-quality steel of a Sandvik scraper blade produce a much cleaner burr that keeps cutting long after others are dull. Because most people buy only one or two blades in a lifetime, it is a good investment to buy the best. I like to keep two blades ready — one for all-purpose work and one just for scraping lacquer and shellac.

The working edge of all scrapers is a burr, which, when magnified, resembles a small hook running the length of the edge. It's not hard to sharpen and maintain a scraper, but it takes a lot of practice to get right. Many people get frustrated and give up, which is one of the reasons you don't see scrapers used more often. Once you learn to sharpen and maintain the proper edge on a scraper blade and a cabinet scraper, however, you'll wonder how you ever did without them.

In sharpening a scraper blade, first file the long edges square with a fine, flat mill file. Clamp the blade in a vise and curl your fingers around the file for control **(4)**.

Hold the file square to the edge and draw it along in long, even strokes **(5)**. Let the file cut only when you push it forward; if you try to cut on the pull stroke, the file will chatter and mar the edge of the blade.

As you can see, the file leaves shallow marks on the edge **(6)**. It isn't necessary to remove these marks for rough work, but it is for fine work, such as scraping finishes. To remove the file marks, use a medium-grit wet/dry carborundum stone without oil. To prevent making a groove in the stone, which would round the blade edges, work on different areas of the stone **(7,8)**, not in any one spot. Using the edge of the stone **(9)** will help prevent ruining the face.

4

5

6

7

8

9

10

11

12

Now you can remove the few remaining fine scratches with a Belgian clay waterstone and water **(10)**. I don't like to use oil because it mixes with particles from the stone and gets on my hands and the bench. Before I know it, the work gets oily, too. The edge a waterstone produces is just as good as an oilstone's, and it cuts the metal faster. Don't rock the stone — the blade edge must remain flat and square. Again, make sure to work on different areas of the stone so grooves don't form in it.

When honing, give the edge about ten strokes, and then hone the sides of the blade ten strokes each. Repeat the process, this time with nine strokes, and continue until you get down to one stroke on each side. Use your finger to steady the blade when honing the sides, as I do here **(11,12)**.

Now you are ready to give the blade its cutting edge. This is done by stroking with a burnisher, which is a piece of steel, harder than the blade, that puts on the cutting burr. Burnishers come in different sizes and shapes — triangular, round and oval — but I think the back of a chisel works just as well as anything and then I don't have to buy another tool.

If you buy a good scraper blade to begin with, such as the Sandvik, you won't have to go through the filing and honing steps the first time. The blade will be ready for the burr as soon as you bring it home.

Before putting on the burr, place a few drops of machine oil on the scraper blade and the back of the chisel **(13)**. The oil prevents the chatter of steel on steel, which will nick the burr once it's made.

Hold the chisel at an angle of about 85° to the face of the scraper **(14)** and draw it toward you in a smooth stroke that is the full length of the blade **(15,16,17)**. Pulling the chisel lets you keep the pressure, which should be very light, consistent — never push. Tilt the chisel so that you only use the back edge. In this photograph **(16)**, the angle is exaggerated to show how to hold the chisel. If the chisel is 1 in. wide, the gap in front should be about 1/32 in.

13

14

15

16

17

After two or three light passes you should have a small, even burr. Move your finger across the face of the scraper after each stroke to feel how big the burr is **(18)**. When you're finished, you should barely be able to feel it. Don't cut yourself.

Most people usually get too excited and burnish too hard the first time they sharpen a scraper blade. The result is a big hook that digs too far into the wood. This is okay for rough work, like scraping glue, but for fine finishing you need a light touch when burnishing the cutting edge.

When the burr feels right, put one on each of the remaining three edges. Then try the blade to see if it cuts; if it doesn't, go over it once or twice more until it does.

When a scraper blade gets dull, there's no need to refile and hone each time. Simply recondition the burr. First put a little oil on both faces of the scraper and on the back of the chisel **(19)**. Then smooth the oil with your finger—which finger to use is up to you. Burnish the old burr down, and then pull it back up again.

Lay the blade flat on the edge of the bench. Be sure the chisel is flat **(20)**, not as it is here **(21)**, because the cutting edge would be ruined if you did it this way. Let your index finger slide along the edge of the bench so you don't cut into your other hand. With your thumb holding the chisel flat against the surface of the blade and the chisel tilted slightly in the direction in which it is moving, go the full length of the blade with every stroke. Use light pressure in the beginning. As you go along, you can get more and more excited and put more and more pressure on until the burr is flattened.

The chisel can be moved back and forth in this case, but be sure to go the full length of the blade each time and to tilt the chisel slightly. Now you're ready to raise the burr, as before. You can do this five or six times before having to refile and hone.

For rough work and even for use before sanding, I simply file the edge, without stoning. I leave on the burr produced by the file, burnish it flat and raise it back up again. An edge treated this way will cut as well as if it were stoned, but it will have microscopic nicks. Since sandpaper will remove any nicks in the work, this is okay.

With the scraper blade sharpened, it's ready to be used. If it is sharpened correctly, it will make fine shavings, not dust.

18

19

20

21

You can either push or pull a scraper blade, but pulling is better because you have more control. For rough work, such as removing glue, paper or old finish, it's okay to push.

When pushing, curl your fingers around the ends of the blade and press your thumbs in the center to bow the blade slightly **(22)**. When pulling the blade toward you, your four fingers of each hand will support the back of the blade and keep it straight. Your two thumbs will be in the front, controlling the angle of the blade **(23)**.

When this blade was pushed, it cut only in the center, so the shaving produced was not very wide **(24)**. When the same blade was pulled, the cut was as wide as the blade **(25)**.

22

23

24

25

26

27

Don't hold the blade at too shallow an angle **(26)**, as it will scrape instead of cut and dull quickly. Held at the correct angle, about 80° **(27)**, the blade will last for a long time. It will also cut better and more evenly if held askew to the grain direction but moved parallel to the grain **(28)**. Reverse the angle of the blade to your body after each stroke **(29,30)**. If the blade were to dig down a little, making a slight groove, and you worked the blade the same way every time, the groove would get bigger and bigger. Think of a road with a small hole; every time a car passes over it, the size of the hole increases slightly, until finally there is a large pothole.

After reading this and trying to sharpen a scraper several times, you might be the most frustrated person in the world. But don't give up. All of a sudden it will work out right, if you don't get too excited. Remember the light touch. ☐

28

29

30

The Cabinet Scraper

A cabinet scraper has many uses. It can remove old finishes, dried glue and paper that is stuck to veneer. Its main function, if sharpened correctly and used right, is to put a fine surface on burled or figured wood or delicate veneer before sanding.

A cabinet scraper has two screws to hold its blade in place **(1)**, and a set screw **(2)** to flex the blade. The blade of a cabinet scraper is sharpened like a scraper blade, except it has a bevel. Also, its burr should be slightly larger.

1

To begin, clamp the cabinet-scraper blade to the bench with its bevel up and overhanging the bench edge. With a flat mill file held in both hands, file the bevel at an angle of 25° to 30° **(3)**. This angle makes the bevel about twice as long as the blade is thick — a quick way to judge if an angle is correct.

File until there is a burr on the back, being careful not to file the blade to a convex shape. It is better, in fact, to file it a hair concave. When the set screw is tightened, the blade will straighten out and take a shaving the full width of the blade. As you file, knock the corners off the blade so they won't dig into the work later.

Make a handle for holding the blade when sharpening **(4)**. A piece of scrap wood with a saw kerf in it for the blade works well and will prevent you from cutting yourself too often. Some people sharpen both edges of the blade, but I don't. When you're trying to work with this tool, it is too dangerous to have a sharp edge sticking up.

2

3

4

Remove the file marks from the bevel with a medium-grit sharpening stone **(5)**. I use a wet/dry carborundum stone without oil. Don't turn over the blade to remove the burr because the stone will leave scratches there.

Next, hone the edge on a fine-grit stone. I use a Belgian clay waterstone. Move the bevel back and forth over the stone ten times, then flip the blade and do the other side about ten times **(6,7)**. Do each side nine times, then eight, and so on, until you get down to one time each. The burr should be gone. (In these pictures it looks like I'm losing fingers but don't worry, they're just tucked out of the way.)

5

6

7

After the edge is honed, put the cutting burr on with a burnisher. The size cutting burr you put on depends on the kind of work the cabinet scraper is going to do. You'll want a larger burr to remove old finishes or glue than you will for finer work. Experience helps here. Try to start out with a small burr and if that doesn't work, put on one that's a little bigger until it works right.

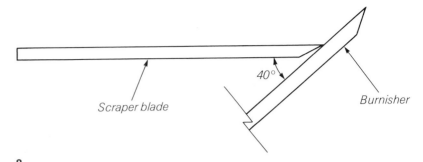

Scraper blade   40°   Burnisher

8

The first step in putting on the burr is to apply a little machine oil to the blade so the burnisher will slide smoothly. Hold the burnisher at an angle of about 40° to the face of the blade **(8)** and draw it toward you until an even burr forms **(9,10)**. When using a chisel for a burnisher, tilt it slightly so that you work with only one edge. Always use a light touch. It is much better to go over the edge two or three times rather than to try to put on the burr with just one stroke.

After each stroke, feel how big the burr is with your finger, but be careful that you don't cut yourself.

Now set the cabinet scraper blade into its handle, making sure that the set screw is out of the way. Put one or two pieces of paper under the front of the scraper sole, depending on how much of a shaving you want to remove, and slip in the blade so it rests on the bench. Push down the blade with your index fingers and use your two middle fingers to tighten the screws that hold the blade **(11)**. Tighten the screws with a screwdriver before using the scraper.

9

10

11

When the blade is secured, tighten the set screw **(12)** so it just touches the blade, which will help prevent chattering. Then make a test cut. If only the two corners of the blade are cutting, tighten the screw a little more until the whole blade cuts a shaving.

Here the blade is set correctly and you can see that the shaving is as wide as the blade **(13)**. With the cabinet scraper set like this, you'll remove a shaving about the thickness of the paper you put under the front of the sole in the beginning.

The cabinet scraper was designed for pushing; the handles were designed to fit the palms of your hands. Many people use this tool by pulling it, but then it chatters and won't cut.

When using a cabinet scraper, use the weight of your body to hold it down and keep it from chattering **(14)**. If the scraper still chatters, the blade is probably set too deep, so take it out and reset it using fewer or thinner papers under the front of the sole.

When the blade dulls, you needn't go through the whole process of refiling and honing. Just recondition the burr. Place the blade on a bench, burr side up, and put a little oil on it and the burnisher. Flatten out the burr with one edge of the burnisher, using a light hand at first, and adding more pressure with each pass **(15)**. About five passes should do it. Make sure to keep the edge of the burnisher flat on the surface, and slide one finger along the edge of the bench to keep from cutting yourself.

When the burr is flattened, pull it back up the same way as before. You can recondition the burr like this five or six times, depending on the job, before you will have to refile and hone the blade. □

12

13

15

14

Carving
Chapter 3

Types of Carving

The term woodcarving encompasses a wide range of specialties including figure, letter and relief carving. Generally, figure carving entails working in the round as when making a bowl or a statue. Relief carving is the process of making shapes stand out from their background, such as carving a shell on the front of a highboy. Letter carving is one of the most difficult types of carving to learn. After you've finally selected the right style of letter to express the message, you've got to do the work without making any mistakes. If the gouge slips when finishing the very last letter, you've got to start all over again.

The best woodcarvers usually possess a good feeling for form and shape along with a sound knowledge of wood as a material. Both are necessary to take full advantage of the natural beauty of the wood. In this chapter, I will show how to carve a simple bowl to illustrate basic techniques, and I will also demonstrate how to use common carving tools. ☐

Tools

If you want to learn how to carve, the first thing to do is to buy some good woodcarving tools. Make sure that they fit comfortably in your hand and that they take and hold a good edge. Carving tools are available in a variety of shapes and sizes, for light or heavy work. Some are especially made for letter or relief carving. It's a good idea to start out with a small set and then add the type of tools for the kind of work you want to do.

Gouges are the most important tools for carving **(1)**. For the type of carving I do, I prefer medium-size tools (about 5 in. to 6 in. long). These are easy to handle, but they can be hit with a mallet.

The drawing **(2)** shows the types of tools I have found necessary for carving. I also use regular flat chisels, for outside carving.

1

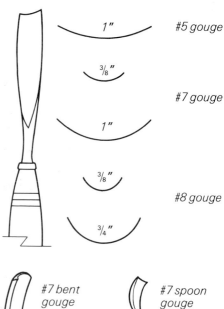

1" — #5 gouge

3/8" — #7 gouge

1"

3/8" — #8 gouge

3/4"

#7 bent gouge

#7 spoon gouge

1"

3/4"

2

To do a good job, a carving tool must be sharp. How often you sharpen depends on the quality of your tools and the type of wood you're working. When a tool starts to dull, it will break, not carve, the fibers off the wood, especially when working across the grain. It's time to sharpen your tools when they stop cutting cleanly. If you don't let your tools get too dull in the first place, they will not take long to resharpen.

The techniques for sharpening carving tools are essentially the same as those for sharpening plane irons and flat chisels. I prefer to use a belt sander equipped with a fine-grit belt (nothing coarser than used, worn-out, 120-grit belts) and a buffer, though there are many different opinions on the best way to do the job.

3

The cutting edge of most carving tools should be beveled to approximately 30°. Lightly hold the tool in your hand and roll it from side to side on the running sander **(3)**, making sure that you keep the tool moving. Don't let the blade get too hot or you will ruin the temper and damage the edge of the blade.

The sanding marks should be 90° to the edge of the chisel, but no less than 45°. Many people prefer to hold the tool sideways **(4)**, which is easier but wrong, because then the sanding marks will go with the bevel. A sanding mark that is right on the edge of the tool **(5)** will prevent the tool from becoming truly sharp.

When you've got a small, even burr on the back of your tool, buff the bevel until the burr is removed **(6)**.

4

5

6

7

You can also use a flat stone to sharpen carving tools **(7)**. Be sure to work over the whole surface of the stone so you don't get a hollow spot in any one place. Sharpen as you would on the belt sander until the edge has a small burr on the back.

To remove the burr, you will need a stone that fits the shape of the back of the gouge. Here are a few of the stone shapes that are available **(8)**. The most commonly used is the gouge slipstone **(9)**. It is concave on one side, convex on the other and tapered, so you can usually find some place on the stone that will fit the tool **(10,11)**. With the stone in hand, remove the burr from the gouge, being careful not to bevel the back edge. □

8

9

10

11

Carving a Bowl

Draw the shape of the inside of the bowl on the wood **(1)** before cutting into it. How you orient the bowl on the wood depends on the type of grain you want the bowl to have. If positioned as shown here **(2)**, the grain will be very strong, with the annual rings cut at a great angle. Oriented like this **(3)**, the grain will be straight, since the rings will be cut at about 90°.

Carving and sanding on the inside of a bowl should always be completed before work on the outside is begun, because the work is much more easily clamped in a vise when it is still a block. As you start to carve, work either across the grain or at an angle to it. Don't go with the grain **(4)**, because you won't have much control, and the wood might split and run in any direction. For the best control, use a deep gouge **(5)**. A gouge that is too flat will split the wood, as will one the full width of the cut to be made. When starting, use a mallet to strike the gouge.

1

2

3

4

5

6

7

To speed up roughing out, drill holes with a Forstner bit approximately to the depth of the inside of the bowl **(6)**. A Forstner bit has a very short point **(7)** and is used where a clean, flat-bottomed hole is needed. With the holes drilled, you can carve in from any direction without splitting the wood, as long as you carve toward a deeper part of the bowl **(8)**. Carving uphill will result in loss of control, and the wood will split.

When roughing out is complete, switch to shallower gouges that approximate the shape of the bowl you want to produce. Instead of a mallet, use the weight of your body to force the gouge down. This is more difficult to explain than it is to do: Your right hand will push down on the gouge while your left hand will hold it back. If the gouge slips, the left hand will prevent it from causing any damage. In other words, your left hand acts as a pivot or an anchor, while your right hand directs the tool. For example, if you want to make the side of a bowl concave toward the bottom, let the bevel of the gouge slide on the wood being cut **(9)**, then slowly move your right hand down **(10)**. After you slip a few times, you will learn to control your tools. As you carve, don't try to steady the work with your left hand — keep both hands behind the tool edge so you will have no chance to cut yourself.

8

9

10

For cutting out the center of the bowl, where the cut angles from the bowl's top toward its lower part, use a gouge and cut with the grain **(11)**. As you carve, keep moving your hand over the work to feel for high and low spots that you might not see **(12)**.

After final carving is done, you're ready to smooth out the inside, unless you want to leave a textured surface. Sometimes I like to leave the gouge marks on the wood, as in this piece **(13)**, which is smooth on the outside and textured on the inside.　□

11

12

13

Textured Surfaces

If you want to carve a textured surface, here are two ways. Starting the gouge at the top of the bowl **(1)** and letting the bevel of the tool slide down the side of the bowl to the bottom **(2,3)** will give you a sweeping cut as on the left side of the bowl in this photo **(4)**. As you slide down, move the tool handle back to control the shape.

For a fishscale effect, as on the end of the bowl in the photo, start to carve from the bottom **(5)**. Then slide up the wood on the tool bevel as you move the handle back **(6)**. Move up the bowl wall and repeat.

Sometimes combinations of different gouges and techniques can be quite effective. Make sure you work with sharp tools when carving a textured surface, because you won't be able to rely on sanding to correct marks left by dull tools.   ☐

1

2

3

4

5

6

Smoothing Out

If you choose an untextured surface, start the smoothing process by using carver burrs in a portable electric router. Here are a few examples of the different shapes available **(1)**. Smaller, more flexible tools are also available for smoothing, but I have found that the router works fine.

Hold the router firmly and don't take off too much wood at one time. Whenever possible, rest your hand against something or let one of your fingers slide against the edge of the bowl **(2)**, for guidance and safety.

The router works fast but takes skill and care to use. A slower but safer tool is a wood riffler. A riffler is a curved, half-round rasp at one end and a curved, half-round file at the other **(3)**. Rifflers, like carver burrs, are available in several different shapes. I have found the half-round shape best for my work, as there is usually a place on the tool that will fit the work **(4)**.

Use the carver burrs and router, a riffler or a combination to remove the gouge marks.

1

2

3

4

5

Next remove the marks left by the router or riffler. A gooseneck scraper blade is the best tool for this job **(5)**. This is an oddly shaped piece of steel that cuts with a burr on its edge. Because of its shape, there will always be some part of the curve that will fit your bowl **(6)**. Scrape with the grain until the surface is clean. (For more information on scrapers and how to sharpen them, see chapter 2.)

The final step is sanding first with medium and then fine-grit paper. Very little sanding will be necessary after scraping.

A chalkboard eraser made out of felt strips makes an excellent sanding block **(7)**. It will conform to the shape of the inside of the bowl and save the ends of your fingers. ☐

6

7

Carving the Outside

Carving the outside of the bowl can be done in several ways. I prefer to start by roughing out the shape with a bandsaw and a chisel.

First draw the shape you desire on the outside of the bowl **(1)**. Notice that the walls of the bowl are not the same thickness all around; it is not necessary to make them uniform. The appearance of a bowl can sometimes be made more interesting by varying wall thickness, which results in different but related shapes on the inside and outside.

Tilt the bandsaw table to an angle that approximates the angle on the inside of the bowl **(2)**. You can do this by eye. Then bandsaw out one side **(3)**. Next, cut both ends **(4,5)** and, finally, the last side **(6)**. Because the angles on the inside of a bowl aren't always the same, the table will usually have to be set differently for each cut.

1

2

3

4

5

6

7

Save the scrap from the last cut **(7)**. You will need it to tape back on the bowl, to keep the bowl square on the table **(8)**.

Now mark the shape of the bottom of the bowl and bandsaw it out **(9)**. Once you've roughly shaped the bowl on the outside **(10)**, you're ready to start in with hand tools.

8

9

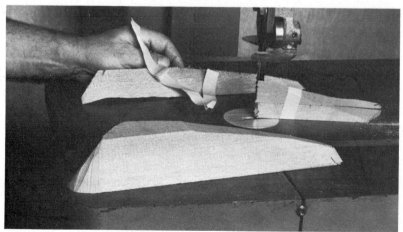

10

By planing, filing, sanding and spokeshaving, finish the top edge of the bowl first **(11,12)**. Working with the bowl resting on this edge later will help you know what shape you're working toward. Sand the surface with 80-grit sandpaper when it is the right shape **(13)**. With the top edge finished **(14)**, the rest of the outside of the bowl is ready for shaping.

11

12

13

14

15

Clamp the bowl to the bench, letting the part being cut hang over the edge wherever possible so that you can feel the thickness of the walls. If this isn't possible, be sure to have some scrap wood underneath the bowl so you don't carve into the bench. Use a chisel to rough out the part of the bowl with end grain (**15**).

Continually check wall thickness as you work (**16**), being careful not to cut through. Also watch for tear-out as you work near the top edge. When the thickness of the walls seems right, begin the smoothing process. □

16

Smoothing the Outside

For smoothing you can use a router with carver burrs; a Surform, rasp and file; a block plane and spokeshave; or a combination of any or all of these tools.

A Surform (1) is like a rasp with holes in the teeth. The chips go through the holes so the Surform won't clog up. It works fast, stays sharp for a long time and is inexpensive. Surforms are sold in several shapes and sizes; the one that takes both a flat and half-round blade is the best for my work.

A rasp is similar to a Surform but a much older style of tool (2). The rasp usually has finer teeth and, of course, no holes. It tends to clog when used on soft wood, but on hard wood it gives a nice, smooth surface. I use half-round and round patternmaker's rasps.

Wood files are just like rasps except their teeth are continuous and run at a slight angle across the width (3). Some files are double cut, which means that there are two rows of teeth running at angles to one another. I use two wood files about the same shape as my rasps, but they give a much finer cut.

Clean the teeth of rasps and files with a file card. File cards are small brushes with wire on one side and bristles on the other (4). Brush the teeth with the wire side first and then the bristle side.

A good way to clean a rasp or a file is to put a little alcohol on one side and light it with a match. The shavings clogging the teeth will absorb the alcohol and burn up without hurting the steel. Then you can use the file card to remove the ashes. Be careful to do this in a safe place.

1

2

3

4

5

A block plane **(5)** is an excellent tool to use if the bowl has some straight or slightly rounded parts on the outside.

Spokeshaves can be used on many shapes **(6)** and are available in many designs: This one **(7)** is straight with a flat sole and is the one I use most. I also have one with a round sole **(8)** for concave work. I prefer spokeshaves with adjustable blade screws.

6

7

8

Spokeshave handles fit the palms of your hands and have two indentations for your thumbs; hold the spokeshave with those **(9)**. To avoid chattering, push the spokeshave instead of pulling it. Some spokeshaves have one handle in the front for pulling, but these are designed for rough work.

If you have difficulty holding the blade for sharpening because it is too small, make a handle for it as you would for a cabinet-scraper blade.

I begin smoothing with a Surform **(10)**, and next use a rasp and file **(11)**. On long grain, work in any angle, but on end grain, always work in the direction of the grain.

9

10

11

The two final smoothing steps, as when working on the inside of the bowl, are scraping **(12)** and sanding **(13)**. Again, a chalkboard eraser helps in sanding.

Now the bowl is sanded smooth and ready to be finished **(14)**. ☐

12

13

14

Spindle Turning

Types of Turning

The woodturning lathe is the oldest of woodworking machines and the only one in which the work rather than the tool is driven by power. Skill is more important in turning than in any other machine process, although a beginner can do adequate work.

Woodturning traditionally was a trade in itself. Today woodworkers are rarely so specialized and are expected to be proficient in most areas of the craft, including turning. In this chapter, I will cover the basics only, for discussing the subject in depth could easily take a whole book.

There are two basic types of woodturning. In spindle turning the work is supported at both ends and driven at one. This is the method used for making round or partly round chair legs, table legs and other similar shapes. In faceplate turning, the method used to make bowls and round boxes, the work revolves on a faceplate secured only to the headstock of the lathe. Occasionally the two types of turning are combined. □

The Lathe

Lathe size is determined by the maximum diameter of the work that may be turned. Therefore, a 12-in. lathe will measure 6 in. from the center of a spindle to the lathe bed. A lathe of this size will usually take spindles up to 3 ft. long.

A ¾-HP motor will furnish enough power for a 12-in. lathe, but a 1-HP motor is better. A motor with a speed of 1725 RPM used with a four-step pulley on the headstock typically will give the lathe a range of speeds from 900 to 3200 RPM, depending on the size of the pulleys. I prefer machines equipped with a four-step pulley because they experience less belt slippage and speed loss than some other types. For example, lathes having a belt with expansion pulleys for speed variation tend to have problems with slippage and slowdown, although they are safe and easy to use.

If you are serious about turning, consider a lathe that has direct drive with a variable-speed motor. These are safe and good, although they can be expensive.

Here is a typical lathe **(1)**. The headstock, driven by the motor, is to the left of the lathe. (The headstock is considered a live center because it always spins with the work.) This headstock is equipped with faceplates for both inboard and outboard turning (p. 85). The gap in the bed next to the headstock allows inboard turning of thin objects of large diameter. The tailstock is to the right. It moves along the lathe bed to accommodate work of varying lengths.

1

A spur center inserted into the headstock drives the wood for spindle turning **(2)**. New lathes are usually furnished with a stationary cup center, or dead center, for the tailstock **(3,4)**. The friction created between the spinning wood and the stationary cup center, however, causes a buildup of heat that can burn the wood. To prevent this, apply a coat of wax to the end of the wood. Many people use oil for this purpose, but the oil is absorbed by the wood and does not do the job as well as wax.

To avoid the problem altogether, buy a ball-bearing live center for the tailstock. Here **(5)** are three interchangeable centers that fit into a bail-bearing live center. The one inserted into the ball bearing is the cup center, which is used for turning wood. The point center is for turning metal or plastic. The flat center is for holding wood or any other material that should not be marked, such as the lid for a box during finish-turning. A live center for the tailstock is definitely a worthwhile investment.

2

3

4

5

6

7

The tool rest is a very important part of a lathe. There are different lengths of straight tool rests available, and it is a good idea to have more than one **(6)**. Extra-long tool rests require two bases **(7)** and although they are often helpful, I don't think they are necessary except for production work.

The tool rest clamps into a base that slides along the bed of the lathe **(8)**. Position the tool rest with its top edge below the centerline of the spindle so the tool will be cutting at the centerline **(9)**. The corners of the wood should clear the tool rest by about ½ in. Always check to make sure that the wood will clear before you turn on the lathe. Here **(10)** the tool rest is too close to the work and damage could result.

If you are turning a large piece that is off balance, start the lathe at a slow speed and work the piece until it is balanced. I usually turn an average-size spindle like the one shown, which measures 2 in. by 2 in., at a speed of about 2000 RPM.

As with all woodworking operations, safety must come first in turning. Be sure you don't have any loose clothing, jewelry or hair that could get caught in the lathe. Long sleeves can be dangerous — roll them up. □

8

9

10

Mounting the Work

Some people prefer to cut the corners off a turning blank so that it is octagonal before they put it on the lathe **(1)**. I find it faster to cut off the corners on the lathe. On pieces too big to clear the bed, however, I cut off the corners first on a table saw or a bandsaw.

To mount a piece of wood between centers for spindle turning, first find the exact center of the piece of wood. Do this by drawing two diagonal lines from corner to corner on each end **(2)**. Use an awl to make a hole in the tailstock end of the piece of wood where the two lines cross. In the headstock end, make two diagonal saw cuts **(3)** with a hand-saw. This will make it possible for the spur center to grip the wood and spin it.

Drive the spur center into the saw cuts with a mallet **(4)**.

To secure the wood in the lathe, insert the end with the spur center into the headstock first, then move the tailstock up to the other end and clamp it tightly. Turn the handle on the tailstock until the point of the cup center engages the center hole in the wood. Keep turning the handle until the rim of the cup cuts into the wood. The cup center should be tight against the wood at all times, but not so tight that the work won't turn freely.

Make sure to lock the tailstock with its clamp **(5)** so that the vibrations won't work it loose. During turning, occasionally check that the cup is still tight against the work. □

1

2

3

4

5

1

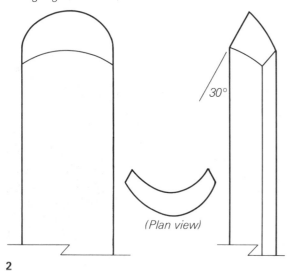

1" gouge (full scale)

30°

(Plan view)

2

Tools

Turning tools are usually sold in sets, but they can also be bought individually, or made. For spindle turning, I use a gouge, a parting tool and a skew. A beginner should have at least four tools to start: ½-in. and 1-in. gouges, a parting tool and a 1-in. skew.

Gouges **(1,2)** come in different sizes and are used primarily for roughing out the work and for cutting coves. Some skilled turners also use a gouge for faceplate turning, but this takes a lot of skill and I don't recommend it for beginners. I will discuss parting tools and skews as they are used.

In general, turning technique is similar to carving technique, but instead of hitting your tools with a mallet, the spinning of the wood supplies the hitting power. □

Roughing Out a Cylinder

To rough out a cylinder, first rest a 1-in. gouge against the tool rest **(1)**, and then slowly and carefully move the cutting edge up into the spinning wood. Always approach the wood in this manner — if you move the tool downward into the wood, there's a good chance that the tool will catch and break either itself or the tool rest. That is an easy way to get hurt.

If you start into the wood with the gouge from the end or in the center, you have little control over the wood splitting. Here **(2,3)** the tool is on top of the piece of wood just to make that point — your tool should always be on the tool rest.

1

2

3

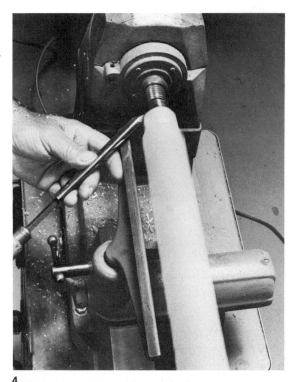

4

To prevent the wood from splitting, approach the work as though it were a pencil and you were trying to sharpen it with a gouge **(4)**. Continue like that, until the corners are removed and the piece is fairly round. Then let your finger and the tool slide along the tool rest **(5,6)**, until the piece is completely round. You don't have to stop the lathe each time to check if the piece is round. After you have some experience, you can simply rest the center part of the back of the gouge lightly on the wood while it is spinning **(7)**. If the wood is round, there will be no noise, but if there are still a few flat spots, the tool will bounce audibly. Of course, you shouldn't try this when the wood is still square.

With one end of the spindle rounded, shut off the lathe, move the tool rest over to the other end and continue turning. Use the gouge in the opposite direction without changing hands. Get used to using the tools in both directions because this will help you to do more consistent work.   ☐

5

6

7

Dimensioning a Cylinder

When you think the cylinder is round and has no flat spots, make it the same diameter along its entire length. For this you'll need a parting tool and an outside caliper.

A parting tool **(1,2)** is used in general for cutting grooves and in particular for dimensioning and marking the spindles to length. The best parting tools are thicker in the center than they are at the edges and thus they clear the sides of the groove they cut. This prevents the tool from heating up and becoming damaged and from burning the wood. All parting tools are available in thicknesses of ⅛ in. and ¼ in. I prefer a ⅛-in. parting tool.

An outside caliper **(3)** is used to measure thickness and outside dimensions.

To dimension the cylinder, hold the parting tool in the right hand at 90° to the tool rest. Set the caliper to the desired diameter (plus a little extra to allow for finish-turning and sanding) and hold it in the left hand. With the lathe running, move the parting tool into the wood and let the caliper rest in the groove until it slips on **(4)**. Then stop cutting and pull the caliper off that spot.

In this manner make several grooves along the length of the cylinder. Remember to make sure that the cylinder has no flat spots before doing any of this, because the caliper will get caught on these.

¼" *parting tool (full scale)*

(Plan view)

25°   25°

1

2

3

4

5

6

7

Remove the wood between the grooves with a gouge **(5)**. Finish off with a skew **(6)**.

The skew **(7)** works like a smoothing plane, but unlike a plane's edge, the cutting edge of a skew is sharpened on both sides **(8)**. Skews are available in different widths and are also used for cutting some *V*-grooves and for making rings and beads.

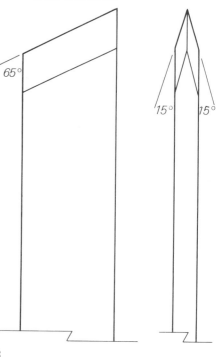

1" skew (full scale)

65°

15° 15°

8

The skew is an important lathe tool but very difficult to learn how to use properly. First of all, watch out for that top corner — if it catches, the work is ruined **(9)**.

To use a skew correctly, be sure that its bevel rests against the cylinder **(10)**. Then slowly move the skew into the work by raising the handle. If the skew bevel doesn't rest on the work when you're starting **(11)**, it will definitely dig right in. Once you've gotten off to a safe start, you can move the tool from the center of the cylinder toward the ends.

9

10

11

12

13

Here (**12,13**) I am going from the center to the left. Notice that I hold the end of the skew in my right hand against my hip. In the beginning, it's a good idea to do it this way, although when you are more experienced, you shouldn't have to. Without moving your feet, move your upper body and hips toward the left.

Here (**14,15**) I am moving from the center to the right. Notice that here again I don't change the position of my feet, but instead I move my hips and upper body.

Be sure to cut with the middle of the cutting edge (**16**). Watch out for that top corner. ☐

16

14

15

A Dimensioning Jig

For a precise cylinder, use a plane with a jig made for the lathe **(1)**. When the jig is placed on the lathe upside-down, you can see that it is made like a miter box **(2)**. The piece that is nailed and glued to the bottom fits snugly into the groove in the lathe bed **(3)**. Notice the blocks with *T*-nuts are positioned to slide through the groove. When the box is in place, turn the blocks to secure the box to the bed.

The rough-turned cylinder is mounted between the headstock and the tailstock, inside the box **(4)**.

With the lathe running at slow speed, rest the plane on top of the box and shave off a small amount of wood until the plane won't cut anymore **(5)**.

You can build the jig so that its sides adjust to accept work of different diameters, but I have found it is better to screw the box together at one size and then drill new screw holes as necessary. □

T-nuts

1

2

3

4

5

Scraping Versus Carving

There are two techniques used in spindle turning. Scraping is the method used by most beginners. Carving is the method used by skilled turners. Carving requires skill, experience and practice, but it is well worth learning from the beginning because you'll save lots of time in the long run.

Here is a brief description of the differences between the two methods:

Scraping is the easy way to turn — just rest the tool at 90° to the tool rest and scrape the wood **(1,2)**. The shavings fly right at your face because in scraping, the fibers of the wood are pulled off, not cut off.

In carving, the tool is tilted and held at an angle to the work. Shavings will not fly up into your face with this technique. Explaining the correct angle at which to hold the tool is impossible. To learn the right way, stop the lathe, put your tool on the tool rest and experiment, using your tool the way you would use a carving chisel. The way that allows the cleanest cut is the best way to hold the tool. Now start the lathe and work. You will find that the tool cuts beautifully **(3)**.

Here is the difference between scraped and carved wood **(4)**. The left side is carved and the right side is scraped. The work could be sanded so that both sides are smooth, but the minute the finish was put on, the fibers on the scraped surface would raise.

1

2

3

4

Here is another example **(5)**. Notice how sharp and clean the carved cut is on this ring. The same shape scraped on the same piece of wood is fuzzy and rough **(6)**.

Here's a cove cut that has been carved **(7)** and one that has been scraped **(8)**. When carving a cove, carve halfway down from each side so that you will always be cutting with the grain **(9,10)**.

5

6

7

8

9

10

11

12

To carve a *V*-cut, use the upper point of a skew. Hold it 90° to the tool rest **(11)**. This is the only time you should use the point of the skew. For rounding off the end grain, use the lower corner of the skew **(12)**, and as you carve, roll it.

When turning from a rectangular section into a round **(13)**, use a skew. First make a *V*-cut with the upper corner **(14)**. Then, using the lower corner, roll the skew as you cut **(15,16,17)**. ☐

13

14

15

16

17

Off-Center and Half-Round Turning

Spindle turnings do not always have to be round in section. By offsetting the centers, it is possible to turn a wide range of shapes such as ovals, triangles and even rounded squares. Here **(1)** is a spindle that is square on one end, round in the middle and triangular on the other end. These techniques require some practice, so it's best to make sure that you are in complete control of your tools before trying off-center turning.

To turn a piece that is round on one end and triangular on the other, first make a full-scale drawing **(2)** of the end of the piece of wood you will be using, in order to locate the points for the cup center. Then transfer the markings to the wood. Turn it as a cylinder and sand.

Insert the cup center into one of the points of the triangle **(3)**. Before starting the lathe, rotate the piece by hand to make sure it clears the tool rest.

1

A, center for cylinder
B, C, D, centers for triangle

2   3

For this operation, use only a gouge **(4,5)**. Do not use a skew because it will catch. Turn the wood as cleanly as possible. Repeat the procedure until you have used all of the points to turn the wood. Here is the turned piece **(6)**.

When sanding an off-center piece, always use a sanding block. I find that a piece of cork (p. 175) makes a good block.

You can also make identical half rounds or quarter rounds easily by spindle turning.

To make half rounds, glue two pieces of wood together with brown paper between them using hot glue **(7)**. If you use a slow-drying glue, the paper will absorb some of the glue and the pieces will not separate later. Don't put too much glue on and don't use glue so thin that it will penetrate the paper. Don't use newspaper, because the glue will go right through it. The pieces should not be clamped — by pressing them together with your hands you can give just the right amount of pressure.

As a safety precaution, make the pieces longer than you need and either put a screw in each end or wire them together as I have done here **(8)**. Making a saw cut or a groove for the wire helps prevent it from slipping. With the ends bound this way, the pieces won't fly apart even if the glue joint fails.

Another good safety precaution is to cut the corners off the piece after it is glued up, so that it becomes an octagon.

4

5

7

6

8

9

10

After you've turned and sanded the piece, split it apart with a chisel **(9,10)**. Cut the ends off, and the turnings are complete **(11)**.

A few final pointers on spindle turning: Whenever possible, make any joints or holes in the wood before you turn it. The holes will not interfere with the turning; just be careful when you sand the work, and use a sanding block if you can.

If there are to be any square sections on the spindle, pencil them out carefully on all four sides before you begin turning **(12)**.

If any saw cuts have to be made on the piece after it is turned, try to leave the ends square for reference **(13)**. □

11

12

13

Sanding

Most of the time you will need to sand the work you have turned. This is easiest while the work is still on the lathe.

Before you start to sand, always remove the tool rest so your fingers won't get caught between it and the turning work **(1)**.

For better control of the sandpaper, fold it over three times so that it won't slide **(2,3)**. Sandpaper folded this way can easily be formed into certain shapes **(4)**.

1

2

3

4

5

When you are sanding a straight cylinder, a blackboard eraser makes a fine sanding block because it has just the right amount of flexibility **(5)**. But always use a regular sanding block when you are sanding an off-center piece **(6)**. Sanding blocks, however, are often not suitable for what you need to do, so you will have to use your fingers sometimes. The most important thing to remember is to be careful. For example, when sanding a piece that goes from square to round, don't put on pressure with your fingers in the center of the sandpaper. Keep your hands out on the end **(7,8)** so that your fingers won't get cut by the sharp corners. By the way, it's a very good idea to wear gloves when sanding. □

6

7

8

Faceplate Turning
Chapter 5

1

Mounting the Work

Only the headstock of the lathe is used in faceplate turning, although sometimes, if the wood is off balance or heavy, or when turning without a scrap plate, the tailstock is used to support the work temporarily. A faceplate **(1)** is a steel disc that threads onto the headstock. All faceplates have threads going in a direction opposite to the spinning of the motor so that they will not come loose while the lathe is running. Faceplates for inboard turning are thus threaded differently than those for outboard turning. Some faceplates have double threads so that they can be used both inboard and outboard.

Faceplates have holes in them through which the turning blank can be screwed, but most people screw the faceplate to a plate of scrap wood that is glued to the bottom of the turning blank. The scrap plate allows you to make full use of the wood to get a deeper

bowl, as well as to avoid having screw holes in the work. Always make the scrap plate about ½ in. larger than the diameter of the faceplate — screws too close to the edge might split the wood. Cut the plate round on a bandsaw or with a sabersaw, or at least cut off the corners and make it octagonal. Do this also to the turning blank. Square corners are dangerous.

To make sure the work will be perfectly centered, use the center mark of the scrap plate, which is glued to the square block to be turned, to draw out the bowl **(2)**. I suggest beginners glue the scrap plate directly to the turning blank with Titebond and then cut or chisel the plate off after turning. More experienced turners can glue a piece of brown paper between the plate and the blank so that the two will separate easily after turning. I discuss this technique and other ways to mount the work later in this chapter.

When the scrap plate has been glued to the turning blank and the faceplate is screwed onto it **(3)**, you're ready to thread the assembly onto the headstock. If you like, you can center the work at this point instead of earlier: Mount the assembly on the lathe and spin it by hand while marking out the bowl with a pencil held securely on the tool rest. Then unscrew the assembly from the headstock and bandsaw out the bowl.

When mounting the faceplate to the lathe, make sure to screw it on securely. Most lathe motors have a brake on them and, with the motor stopping and the spinning piece of wood acting like a flywheel, the wood will continue spinning until it unscrews itself and flies off. This is particularly a problem when working with large pieces outboard. ☐

2

3

Tools

Faceplate turning takes less skill than spindle turning because it is done mostly by scraping — the tool has to cut both with and across the grain. For tools I use diamond-point and round-nose chisels, which are designed for faceplate turning only **(1)**. Some professional turners use gouges for faceplate turning, but before you do this you'd better get proper instruction. I tried this a few times and almost killed myself.

Because diamond-point and round-nose chisels are designed for scraping, I don't hone them but leave on the burr, which is the actual cutting edge, as on a scraper blade. The chisels cut better this way. Many people use these tools for spindle turning because they are easy to use. The result is that the wood needs much more sanding afterward, and the cut is neither accurate nor controlled.

Most available diamond-point and round-nose chisels are made from too-thin steel that bends easily if caught in the wood **(2)**. Tools made from this steel also vibrate when used to make deep cuts where the tool rest can't reach, as when cutting the inside of a deep bowl. My students and I make our own tools out of 18-ft. lengths of unhardened ½-in. by ½-in. oil-hardening steel. We cut the lengths to about 15 in., grind them to shape and then send them out to be hardened. Finally, we turn the handles. Excellent 12-in. long-and-strong tools are the result **(3)**. (If you plan to turn much abrasive wood, such as teak or rosewood, you might consider investing in carbide-tipped tools.)

1

2

3

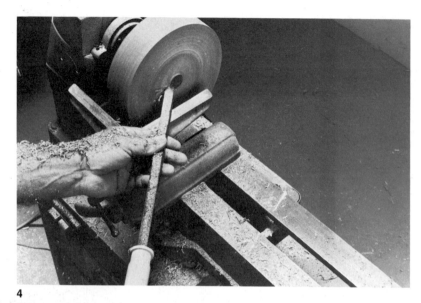

Use a diamond-point chisel to shape the outside of most bowls; use a round-nose chisel for bowls having coves or cavities. Set your tool rest so that the point of the chisel is right in the center of the bowl **(4)** when the tool is held 90° to the rest **(5)**. This is the correct way to hold both diamond-point and round-nose chisels. You can tilt the handle up a little **(6)**, but never hold it as you would a gouge or a skew **(7)**. If you do, the tool will dig right in, which results in either a split bowl, a broken tool rest or a bent chisel.

In these photos I am using a right-angle tool rest, which does not have to be readjusted for outside and inside turning when making small bowls. One of these is not really necessary unless you plan to make a large number of small bowls or plates.   □

4

5

6

7

Turning a Bowl

As in spindle turning, start faceplate turning slowly. First, balance the work at slow speed. The larger the piece you are turning, the slower the lathe speed should be. At any given speed, the outside edge of a larger circle of wood will move into your tool faster than that of a smaller piece of wood.

Use only the tip of the diamond-point chisel for scraping **(1)**, and make sure the back of the chisel sits flat on the tool rest. Do the same when using the round nose. When the outside is perfectly round, true up the top of the bowl **(2)**. Then step up the speed and shape the outside of the bowl **(3)**. For the final cut, run the lathe at high speed, about 1500 RPM, depending on the size of the bowl. Take a very fine cut so there will be little sanding to do. If much sanding is necessary, the bowl might end up oval. The sides of the bowl are made up of both long grain and end grain, and of course end grain won't sand as fast as long grain.

To sand, remove the tool rest and run the lathe at about half the speed of the final cut. Use coarse paper first, about 60 grit, and then sand through 80 grit, 120 grit and 180 grit to smooth out the scratches **(4,5)**. Finish with 220 grit. Keep moving the sandpaper back and forth to prevent deep scratches.

1

2

3

4

5

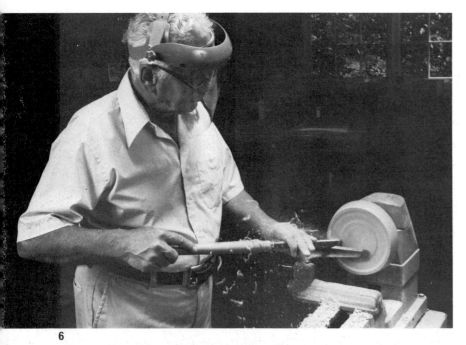

6

Now you are ready to turn the inside. This is usually done with a round-nose chisel, but you might need to use a diamond-point, depending on the shape you desire. The techniques for inside turning **(6,7)** are the same as for outside turning, but here are a few tips.

When turning the inside of a bowl, try to avoid having the sides and the bottom meet in a sharp corner **(8)**, for this shape is very difficult to sand. Try instead to have the sides and the bottom meet as shown by the dotted line.

Keep track of the depth of the bowl as you work, stopping the lathe occasionally to check it **(9)**. Don't try to make a bowl 2⅛ in. deep with stock that's only 2 in. thick.

When turning the inside, you should always work from the outer edge to the center, to go with the grain **(10)**.

7

8

9

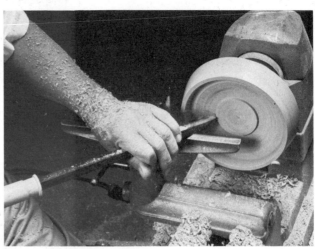

10

Use outside calipers to check that the sides of the bowl are the right thickness **(11)**. Use inside calipers to check that inside dimensions are correct **(12)**.

Sand the inside of the bowl the same way that you sanded the outside **(13)**. Wear gloves to protect your fingers.

If the diameter of the piece to be turned is too big for inboard turning, you'll have to turn outboard **(14)**. For that you'll need a floor stand to hold the tool rest. You will also need a faceplate with the correctly reversed thread. Techniques for outboard turning are the same as for inboard turning. Turn the outside first **(15)**, then the inside **(16)**.

Beginners should not attempt the outboard turning of pieces larger than 18 in. in diameter. Instead, work with a router rigged on an arm on a center pivot. If you do turn pieces larger than 18 in. on the lathe, make sure lathe and tool rest are secure. If necessary, brace the lathe to your shop floor, wall and ceiling. □

11

12

13

14

15

16

1

2

Another Way to Mount the Work

Here's a fast, easy way to make plates and small bowls without screwing the work to the faceplate. Instead, screw a piece of ¾-in. plywood to the faceplate **(1)**. Make sure it does not wobble (if it does, turn it so the surface is perfectly flat and the edge perfectly round), and then glue on a piece of 40-grit sandpaper. This will drive the work.

Plane the back of the plate to be turned and bandsaw it to the approximate shape **(2)**. Remember to mark the center on the top of the plate when drawing the circle.

Now, put the planed side against the sandpaper and move up the tailstock, into which a live cup center has been chucked, until the cup center touches the center mark on the plate **(3)**. The plate should sit firmly against the sandpaper. Be sure to lock the handle before turning on the lathe.

Switch on the lathe and turn and sand the outside and inside of the plate **(4,5)**. Of course, you cannot turn the very center of the inside because the tailstock is in the way.

3

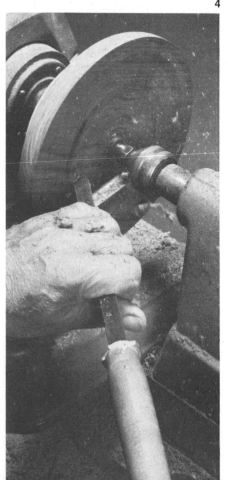

4

5

When the plate is completed, remove the remaining center piece **(6)** with a Forstner bit in the drill press or with a chisel **(7)**. Smooth with a scraper blade **(8)**, and then with a sanding block and sandpaper going with the grain **(9)**.

The plate is finished **(10)**. Sign it and you can charge more if you have the right name.   ☐

6

7

8

9

10

1   2

3

4

Turning Bowls with Bases

If your bowl will have a foot or base, turn that first.

Screw the faceplate directly to what will be the top of the bowl **(1)**. Rough-turn the outside of the bowl, finish-turn and sand the base **(2)**, and then cut a scrap plate to glue onto the bottom of the bowl and screw a faceplate to it.

Apply a small amount of hot glue to the outside edge of the base of the bowl **(3)**. Try to avoid getting the glue on the inside edge because it will be difficult to clean off later. Apply the glue to the edge of the scrap plate, too, and put on a layer of brown paper.

Now move the tailstock up, place the faceplate in front of the live center and tighten the tailstock **(4)**. The live center is tapered and will automatically center the faceplate. To check, turn on the lathe. If the scrap plate is slightly off center, it will be able to center itself because the glue is not dry. To prevent the glue from setting up too fast, it might be a good idea to take the chill off the plate, but don't make it too hot.

Remove the bowl from the lathe after about a half hour and set it aside for curing. When the glue has cured, which takes about 24 hours, remove the faceplate that is on the top of the bowl and place the bowl back on the headstock (5). For safety, move the tail-stock up to prevent the bowl from flying off. Turn and sand the outside.

Turn the inside, but leave the tailstock in place until the walls are the right thickness and the bowl is the right depth (6). Then re-move the tailstock, turn down the center plug (7) and sand the inside of the bowl (8).

5

6

7

8

10

To remove the bowl from the scrap plate, put a chisel right in the glueline and hit it lightly until the bowl starts to separate **(9)**. Carefully pry with the chisel, and then pull the bowl off with your hand **(10,11)**.

Here the bowl and the scrap plate are separated **(12)**. Notice that the brown paper split in half. Don't use newspaper because it will absorb the glue and prevent the bowl from separating cleanly. Sand the bottom of the bowl to remove the paper and the bowl is ready to be signed and finished **(13)**. I usually use salad-bowl finish for bowls that will come in contact with food. □

9

11

12

13

Off-Center Turning

Off-center turning can be done by faceplate turning as well as spindle turning, but don't try it until you have mastered regular faceplate turning. Using a wedge between the faceplate and the wood is another, safer way to do the work and still produce some interesting shapes.

First, turn and sand the outside and rim of your bowl **(1)**. Then loosen the screws in the faceplate and insert a wedge. Remove one screw at a time, replacing each with a longer screw of the same number **(2,3)**. Put the piece back on the lathe. The piece will wobble **(4)**, so start off slowly.

Remove the high spots on the bowl and increase the speed. Continue turning until you get the desired shape **(5)**, then sand.

2

3

1

4

5

6

Here is the piece rough-sanded **(6)**. It is deeper on one side than the other, a shape that would be good for a stool seat or a platter for carving.

But the bottom has three screw holes that still have to be plugged. To do this, use a plug cutter **(7)** mounted in a drill press. You can cut across the grain to make plugs or with the grain to make dowels.

When cutting plugs, don't let the cutter go through the full thickness of the board or you'll have to stop the drill press each time and remove the plug from the cutter. It's easier to leave the plugs on the board and chisel them off later **(8)**.

Redrill the screw holes in the bottom of the bowl so that the plugs will fit snugly. Put glue in the holes and hammer in the plugs, making sure that the grain of the plugs goes in the same direction as that of the bowl **(9)**. When the glue is dry, chisel off the excess and sand the bottom of the bowl **(10)**.   □

7

8

9

10

Turning Large Bowls

Stacking   Finding dry wood from which to turn bowls more than 2 in. or 3 in. deep is difficult, and if you do find some, it will be expensive. But there are several other ways to make deep bowls. You can stack them, turn them green or bricklay them.

Stacking wood for large bowls is often a great waste of materials and labor. The most common way is to glue several pieces on top of one another (1). Frequently, pieces are sandwiched together with the grains at 90° to each other (2). After a short time, a bowl built this way will split apart.

Here is one way to make a stacked bowl with less waste. Draw to full scale the shape of half the bowl. Draw in the thickness of the layers and mark the width of the rings. Add ⅛ in. to each side to be sure that you'll have enough wood if you find, when turning, that the bowl is a little off center (3).

With a compass, take all the different radii from drawing **3** and draw the rings (4) onto the wood. Make them in two half circles, bandsaw them out and glue them together. Or, cut out a full ring with a jigsaw. If you do this, you could use the waste from the center to make smaller bowls. If you're making only one bowl, as is the case here, you could use the center piece from ring 1 for ring 4; ring 5 could be made from ring 2.

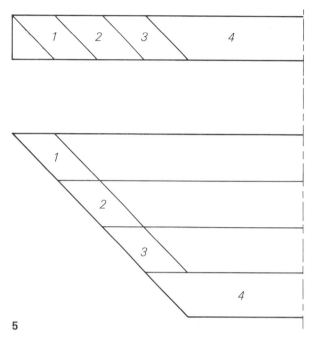

The most economical way to make a stacked bowl is to bandsaw the half rings out of two boards with the table tilted 45°. The only drawback is that very little variation of shape is possible with this method.

Again, make a full-scale drawing of half the bowl **(5)**. Then draw in the layers. Here I use 1-in. thick boards, so the width of the rings also has to be 1 in. Using 1-in. stock gives me room to shape the bowl a little. If I used 2-in. stock, the possibilities for shaping would increase, but so would the waste. If the bowl was to have straight sides, not rounded, I would use ¾-in. thick boards.

Joint the edges of the two boards you are going to use, because they will be glued together later. With the boards together **(6)**, draw the circles and bandsaw them out with the saw table tilted 45°. The only waste is the sawdust from the kerf, and the two outside pieces **(7)**. The two inside pieces will become the bottom of the bowl **(8)**.

5

6

7

8

Now glue the pairs of half pieces together, clamping one half ring to a flat board. Don't use hot glue if the bowl will be washed in water, and place a piece of paper under the joint so it won't stick to the board. Put glue on the ends of both pieces and press them tightly together. Then put on the two other clamps **(9)**.

When the glue has dried, clean off the excess with a chisel, plane or belt sander. Then stack the rings and glue them together. Lining up the joints might look best **(10)**, but I prefer to offset the joints a little for more strength. Here **(11)** they are offset about ¾ in., not enough to make the bowl crack. An offset of 2 in. would be too much.

After stacking is complete, glue on a scrap plate to accept the faceplate. Because the base of this bowl is quite small, I would not use paper between it and the scrap plate. When turning is finished, saw the plate off.

Here's the bowl glued together, ready for turning **(12)**, and after turning **(13)**.

9

10

11

12

13

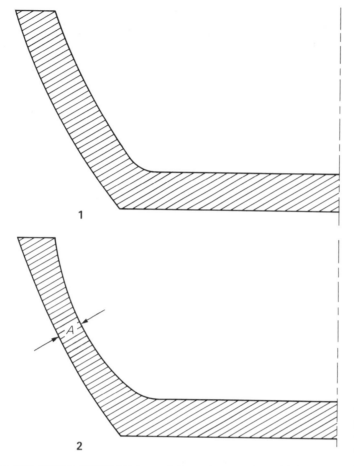

Green wood It is easiest and fastest to turn green wood, but in between rough-turning and finish-turning the wood has to dry, and the long drying time is a disadvantage.

Green wood turns very fast and its smell is not always pleasant. Bowls turned from green wood are worked the same way as those from dry wood, with the same tools. You must, however, screw the faceplate directly to green wood, because glue will not stick to it. In addition, the walls of green-turned bowls have to be left thick because once the wood is dry the bowl will have to be finish-turned. The walls must be the same thickness all around **(1,2)** or else the thinner areas will dry faster and shrink more than the thicker ones, causing the wood to crack, especially on end grain. Remember, the log's pith will crack when it is dry, so don't try to turn a bowl out of wood containing it.

There are many opinions as to the best way to dry green-turned bowls. I store mine in an open shed so air can circulate around them. (Don't put them in the sun or they will crack.) Before storing, weigh the bowls and label each with the weight and date. Then, every week or two, depending on the size of the bowls, record the current weight. When the bowls have been the same weight for several weeks, they're probably dry. I usually take mine inside the shop for a couple of weeks before finish-turning so they'll reach equilibrium with the shop atmosphere.

Some people prefer burying green-turned bowls in sawdust to draw out the moisture. This is a good method but time-consuming.

As green bowls dry, they will shrink in both width and thickness. The bowl here **(3)** was 9 in. in diameter when turned. It still measures 9 in. going with the grain, but across the grain it is 8¹¹/₁₆ in. wide, ⁵/₁₆ in. less **(4)**.

This bowl **(5)** was made out of half a tree trunk and measured 3½ in. tall when green. It shrank at different rates because the old wood (the heartwood) shrank less than the new (the sapwood) **(6)**. The middle of the bowl now measures 3⅜ in. **(7)** and the sides measure 3¼ in. **(8)**. Notice that the middle of the bowl, with the end grain, has the old wood, which has shrunk less than the sides with the long grain and the new wood.

The use of polyethylene glycol (PEG) is becoming more and more popular these days for stabilizing wood and preventing it from shrinking. PEG molecules replace the water molecules in wood and remain there when the wood dries, reducing dimensional change. I don't use PEG because I don't like what it does to the color of the wood.

5

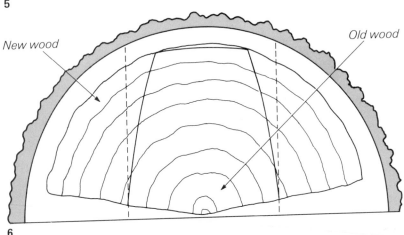

New wood   *Old wood*

6

7   8

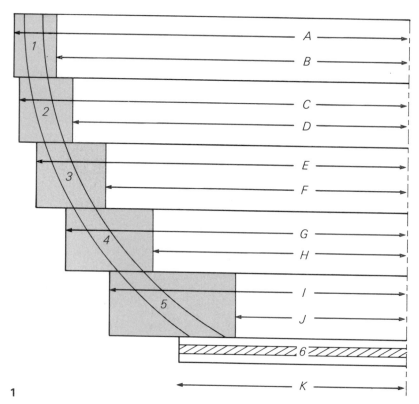

A

B

C

D

E

F

G

H

I

J

6

1

K

Bricklaying Bricklaying is a technique that has been used for years to make such things as large wooden pulleys for belt-driven machines and frames for upholstered furniture. Patternmakers also use bricklaying to make complicated objects. It is a good way to make a stable bowl of any shape, with little waste, and can be attractive, too.

Circular bricklaying might seem difficult and complicated, but it isn't. It is more difficult to explain than it is to do. You can make the joints by hand using a miter box and a block plane, but that is time-consuming. The best and easiest way to make the joints is to use a table saw.

First, draw the shape of half the bowl from the side view in full scale, and then draw in the rings—as many as you want **(1)**. Then mark the width of the rings, adding ⅛ in. on each side of the bowl walls to be sure to have enough wood if the bowl should be a little off center when mounted on the lathe.

In this case, there are five rings plus a bottom. The rings are 1 in. thick. The bottom is made of three layers of wood with the grain of the center piece going 90° to that of the outside pieces. Although I have said that wood should not be stacked this way, it is okay here because the layers are thin, and better than having a solid-wood bottom. The grain in the rings runs around the circumference, so the wood will move up and down, but the circumference will not change. A piece of solid wood on the bottom would shrink and eventually break. As it is, the last layer of the bowl bottom will probably get small checks.

Now construct a drawing such as drawing **2**. In this bowl, each ring is made up of eight pieces. First, draw a straight line on your paper and then a line perpendicular to it. From the point where the two lines cross, the center, draw lines at 45° to divide the four quarters into eighths.

Now, set your dividers exactly the length of *A* from drawing **1** and draw an arc on drawing **2** as shown. Then set the dividers the length of *B* and draw another arc. Draw a straight line *B1* and then, parallel to it and just touching the outside arc, draw line *B2*. Continue until you have drawn the length and width of all eight pieces for the five layers.

After drawing **2** is finished, cut the pieces of the rings to width and roughly cut the lengths to angle. Drawing **3** shows a way to cut the wood without waste, flipping the wood after each cut. Then set the miter gauge, taking the angle from the drawing. With eight pieces, the angle of each is 67½°. (Because you are working with a circle, all the pieces have the same angle, only the lengths of the pieces are different.)

After setting the miter gauge, cut the angle on eight pieces of scrap wood that are the same width and length. If the miter is off a fraction of a hair, it won't show up if you just check two pieces. If the angle is not correct, reset the miter gauge and try again. With the miter gauge set to the exact angle, you are ready to cut the pieces.

First, cut an end off each piece. Then for each ring put a stop on the miter gauge and cut the eight pieces to the exact length in the drawing (**4**). Notice that the corner of the stop against the fence has been cut off, so no debris will be trapped there. An accumulation of sawdust and dirt would cause an inaccurate cut.

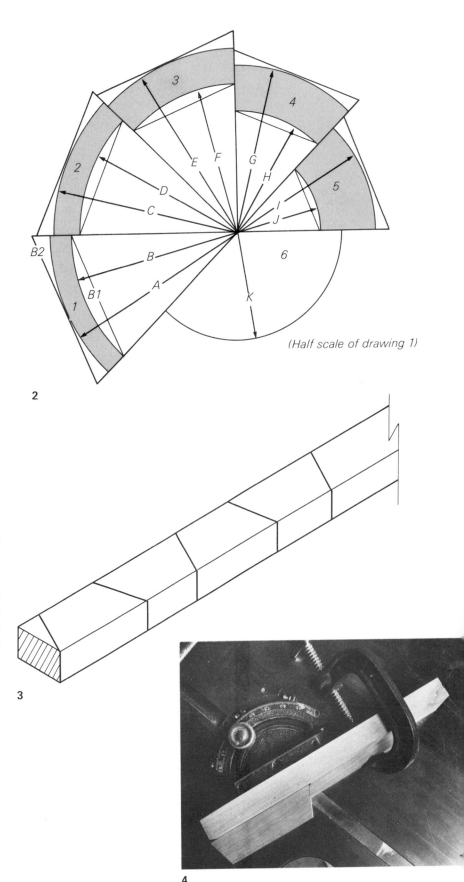

(Half scale of drawing 1)

2

3

4

5

6

When all the pieces are cut, glue them together in pairs with hot glue **(5,6)**, even if you're making a bowl that will have to be washed. Later on you can use a water-resistant glue such as Cascamite to put the rings together, and the joints glued with hot glue will be sandwiched in between the rings. Make sure to use glue on both ends and have paper underneath, so the wood won't stick to the bench. Rub the two pieces together to squeeze out the glue; after about a minute, the glue should be cold enough for you to let go. Set the pieces aside to cure.

When the pieces have been glued in pairs **(7)** and the glue has cured for about fifteen minutes, glue the pairs together **(8)**.

After about two hours, check to see if the two halves fit together **(9)**. If they don't, making them fit is not too difficult, but you'll need to make a jig for the table saw **(10)**.

To do this, cut out a piece of wood with sides that are exactly parallel and draw a line through the center. Put the center joint of one of the halves right on the line, and then check that distances A and B are exactly the same. Trace the piece to be cut on the jig and bandsaw out the jig carefully. After cutting on the table saw, distances C and D will be the same.

7

8

9

10

11

Set the fence so the blade just touches the joint (**11**). Cutting too much off will make the circle into an oval.

Pull the jig away from the blade, then start the saw and make the cut (**12**). Continue pushing the jig through and cut the other end (**13**). Cut the other half the same way. The joint comes out perfectly. Now put the halves together using hot glue.

When you've assembled all the rings, let the glue cure about ten hours. Then clean the excess from both sides with a smoothing plane. You could also use a 6-in. belt sander for this, but that takes more skill and guts.

12

13

Before building up the bowl, find the center of each section of each of the rings and mark it. Square it across with a pencil **(14,15)**. Then stack the two lowest rings, alternating the alignment of marked centerlines and glue joints **(16)**.

When these rings are in position, mark the inside of the lowest ring for three or four brads **(17)**. The brads prevent the rings from slipping when they are being glued together. Don't put them in too deep. Because there is the extra ⅛ in. left on each side of the bowl walls, the brad marks will be removed when the bowl is turned.

Mark the next ring and proceed that way until the bowl is built up **(18)**.

14

15

16

17

18

19

To center the bottom of the bowl, cut a piece of scrap wood to fit snugly inside the last ring. Find its center by measuring from one inside edge of the ring to the other **(19)**. Then do the same thing, turning the ruler 90°

Now set a compass to the radius of the bottom of the bowl **(20)**, and draw out the circle on the last ring **(21)**. Here again, use brads to prevent the bottom from slipping.

20

21

Next, mark out a scrap plate for the faceplate. The scrap plate should be ½ in. larger than the radius of the faceplate. Measure the diameter of the faceplate **(22)**, mark it on the scrap plate **(23)** and bandsaw it out. Center the scrap plate on the bowl bottom **(24)**.

With everything in place and marked, you're ready to glue the assembly together **(25)**. You can do this in one step but I prefer to glue up the rings first, and then the bottom and scrap plate. Beginners should glue two rings at a time.

Glue the scrap plate directly to the bowl without brown paper between. Because of the sharp corners and the danger of chattering, it's too dangerous to do otherwise. Remember to remove the brads before you start turning, and be careful not to turn through the first layer of the bottom of the bowl, because then you will be able to see the glueline and it looks awful.

When the bowl is finished, cut the plate off using a handsaw and sand the bottom. In this photo **(26)** the bowl is finished and oiled.

22

23

24

25

26

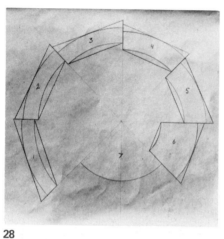

The way that I have shown for bricklaying a bowl is the fastest way. It is also a safe way, if you know what you are doing. Now I will tell you another way. This takes a bit more time but is safer, especially for a beginning turner. In this method, the rings of the bowl are bandsawn out and then glued on top of each other.

You'll still need to make full-scale drawings first **(27,28)**. Cut and glue the pieces together as before, into half sections, but don't glue the halves together until after bandsawing.

Here's a good way to mark the circles exactly. Glue a piece of wood in the center of a piece of cardboard—make the wood the same thickness as the rings so that a compass can rest on it **(29)**. From the drawing, take all the outside radii of the rings and draw the circumferences on the cardboard **(30)**. Then place each pair of halves on the cardboard so they fit inside the circumference of a particular ring **(31)**.

27

28

31

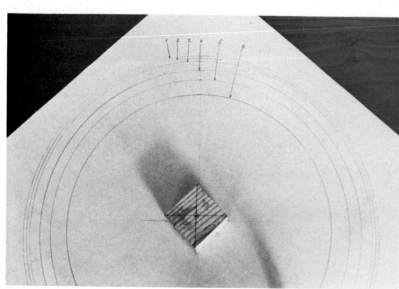

30

29

From your drawing, take the outside and inside radii **(32,33)** and transfer them to each ring with a compass. Because the halves are not glued together yet, it's best to have an extra pair of hands when doing this **(34)**.

Bandsaw the halves to the desired curve and then glue them together **(35)**. When the glue is dry, plane or sand the rings so that they are flat. This particular ring is the last one before the bottom.

32

33

34

35

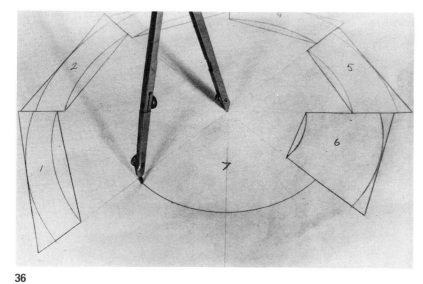

36

Now take the radius of the bottom of the bowl from the drawing **(36)**. In this case, the bottom of the bowl, which is laminated from three layers of walnut, measures 6 in., the same as the diameter of the faceplate. Because the scrap stock is already glued to the bottom stock here, just mark the bottom **(37)** and bandsaw it out.

Leaving the compass at the radius of the bowl bottom, put the last ring back on the cardboard and mark it for the bottom **(38)**.

Now stack the rings. Use a ruler to check the overhang and ensure that each ring is placed correctly **(39)**, or you might put each ring back on the cardboard and mark out the next ring on it before stacking.

37

38

39

Also check that the joints on alternating rings line up **(40)**. Then mark the rings for the brads **(41)** — each should have four. Glue up everything, including the bottom and scrap plate **(42)**, with water-resistant glue.

When the glue has dried, screw on the faceplate **(43)** and turn the bowl. Make sure not to turn through the first layer of the bowl bottom. If you do, you'll reveal the glueline. Here **(44)** I went through on purpose and you can see the ugly blotch that results.

41

40

42

43

44

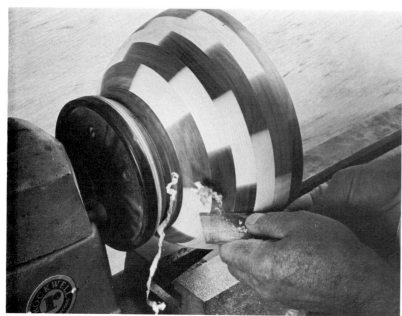

45

A bricklaid bowl has no end grain, so before sanding the outside, use a scraper blade (it's much faster) instead of a coarse grade of sandpaper **(45)**. Use a gooseneck scraper for the inside **(46)**.

In this bowl I used ash and walnut to emphasize the bricklaying **(47)**. When using different woods, be sure to pick woods of similar density so that they will move together. For example, if the walnut in this bowl were ebony, which does not shrink much, there would be conflict between its rate of shrinkage and that of the ash, and the bowl would eventually fall apart. □

46

47

Plywood and Veneer
Chapter 6

History

The art of veneering has had a checkered career. It was practiced in Egypt 3500 years ago, as well as in ancient Greece and Rome. During the Middle Ages, there seems to have been less veneering in furniture construction; but veneering made a comeback in Italy during the fifteenth century, and the art spread through Europe, reaching a climax in skill and artistry in eighteenth-century Germany, France and England. Interest in the art of veneering declined again, however, in the nineteenth century, with the introduction of production machinery.

Throughout history, the lack of glues resistant to water and heat has been the biggest problem in veneering. Today there is a resurgence of interest in veneering, which, I think, is largely due to modern adhesives and the development of plywood.

Many people talk about plywood as "that modern glued-up stuff," but this is ridiculous when you consider that the basis of plywood construction is the age-old process of veneering. Because plywood makes an excellent ground surface on which to veneer, craftsmen should at least know how it is made and used, so I'll talk about that first. □

Plywood

Plywood is made by gluing together several thin layers of wood with alternating grains. It has distinct advantages and disadvantages, so there is usually little doubt about where and when to use it instead of solid wood.

Its biggest advantage is that it is more stable and won't change dimension, except in thickness. The crossply construction in veneer-core plywood gives about 50% long-grain to long-grain gluing surface, allowing the use of less complicated joints in some applications. There is also less waste for the craftsman, because there are no knots, checks or other defects that must be cut out. Plywood is also economical to manufacture, since almost all of a tree can be used, and it is often more economical to work than solid wood because it's ready to be cut up and joined. Solid wood has to be edge-joined, thickness-planed, and so forth, before joints can be made.

The greatest disadvantage of plywood is that it is more difficult to repair than solid wood. This is because the veneers are so thin. Also, the joints usually have to be hidden and the edges faced. Besides that, plywood cannot be shaped or carved. Along the grain, solid wood is much stronger than plywood, while across the grain, veneer-core plywood is stronger.

The first fumbling efforts to use plywood in the mass production of furniture were in the 1920s, and since then plywood has become indispensable. The flush corners and edges of modern furniture and the development of frame-and-panel construction into plain, unbroken surfaces would have been impossible without the dimensional stability of plywood. Even architecture has been revolutionized by the availability of standard-size sheets of wood that are stronger than ordinary lumber. □

Plywood Manufacture

Veneers for plywood are cut in one of four ways, depending on the species of the lumber and the use to which the veneer will be put. I will describe these methods briefly before getting into plywood construction to give an idea of how veneer is prepared.

Most veneer is rotary cut (1). This method requires first removing the bark and steaming the log. Then the log is placed between centers on a large veneer lathe and revolved into a knife. As the log turns, the knife automatically advances into the stock at a controlled rate, which determines the thickness of the veneer.

Rotary-cut veneer doesn't have the fine figure of sliced veneer, because when it is cut the veneer is peeled off the log like a sheet of paper toweling pulled from a roll. Because the cuts are always parallel to the annual rings, the grain of the veneer looks unnaturally stretched and doesn't have much character. This mahogany (2) has been rotary cut. Some of the color of the wood is also destroyed during steaming. Rotary-cut veneer is used mostly for core stock in hardwood plywood, for crossbanding and as facing on cheap plywood.

For face veneer, the finest hardwood logs are used and the veneer is usually sliced instead of rotary cut. Here again, the log is steamed first. There are several ways to slice veneer. Most often the log will be pushed into a fixed knife and then automatically advanced between cuts so each slice is the exact same thickness, usually 1/28 in. The pieces are kept in order as they come from the machine so they can be matched. Sliced veneers are sold in flitches, bundles containing all the stock from one log or from one section of a large log. This makes it possible to panel a whole room with face veneer from the same tree and to match the grain from one veneer leaf to the next.

Half-round veneer is similar to sliced veneer, but it is cut on the veneer lathe. The log and the staylog to which it's bolted in eccentric chunks are mounted on the lathe. As the staylog revolves, it presents only a small part of a large circle to be sliced into veneer. Veneer cut this way has interesting figure.

The fourth and oldest method of producing veneer is by bandsawing with a thin blade, which makes a narrow kerf. Even so, as much wood is wasted as is saved. Because this method produces so much waste, it is not often used commercially. It's still the best way, however, for a woodworker to make his or her own veneer.

All veneer must be dried carefully after cutting. In drying, the veneer passes between rollers and heated platters that are arranged to keep the veneer as flat as possible. □

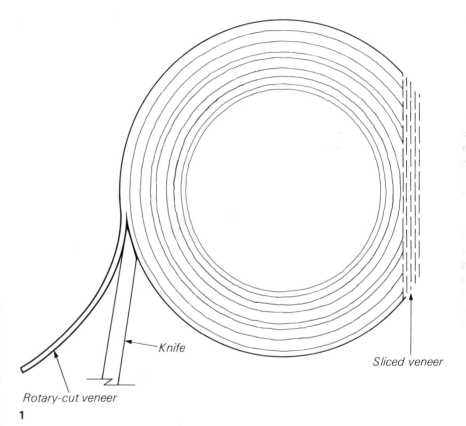

Knife

Sliced veneer

Rotary-cut veneer

1

2

Face veneer

Crossband

Lumber core

Crossband

Face veneer

Glued

1

2

3

Plywood Construction

Plywood is always glued up of an uneven number of plies of various thicknesses, depending on the final thickness of the sheet itself **(1)**. But whatever the thickness, the grain direction of any ply must run at right angles to that of the adjacent plies. This crossing of the grains gives plywood its uniform strength and dimensional stability.

In Europe during the 1930s, synthetic resin glue was developed. This glue provides a strong bond and has a great resistance to moisture. Today plywood is usually glued with a synthetic resin glue.

The two outside veneers on a piece of plywood are called the face veneers and are usually $\frac{1}{28}$ in. thick. The layers under the face veneers are called crossbands and in good plywood are usually thicker than the faces. The wood between crossbands, which constitutes the center, is called the core. Plywood is available with either a veneer core or a lumber core.

Veneer-core plywood is the best known, most popular plywood. The thinner the veneer used to build up the core, the greater the strength of the plywood. I would never use, for example, three-ply $\frac{1}{4}$-in. plywood. In most cases such plywood is made of cheap materials, especially in the core, so any imperfection telegraphs right through the face veneers **(2)**. Assuming that the face veneers are $\frac{1}{28}$ in. thick, the core will be about $\frac{1}{5}$ in. thick, and because the grain of the core crosses the grain of the faces, the plywood is weak and breaks easily. If $\frac{1}{4}$-in. plywood is made with five plies, the center ply and the face veneers will run in the same direction, making the plywood stronger and more stable. This photo **(3)** shows both types of $\frac{1}{4}$-in. plywood.

The quality of veneer-core plywood varies greatly. This **(4)** is the cheapest type, where anything goes in as long as it is wood. It's full of cracks and voids. Voids make the face veneers weak in those places because there is nothing to back them up.

Baltic birch plywood, made in Russia, is a better veneer-core plywood **(5)**. When it was first imported the Russians and Americans were not on friendly terms; so rather than call it Russian plywood, the Americans named it after the Baltic sea, to which the Russians have access. On the west coast of the United States, Baltic birch plywood is called Russian plywood. In some areas it is also called Finnish plywood.

Baltic birch plywood is made to metric dimensions: Standard sheets are 150 cm. by 150 cm. (roughly 5 ft. by 5 ft.). It is birch the whole way through and has no knotholes. Its edges, which are very clean, can be exposed. The plies are very thin — a ¼-in. thick piece of Baltic birch plywood will have five plies. Disadvantages are that it twists if not held down and lately I have found that sometimes the plies separate.

Another good veneer-core plywood is made in the Philippines and sold under the commercial name lauan. It is very stable and has a good core, free of knotholes **(6)**. The core veneer is thicker than that of Baltic birch, but because lauan moves very little, this is fine. A piece of ¾-in. plywood will have seven plies, including the face veneers. Lauan is close in color to mahogany. A similar product made out of shina (another commercial name for limewood) is much lighter in color.

Lumber-core plywood is made up of two face veneers, two crossbands and a solid-wood core. Because the core is considerably thicker than the crossbands and has grain running in the same direction as the face veneers', it has great strength lengthwise.

The core of most American commercial lumber-core plywood is made up of edge-joined strips, commonly of poplar or basswood, although mahogany is better. These strips vary in width, but 3 in. is usually the maximum. They are glued together and dressed to the necessary thickness, and then the crossbands and face veneers are glued on. Lumber-core plywood can twist because the glued-up core acts like one piece of wood.

4

5

6

Imported lauan plywood is also available in lumber core. The difference between the lauan lumber core and the ordinary commercial kind is that the core strips in the lauan are not glued up into one solid sheet. They're held together by the crossband plies, with small spaces between the strips **(7)**. This allows each strip to move independently, making the plywood more stable and more suitable for cabinetmaking.

When I was an apprentice in Denmark, most lumber-core stock was constructed without face veneers and craftsmen put on their own. Now this unfaced lumber core is available in the United States, in 8x4 sheets. Unfaced veneer-core plywood is also available in the same-size sheets. Both are called platform stock and come in lauan and shina.

7

Beware of plywood having face veneers of different woods because, with plywood, the cardinal rule is that what is done to one side must be done to the other. If walnut is on the front face and poplar is on the back, for example, the woods will expand and contract differently and cause the whole sheet to twist. Sometimes it is okay to use plywood that is faced with different species, as when making panel walls or drawer bottoms. In these applications, the backs won't be seen and the plywood will be locked in place, unable to move. Plywood having the same species of face veneer front and back is available, although usually the quality of the front face is better and has fewer defects.

Because most plywood is made for builders, not cabinetmakers, manufacturers sometimes try to cut costs by using a core of fir. Never veneer directly over fir plywood or buy plywood where the face veneers are bound directly to fir — the grain of the fir will eventually telegraph through because of the difference between the wood's spring and summer growth.

I think it is always worthwhile to buy the highest-quality plywood possible. For a craftsman to try to save a few dollars on material doesn't make sense when you consider all the hours invested in making a piece of furniture.

Plywood grading The U.S. Department of Commerce has established voluntary standards for grading hardwood plywood. This grading system is different from the one used to grade softwood plywood. Premium-grade veneers are given the symbol *A*, while other-quality veneers are designated by a number: good grade, *1*, sound grade, *2*; utility grade, *3*; backing grade, *4*. There is also a specialty grade, *SP*. Any combination is possible, the first symbol representing the quality of the face veneer and the second the quality of the back veneer. Plywood grade *A-3*, for example, has a premium-quality face veneer and a utility-grade back veneer. The best would be *A-A*.

When ordering hardwood plywood, always give the dimensions in the order of thickness, width and length. This way, you'll be sure the grain on the face veneer will run along the length. ☐

Other Materials

There are other materials that can be veneered or that come already faced with veneer. These are sold under the commercial names of particleboard and fiberboard. There are both advantages and disadvantages to using them.

The greatest advantage is that veneer can be applied to them with its grain going in any direction, because particleboard and fiberboard have no grain direction of their own. These materials are also less expensive than plywood. A disadvantage, however, is that they are not nearly as strong, and they're not easy to join together, either, because the joints must be reinforced with splines made out of some other material.

Particleboard is made out of wood flakes, chips or sawdust coated with glue and pressed into sheets. Consequently, its edges are not very attractive **(1)** and usually a facing must be glued on. The surface of particleboard also is not very smooth **(2)** and is not good for painting.

Fiberboard is made out of wood fibers coated with glue and pressed into sheets. It has edges that are very smooth **(3)**, and they stay that way even after being shaped **(4)**. The surface **(5)** is smooth enough for painting, but a drawback to using fiberboard is that it is quite heavy.

The major disadvantage of particleboard and fiberboard is that they will bow if used to make doors that slide in a track on the bottom. This is because there is no grain direction to support the weight. If you are making doors more than 3 ft. tall, either put a wide solid-wood facing on both edges of the doors or hang them from a frame on the top, so they won't warp.

If you are making doors that hang, put a solid-wood facing on both sides for the hinge screws. Do this also if making tall cabinets. Get a shelf or stretcher going across every 2 ft. or 3 ft. or else use a wide facing in the front or the back. If the back is screwed on, a wide facing might not be necessary there.

When screwing into particleboard or fiberboard, I always put glue on the screw thread to give it more strength or I glue in dowels for the screw to penetrate. Here **(6)** a hinge is inserted right into the particleboard without a facing. The screws will go through the dowels and hold the hinge securely. This makes a nice detail, but if you choose to paint the door, the dowels won't show.   □

1

2

3

4

5

6

1

2

3

4

Veneering

If you are building a veneered cabinet where the veneer has to match the whole way around and from top to bottom, you will usually have to do your own veneering. Here are four rules to follow:

First, always take the pieces of veneer from the top or the bottom of a flitch **(1)**. If you pull out some sheets from the center, the grain can no longer be matched perfectly and the flitch will lose its value. This is the reason you pay twice as much for small quantities of veneer as for a whole flitch.

There are two ways to match veneer on a panel. One is called bookmatching, because the first two pieces of veneer are opened like a book **(2)**. Then the next two are opened the same way and the four pieces are put together **(3)**. This is usually how good-quality sheets of hardwood plywood are faced. The other way of matching is to use veneers in the order they come off the flitch without flipping them **(4)**. This is called slipmatching.

Trees for face veneer are hard to find and very valuable. If you have a nice walnut, cherry, oak or any other hardwood tree, don't cut it down for firewood, because it might be worth a great deal of money.

The second rule in veneering is that you should never use veneer thicker than $\frac{1}{28}$ in.; veneer that is too thick will definitely crack. For example, assume that the face veneer in the drawing **(5)** is $\frac{1}{4}$ in. thick and 48 in. wide. The glue will hold the bottom of the veneer at 48 in., but the top of the veneer will shrink as it dries. The edges will bend in at first, but after that, the veneer will start to crack.

Glued   *Lumber core*   *Crossband*   *Face veneer*

5

Third, always cross the grain direction of the face veneers and the crossbands **(6,7)**. The angle doesn't have to be 90°, but it should be no smaller than 15°. If you place the grain of the face veneer parallel to the crossband's, the veneer will crack later on.

If the grain of the face veneer has to run in different directions **(8)**, either the plywood has to be cut so the grain is angled at 45° or some inexpensive veneer has to be applied to both sides as crossbanding that runs at an angle of 45°. Particleboard or fiberboard, neither of which has any grain direction, could also be used.

This rule changes, however, when applying face veneer to solid wood, where the grain of the wood and of the veneer should run in the same direction so the two layers of wood can move together as a unit. You can also use thicker veneer on solid wood.

The fourth rule of veneering is that you must always do the same thing to both sides of the ground surface. If you don't, the piece will definitely bow and twist.

This piece was veneered only on one side and the pictures **(9,10)** show what happened. The veneer absorbed the moisture from the glue and expanded before it was clamped down. When the piece came out of the press, the veneer started to dry and shrink, twisting the plywood.

6

7

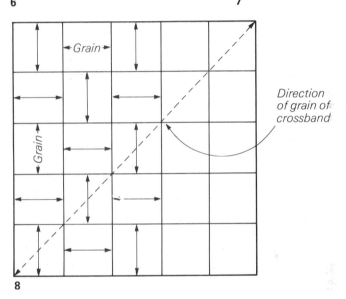

Direction of grain of crossband

8

9

10

Knowing that veneer will shrink when drying, I started to experiment to see if I could take advantage of that to make tubes without a form. I was lucky and it worked. Here's how it happened.

I took two pieces of mahogany and one of rosewood. The grain of the mahogany was 90° to the grain of the rosewood **(11)**.

The mahogany veneer measured 19¹¹/₁₆ in. in width when it was dry **(12)**. I soaked it in water for a minute or two. Then I placed it between two boards with five layers of newspaper on each side to absorb some of the water, but I did not put pressure on. After ten to fifteen minutes, I removed the boards. The mahogany measured 20⅜ in. — it had expanded ¹¹/₁₆ in. **(13)**.

For gluing I used Cascamite mixed very thick because the mahogany veneer was already moist. If the glue had been mixed to the regular consistency, it would have been too thin for this job and the pieces would not have stuck together.

I glued the wet mahogany to the dry rosewood and placed the piece between two boards with six pieces of newspaper on each side **(14)**. I left it for about six hours; the time depends on the room temperature.

11

12

13

14

The minute I took it out of the press, the piece started to roll up, so I had to hurry to scrape and sand it while it was still relatively flat **(15)**. Then I placed the ends of the piece on two boards so that the veneer would be pulled down by its own weight and would dry faster **(16)**.

I rolled up the piece **(17)** when it was fairly dry. (Don't let the glue dry completely or the piece might break.) I overlapped the ends and clamped them between two boards **(18)**. After drying there was no springback **(19)**. □

15

16

17

18

19

Glues and Gluing

I use three kinds of glue for veneering, depending on the job. They are hot glue, Titebond and Cascamite. The glue you use is as important as the way you use it. I would never use a new glue on a piece without testing it for a couple of years first. It is very important to test new glues on a regular basis because there are so many different ones on the market today, all claiming that they can glue everything but broken hearts. Each craftsman has a favorite, and if it works, that's fine. To me the most important thing about a glue is how it holds over the years.

This is the main reason I like hot glue. It goes way back to the Egyptians, so you know you can rely on it. Hot glue is made from animal hides, blood and bones. It is made liquid with water and heat. I use hot glue for hammer-veneering (p. 126) and anywhere I can apply heat to the work after it is clamped up, such as when using sandbags (p. 156). The advantage of hot glue in this case is that the veneer doesn't get a chance to absorb moisture and expand. This is because the glue is applied to the ground stock and allowed to cool before the veneer is applied. The veneer is then clamped up and the glue remelted. I also use hot glue for vacuum-forming. Another of its advantages is that the work can be taken out of the press after a couple of hours when the glue is cold. But hot glue is not suited for use in warm and humid climates.

Hot glue is melted in a glue pot, which is like a double boiler. When buying a glue pot, get one that will hold water between the glue container and the outer container. Because water constantly evaporates from the glue, hot water has to be added frequently to maintain the glue's consistency, and it's nice to have some right in the pot. Also, in hammer-veneering, after the veneer is glued down and has to be trimmed, the veneer saw has to be submerged in hot water so it will be warm and wet. If you can't get your water from the glue pot, you have to keep an extra container with hot water nearby.

Judging whether your glue is the proper consistency is something you have to learn to do through experience, but if the glue drops from the brush like honey it is probably right. You will know the glue is spoiled if it stays liquid after it is cooled.

To check that the glue is made correctly and is ready to use, put a drop between your fingers and rub them together, applying pressure. You should be able to squeeze out all the excess easily after about a minute. If the room is around average temperature, about 60° to 70° F, your fingers should start to stick together as the hot glue gets cold and starts to bond. The glue won't reach full strength, however, until it has dried completely, which takes about 24 hours.

Titebond is an aliphatic resin glue. It is a good strong glue, water and heat-resistant, with a short setup time. I use this glue when I'm not gluing up too many pieces and have enough time to get everything in the press before the glue dries. Titebond doesn't have to be mixed or heated so it's always ready to be used, and it has a long shelf life. Brushes and rollers used with it are fairly easy to clean with water.

Cascamite is a plastic-resin glue that comes in powder form and has to be mixed with water. When you use Cascamite, be sure to stir the powder well before adding the water, to avoid lumps. Because of its long setup time, Cascamite is the glue most often used for veneering. I use it when I have many pieces to veneer or when a piece is large and takes a long time to glue up.

Cascamite is water and heat-resistant but has a short pot life, remaining usable after it is mixed for only a few hours. Don't buy large cans of this glue unless you intend to use it up quickly, because each time you open the can you allow moisture to get in. After a while, the powder in the bottom of the can won't be any good.

Unless you become an expert at opening and closing the can without admitting moisture and learn to mix up only the amount you need, Cascamite can be very expensive to use. Some people put flour in Cascamite to stretch it, but I don't like to risk weakening it. This glue is easy to clean off brushes and rollers, however, so you can save some money there by using them over and over again. With some other resin glues, brushes and rollers can be used only once or twice.

One thing to keep in mind when using Cascamite is that it shrinks as it dries. Here **(1)** the can it is mixed in is 2½ in. in diameter. The glue shrank ³⁄₁₆ in. in diameter and the same in height. If glue is trapped under veneer, the veneer will eventually crack. Also, if there is an imperfection in the surface that is full of glue, the glue will pull the veneer down into the hole after a while.

When applying any glue, be sure there is enough on the work and that it is evenly spread. Don't put so much on that it runs all over the work and the bench. Just put on enough so that a little will be squeezed out along the edges. A good way to spread Titebond or Cascamite is with a paint roller, but always put a little extra along the edges to make sure that they will be glued down.

Apply glue only to the surface of the piece to be veneered, never directly to the veneer. This rule pertains to all veneering but hammer-veneering. If you put glue on the veneer **(2)**, one side will expand and the whole piece will roll up like a scroll **(3)** before you can get it into the press.

Never use contact cement for veneering. I've seen it fail too many times and it is just about impossible to repair. □

1

2

3

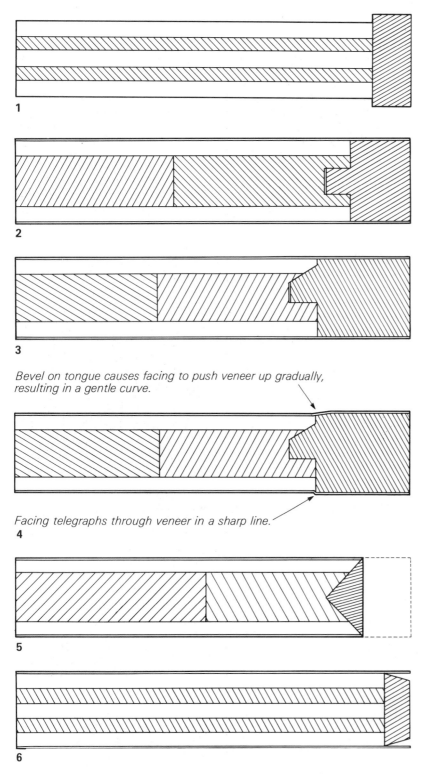

Bevel on tongue causes facing to push veneer up gradually, resulting in a gentle curve.

Facing telegraphs through veneer in a sharp line.

Facings

When using plywood for furniture, you ordinarily have to apply a facing or a piece of veneer to cover up the plywood edges. Of course, if you use Baltic birch, the edges are attractive and can be exposed.

There are several ways to apply facings. They are usually glued on before the face veneer is applied, but you can do it afterward, too — the methods are the same. The exception to this is the beveled tongue-and-groove joint, which should be used only before the face veneer is applied. Whichever method you choose, the facing should be ⅛ in. wider than the thickness of the plywood so it can be planed flush with the surface later.

The simplest way to apply a facing is to glue a ¼-in. piece of wood directly to the edge of the plywood without any joint **(1)**.

Facings ½ in. to 1 in. thick should be applied using a tongue-and-groove joint **(2)**.

Where a facing is 1 in. thick or over and goes across the grain of the veneer, a beveled tongue-and-groove joint should be used **(3)**. If you were to use a regular tongue and groove, the differences in movement between the plywood and the facing would cause the facing to telegraph right through the veneer, especially across the grain, revealing a sharp line. This would not be as noticeable lengthwise. With a beveled tongue, the differences between the two pieces are minimized because the facing pushes the veneer up gradually. Instead of a sharp line, you get a gentle curve **(4)**. The same is the case if the facing shrinks.

If the face veneer is already on and you don't want the facing to show, a good way to apply it is with a *V*-groove **(5)**. This is also a good way to apply facings over 1 in. thick.

After applying the facing of your choice, the next step is making it flush with the surface, using a plane, belt sander or router. Be careful not to round over the facing, because this will keep the edge of the veneer from being glued properly **(6)**.

The fastest, easiest way to get a facing flush is with a router. Screw a piece of wood to one side of the router base and set a flat-bottomed bit flush with its bottom **(7)**. Push the piece of wood down on the work and move the router forward **(8)**. If the facing is thick, trim it in several passes.

Sand lightly after routing **(9)** to be sure the facing doesn't protrude above the surface, being careful not to round over the edge.

When gluing facings on all four edges of a piece of plywood, first fit all the facings without glue. Then remove two of the facings and apply glue to them, leaving the other two to guide the ones being glued **(10)**. As soon as they're clamped in place **(11)**, remove the guide facings so they don't get stuck. Remember to put strips of wood between the facings and the clamps to keep the clamps from marring the work. When the glue is dry, plane the facings flush and then glue on the next two, trimming the edges flush as before.

Now you're ready to apply the veneer. If there are any imperfections in the plywood, such as dents, cracks or holes, fill them with powdered chalk (whiting) mixed with thin hot glue. The mixture should be like putty, so use just enough glue to keep the whiting together. Fill the cracks so that the filler is above the surface. This way, when the filler dries, it can be sanded flush with the surface. If you use too much glue, or plaster of paris instead of whiting, the filler will be harder than the wood and won't sand flush. If properly mixed, the filler will be porous enough to absorb the glue that is applied for the veneer. ☐

7

8

9

10

11

1

2

Hammer-Veneering

Hammer-veneering is the old way of applying veneer to solid wood or to plywood. Hammer-veneering can be done very quickly, but its biggest advantage is that you don't need a veneer press, cauls or clamps. In the method of veneering common today, the size of the work is limited by the size of the veneer press or of the clamps, but with hammer-veneering you could veneer the whole world if you wanted to.

The main tool for hammer-veneering is the veneer hammer, which is not used for hammering at all but for applying pressure. The hammer has a narrow face, so you can transmit the strength of your arm and the weight of your body to a tiny area of veneer. The veneer is held down by hot glue, which sticks as soon as it is cold. You spread the hot glue on the ground surface and the veneer, then use the hammer to squeeze out the glue before it cools off. You can resoften the glue as necessary with a warm iron. Hammer-veneering is usually the easiest way to fix furniture when there is broken veneer or an air bubble under the veneer.

The veneer saw A veneer saw or knife is used to cut the veneer to size **(1)**. It is called both a saw and a knife because it is filed like a saw and sharpened like a knife to make a smooth cut for joining veneers. The curved blade of the saw is only about 3 in. long. The blade can be removed for sharpening and the handle is offset **(2)**, so when you're using the saw against a straightedge you won't scrape your hands.

Both edges of a veneer saw can be sharpened with a small triangular file **(3)**. I file each tooth at 60° to the surface of the blade with no back or front **(4)** so that I can use the saw in either direction. This makes for a slower but smoother cut.

3

After the teeth are filed sharp like a saw's, they are sharpened so that the cross section of each is like a knife's. Rotate the saw along each curve against a stone, holding the blade at a shallow angle but being careful not to lose the points of the teeth **(5)**.

When using the saw, keep a board under the veneer so you don't cut into the top of your bench. Use a straightedge to guide the saw as you cut **(6).**

Veneer saw

4

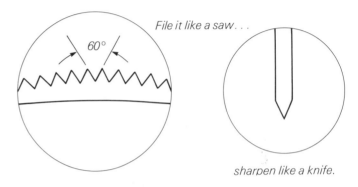

File it like a saw . . .

60°

sharpen like a knife.

5

6

7

Veneer hammer — use a dense hardwood.

1¼"

13½"

Aluminum or brass face

3/16"

¾"

7/8"

1¼"

Grain

5/8"

¼"

3½"

3½"

Aluminum pin

Wedge→

8

Veneer hammers Veneer hammers vary in design. Hammers made out of steel like this one **(7)** are available commercially. If you want to make your own, plan on having a long handle and use a hardwood wedge with an insert of aluminum or brass for the working edge **(8)**. The edge must be straight and about 3½ in. wide, with a round profile to squeeze out the glue from underneath the veneer. Follow the dimensions in the drawing and use a hard, heavy wood such as maple. Before using a new hammer, soak it in raw linseed oil so the glue won't stick to it, but let it dry before using.

Edge veneering It is clumsy and time-consuming to veneer edges with clamps, but it is fast and easy with a veneer hammer. It doesn't matter whether the edge is straight or curved. Cut the strip of veneer to be applied about ⅛ in. wider than the thickness of the plywood. If you cut the veneer too wide, the excess sticking in the air will dry before the glue has cured and will curl away from the edges of the wood.

Wet the veneer on both sides to make it more flexible and also to see which way it naturally wants to arch. Glue it concave side down, so the arch will keep it in place **(9)**. If you do it the other way, you'll have trouble keeping the outer edges stuck down **(10)**.

9

10

Begin by brushing glue onto the edge to be veneered **(11)**, then place the outside surface of the veneer right in the glue. Brush glue onto the other side of the veneer **(12)**. The glue that smears on the outside will help the hammer slide and prevent the outside of the veneer from drying too fast, which might pull up the edges. You can scrape the glue off the outside later.

Now flip the veneer over and hold it in place with one hand — hot glue is slippery. Hold the hammer in your other hand and press down hard to squeeze out the excess glue all along the edge **(13)**. You have to work fast to get all the veneer down while the glue is still hot. The minute the glue gets cold, the veneer will stick. Keep an old iron warmed up and handy, so if the veneer is not glued down right, you can remelt the glue before going back over it with the hammer. Don't have the iron so hot that the glue burns or you will regret it. Burned glue has an unpleasant smell that hangs around for a long time.

11

12

13

14

Use the veneer saw to clean off excess glue and trim the veneer while the glue is still soft. Remove the glue pot from the water jacket and dip the sawblade into the hot water **(14)** so it will be wet and warm and the glue won't stick to it. Then cut off the excess veneer at both ends, holding the work up at an angle **(15)**. Next, stand the work on edge, tilt it a little to apply pressure right at the corner to be cleaned and saw off the excess veneer **(16)**. Dip the blade in hot water after each cutting. After the work is trimmed, put the piece aside to dry for about 24 hours.

It doesn't make any difference if the edge is curved. You can veneer it exactly as if it were straight **(17)**. If the work isn't straight, however, you must wait until the glue is hard and dry to remove the excess veneer and squeezed-out glue and use a block plane or a smoothing plane to clean it off.

15

16

17

Veneering large surfaces　To veneer a large surface you will have to edge-join pieces of veneer, either lengthwise, across, or both. The edge joint must be very accurate. I overlap the two pieces of veneer about ½ in. at the joint, then cut through both pieces at the same time after they are glued down and lift out the waste.

Begin by figuring out how you want the veneer to match, and mark the location of each piece on the work **(18)**. The veneer should overhang the surface to be veneered by about ½ in. on all sides so you can trim the waste off later. Work on one section at a time. Moisten the veneer to see which way it wants to curl. Brush hot glue onto the ground surface **(19)**.

Place the veneer in the glue, concave side up, exactly as in edge veneering. Apply glue to the veneer **(20)**, then flip it over and position it. Use the veneer hammer to secure it somewhere in the center first **(21)**.

18

20

19

21

22

Now use a warm iron to melt the glue under a small section of the veneer **(22)**. Push down with the veneer hammer as hard as you can, using the weight of your body to squeeze out the excess glue **(23)**. Try to avoid going directly across the grain with the hammer, but do hold the hammer at an angle to the grain so that the glue will be squeezed out toward the edges. When that part is glued down, move to the next area and repeat, proceeding until the whole sheet is stuck tight.

Now apply glue to the next sheet of veneer and proceed in exactly the same way. Don't forget to overlap the edges to be joined ½ in. When both sheets are stuck, use a straight-edge and a sharp, warm, wet veneer saw to cut through both sheets at once **(24,25)**.

23

24

25

Remove the scrap veneer from the top **(26)**, carefully lift up the top sheet and pull out the scrap from underneath **(27)**. Butt the edges together, heat with the iron **(28)**, and push hard with the hammer to squeeze out all the excess glue through the line of the joint **(29)**. Here it is okay to use the hammer going across the grain because both pieces are already glued down.

26

27

28

29

30

When the joint is down tight, press a strip of heavy brown paper over it to prevent it from opening while drying **(30)**. After the glue is dry, use a sharp scraper blade or cabinet scraper to remove the paper and excess glue, but set a heavier burr than normal on the blade (chapter 2). A good seam should be invisible.

You must be sure that no air bubbles are under the veneer. If you can't see the bubbles when you push down with the hammer, tap the surface lightly with your finger and listen for hollow spots. If you don't glue down these hollow spots, they will eventually crack. The veneer I used for this demonstration was very curly in one spot in the center and would not stay down, so I covered it with brown paper and clamped on a warm block of wood to reheat the glue and hold the piece down tightly while the glue cooled and dried **(31)**. If you don't notice an air bubble until several days or months later, just use water, heat and pressure to work the piece down. The glue will still hold. If this doesn't work, another way is to cut the bubble with a razor blade or sharp knife, inject some glue underneath and then clamp down (p. 145). □

31

Hard-to-Handle Veneer

Some veneer can be brittle, wrinkled and hard to handle, such as this bird's-eye elm veneer **(1)**. It can be flattened by soaking in water and then pressing between two flat boards with two or three sheets of newspaper on each side of the veneer. The problem is that the water will cause the veneer to expand, and the minute the piece is removed from between the boards it will start to dry and wrinkle again. For small pieces where the veneer can be glued on before it starts to wrinkle, this method is fine.

A better way to treat hard-to-handle veneer is by using the following mixture: two parts Cascamite powder, one part flour, three parts water, one-and-a-half parts glycerin and one part alcohol. Mix the Cascamite and flour together, and add the water slowly so the mixture doesn't lump. Slowly add the glycerin and alcohol. Apply this mixture generously to both sides of the veneer or immerse the veneer in it. Then stand or hang the veneer on end until it is dry to the touch.

Clamp the veneer between two flat boards with three or four sheets of newspaper on each side to make it flat. After two hours, if the temperature in the room is about 70° F, replace the damp newspaper with dry. If left too long, the paper will stick or the veneer might mold. Put the veneer and fresh paper back between the two boards and clamp down. After three or four hours, remove the newspaper and put the veneer back between the boards without paper. Apply light pressure. The veneer should dry in a day. It will shrink a little, but it will still be flexible enough to use without cracking.

Keep the veneer between the boards until you use it. If more than one sheet of veneer from the same flitch has to be flattened, put the sheets on top of each other and double the layer of newspaper in between. After treatment, the veneer will be flexible and handle like regular veneer.

When veneering is done right, the type of veneer used should not make any difference. But regardless of how you treat them, burl and crotch veneer will eventually crack. This is because the grain is going in all directions and in some places it is end grain. Although I know of no way to prevent cracking, there is a way to postpone it. This is by sizing the veneer after it has been applied to its base with very thin hot glue. Experience will teach you how thin to make the sizing. An exact formula is impossible to give because the consistency of hot glue changes constantly as the water in it evaporates, but one part glue to two parts hot water is about right. Check the glue for proper consistency as explained on p. 122.

1

Before applying the sizing, scrape the veneer and sand it with 80-grit sandpaper. Use the palm of your hand to rub the sizing into the veneer. Wipe off any excess glue from the surface.

When the glue is completely dry, which usually takes about 24 hours, lightly scrape the veneer again, sand it with 80 grit and finish sanding with fine paper. The sizing will not discolor the veneer or interfere with the finish. By the way, rosewood will crack eventually, but it takes a long time and I'm not sure that even glue sizing will help.

A coat of glue sizing is also used in veneering end grain, to seal the pores of the wood. Let the sizing dry completely and then apply the veneer, using hot glue. Either hammer-veneer or use clamps. If the wood is soft, such as poplar or basswood, it might be better to size the ends twice, because the first coat will soak in.

When veneering end grain, never position the grain of the veneer across the width of the board **(2)**. The board and veneer will expand and contract in different directions and the veneer will loosen. Have the grain of the veneer going up and down with the thickness of the board if you can. Also, don't veneer the end of any board over ¾ in. thick. When the board changes in thickness, the veneer will come loose.

Glue sizing is also good for repairing cracked veneer when refinishing veneered pieces. Here the sizing should be thicker than usual. Equal parts of glue and hot water will be about right. Before removing the old finish, give it a coat of sizing and rub it in with the palm of your hand. Go across any cracks so you'll fill them. When the sizing dries it will pull down the veneer. After this kind of treatment, the veneer will usually stay down because it is old and will not move as much. When the glue is completely dry, remove the old finish with a cabinet scraper. Do not use a finish remover because it could dissolve the glue. ☐

Shrinkage

Right shrinkage

Wrong shrinkage

2

Preparing Veneer

If sheets of veneer have to be pressed on with clamps or in a veneer press, they have to be joined and taped together first.

To get a straight edge on short pieces of veneer, clamp them between two straight boards **(1)**. You can put as many pieces between the boards as you like. Then trim one edge with a jointer plane **(2)** or run it over a jointer. Reclamp the boards, flipping the veneer over if both edges are to be joined.

To get a straight edge on long pieces, you can make a clamping jig that will hold the veneer tightly while it is being planed **(3,4)**. This particular jig is 6 ft. long but you can make it any length. It will last a long time. The two 2x3s can be used over and over again, but the two 1-in. boards in the center should be replaced when worn.

1

2

3

½" threaded dowel with handle

½" bolt with wing nut and washer

1" boards

Screwed to 2x3

—— 6' 0". ——

4

5

6

Here **(5)** the jig is apart. One board is screwed to a 2x3 but the other is loose. A bolt in each end clamps the ends of the jig together **(6)**. In the top 2x3 there are three wooden screws with handles to put pressure on the center **(7)**.

Tap dies **(8)** for threading wood are available in different sizes. A good set of dies is a little more expensive but does a much better job than a cheaper set. When threading a dowel, be sure it is not too big for the die because the threads will break. Sand dowels that are too big to the correct size using a drill press.

Drill a hole for the female thread with a drill bit that is a hair smaller than the final size you want **(9)**. In this case I used a $\frac{7}{16}$-in. bit for a $\frac{1}{2}$-in. hole. Then I threaded the hole. If you have trouble with the threads breaking, you can fill the hole with linseed oil and empty it before threading.

The wooden thread joint **(10)** is strong, good for pieces that have to be assembled and disassembled repeatedly.

7

8

9

10

Once you've got straight edges on the pieces of veneer, you have to hold them together for gluing. It's a bad idea to use masking tape on the front of the veneer because the fibers might come up when you pull off the tape **(11)**. I used to use masking tape on the back of the veneer to be joined **(12)** and then flip the piece over and glue gum tape on the front. When the gum tape was dry, I removed the masking tape from the back. I found, however, that if I made the gum tape too wet, the veneer would expand and overlap.

I'm now back to doing it the way I learned as an apprentice. I line up the joints and keep the veneer from overlapping with very fine nails or brads. Then I glue on gum tape **(13)**. Wet it, but don't soak it — that's the key.

Use a cabinet scraper to remove the gum tape **(14)** after the veneer has been applied. You could remove the tape as soon as it comes out of the veneer press by soaking it with water and peeling it off, but I prefer to use a cabinet scraper because it is faster, safer and less messy.   □

11

12

13

14

1

2

3

Veneering with Clamps

First I will explain veneering both sides of a ground surface without a commercially made veneer press, because very few craftsmen have one and it isn't really necessary for occasional veneer work. With some pieces of plywood and hand clamps, you can easily glue down veneer.

If the piece to be veneered is too wide for a clamp to reach its center, you will need to make a few sets of clamping boards to get the necessary pressure there. Plane the boards to a slight taper on the edges **(1)**. Make the taper even, so when the two pieces are clamped at the ends, the pressure will be uniform all along the joint **(2)**. An uneven taper will cause uneven pressure **(3)**. This is a good technique, but never veneer more than three pieces at the same time, because you will not get enough pressure.

Spread the glue on one side of the ground surface and apply the veneer, tacking it with veneer pins or tiny brads at each end in the center **(4)** to prevent it from sliding when pressure is applied. Don't tack the veneer in the corners because that will cause it to wrinkle when it tries to expand.

The piece will be clamped between two boards **(5)**, but first put down some paper onto one of them **(6)** so if any glue leaks, the veneer won't stick to the wrong thing. Put the piece, veneer side down, on the paper, and apply glue to the other side. Tack down the other piece of veneer, put on some paper and then cover with the other board.

Clamp the tapered pieces to the board, one piece on the top and one on the bottom **(7)**. Here I used two sets. Don't tighten the clamps too hard, and be sure that the pressure is in the center.

Now clamp boards at each end — they don't have to be tapered because a clamp can easily put pressure in the middle of the end **(8)**. Applying pressure to the center first gives the glue a chance to move out toward the edges and allows the veneer to expand. If the ends were clamped first, the glue would be trapped and the veneer would wrinkle. Up to this point work as fast as you can, but now give the glue a couple of minutes to ooze out. Then tighten up the clamps a little at a time.

Put the side clamps on the end boards **(9)**, making sure that the pressure is still mainly in the center. Slowly tighten all the clamps until the pressure is uniform throughout.

Leave the veneer clamped up for the amount of time recommended by the manufacturer of the type of glue that you use **(10)**. □

5

6

8

7

9

10

1

The Veneer Press

A commercially made veneer press is expensive but a worthwhile investment if you do much veneering, laminating or bending. This press **(1)** has five sections, so it can be used to veneer 4x8 sheets of plywood without the sections being more than 24 in. apart — the maximum distance that allows good pressure. Each section is movable from front to back; the screws on each section are movable from side to side.

This press is extra large (36 in. high and 50 in. wide) so it can be used with large jigs when bending plywood. For regular veneering, I put 7-in. by 7-in. blocks in the bottom of the press to raise the floor. On top of the blocks rest 1¾-in. thick planks. Soak the planks in oil so they won't warp and glue won't stick to them, but let the oil dry before using them.

Place the piece to be veneered in the press so that its end is flush with the press edge and position the sections. You can position the sections by eye or by first standing the piece to be veneered up against the side of the press **(2)**. Now position the screws. Always try to use an uneven number so you can clamp the center first. Place the screws so that the two outside ones are inside the edges of the piece to be veneered **(3)**, then remove the piece from the press.

2

3

On top of the planks, put a piece of plywood or particleboard. The planks and plywood will distribute the pressure uniformly among the sections. Put newspaper on top of the plywood so the veneer won't stick to it if glue should bleed through.

When you put the piece to be veneered in the press, make sure it lines up with the screws you have positioned **(4)**. Handle the veneer and the glue the same way as when using hand clamps. Cover the veneer with newspaper **(5)**.

If more than one piece of the same size is going to be veneered, separate the layers with a piece of plywood that is larger than the pieces being veneered **(6)**, and cover it with newspaper. Never put the pieces to be veneered directly on top of each other. The surface might be uneven, and if the pieces are not aligned exactly, the edges will not be glued properly. Continue stacking until all the pieces to be veneered are in the press **(7)**.

4

5

6

7

8

9

A final piece of plywood or particleboard goes on top of the stack **(8)**. All the plywood used should be smooth, because defects or debris will ruin the work. Then the stack is finished up with a 1¾-in. thick plank **(9)** and pieces of smooth, parallel 4x4s **(10)** to ensure that the pressure will be even. Here two are stacked on top of each other so the screws can reach.

Tighten up the center row of screws a little at a time. From the time you start spreading the glue until this point, work as fast as possible, but now slow down to give the glue a chance to ooze out toward the edges. Continue tightening the center screws a little at a time, but don't overdo it.

Slowly follow up with the outer screws **(11)**. As you work, try to keep the pressure uniform. Each time you tighten the outer screws, return to the center screws and tighten them again.

Many times, veneering will take more than one person and you should always try to get help. But after the center screws are tightened, only one person should finish tightening the other screws so the same amount of muscle goes into each. Don't be in a hurry to tighten the outer screws because the glue might get trapped, which would cause the veneer to buckle.

10

11

After the veneer comes out of the press, clean the edges while the glue is still a little soft. Hit the ends of the veneer with a chisel **(12,13)** to break the fibers so the veneer will be easier to cut. Check the piece for air bubbles by tapping the surface lightly and listening for hollow spots. If you don't locate them and glue them down, they will show up when the finish is put on and will eventually crack. If you can't find any bubbles by tapping, here's a way to be certain there aren't any. Scrape and sand the veneer with 80-grit paper, then apply a little hot water to the surface and keep it damp for a while. The moisture won't hurt the glue, but it will cause the veneer to expand where the bubbles are **(14)**. Mark the spot and let the veneer dry.

Next slice the bubble, going with the direction of the grain, with a sharp knife. Lift up the edge and shoot some glue under the veneer with a hypodermic needle **(15)**. In this photo, the veneer is still wet for clarity. Then put on paper, a block and a clamp, and allow the glue to dry **(16)**.

Stack the veneered pieces so that air circulates around them and both sides dry evenly **(17)**. Although the glue is set and the veneer won't come loose, the glue is not dry when the pieces are removed from the press because no air has circulated between the layers. If one side is covered up, the side exposed to air will dry first, pulling the work into a concave shape. □

12

13

14

15

16

17

1

Blanket

Strips of wood

Hole for wire or string

2

Bending Plywood

In industry, bent plywood is made exactly like flat plywood, except a two-part form has to be made for the curve. Before you can make the form, which consists of a series of ribs nailed to slats, you have to make a full-size drawing of the actual piece you are going to bend. This drawing also includes the form blankets plus the ⅛-in. plywood facings that protect the face veneers. Build the blankets first.

The blankets are made out of many strips of wood of the same thickness, in this case ⅝ in. by ¾ in. **(1)**. Two or three holes are drilled in exactly the same place in each strip, and a string or wire is run through to line them up perfectly **(2)**. When they are strung together, the strips make a flexible blanket that fits on the form and gives it strength lengthwise. Here **(3)** is a half of the form without the blanket, and with the blanket on **(4)**. A blanket is also necessary between the piece to be bent and the top half of the form.

The length of the blanket is not critical as long as it is about 1 in. longer than the form on each end. Blankets can be altered for many different forms by adding or subtracting strips. Make some extra strips when you're milling them and keep them handy.

When the blankets are made, assemble and measure the rest of your materials. Don't assume when you buy ⅛-in. plywood that that's what you get, because all plywood varies in thickness.

3

4

It makes sense to build up the core of the piece you want to bend from thin plywood, not layers of veneer. It costs a bit more in materials, but you save labor and time. Italian poplar is best, as it bends easily and can be soaked in water for severe bends. If you do lay up the core from veneer, use perforated gum tape to join the interior layers. This tape is thinner than regular gum tape so it won't show up in the laminates, and glue can penetrate through the holes.

For this core I used six pieces of 1/8-in. plywood (5). On each side of the core there is a 1/28-in. face veneer followed by a piece of 1/8-in. plywood on each side and finally the 5/8-in. blankets. The plywood evens out the pressure and prevents the sharp corners of the blankets from marring the veneer. The simplest way to add all this is to stack the pieces and measure them. These measure 2 5/16 in. The outside radius of the piece to be bent is 40 in.; the inner and outer radii on the drawing are the radii of the male and female parts of the bending form, respectively.

Usually I glue up the core first and glue on the face veneer later; it's easier to glue and cut the core to size and apply the edge facings before applying the face veneer. If a bend is complicated, it's sometimes good to glue the face veneers on the outside pieces of plywood before laminating the curve in the form, but be sure to get the pieces into the form the same day you get them out of the press, before the glue gets too dry.

Making the form   After you've made the drawing, you're ready to make the form. Plan to make it about 1 in. wider and longer than the finished piece to ensure enough pressure on the ends. More than 1 in. is not good. Maximum distance between ribs should never be more than 6 in.

First nail together the pieces of plywood that will be the ribs of the form. In this case, I used eight pieces of 3/4-in. plywood (6), marked so I could keep them in the same order throughout the building process. Make sure the plywood lines up and is square.

Glue the drawing directly to the plywood with rubber cement (7) and mark the dadoes for the slats that will keep the ribs in place. Mark the centerline on the ends of the form as a reference for squaring up the bent piece and cutting it to width. Bandsaw out the curve, using the widest blade possible, to give a more even cut and fewer bumps and flat spots. When you saw, remember to split the line, keeping the kerf on the waste side.

6

7

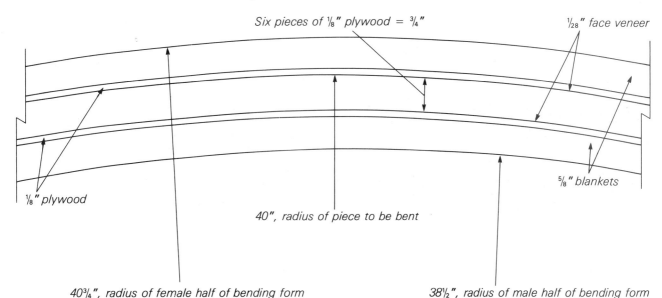

Six pieces of 1/8" plywood = 3/4"

1/28" face veneer

1/8" plywood

40", radius of piece to be bent

5/8" blankets

40 3/4", radius of female half of bending form

38 1/2", radius of male half of bending form

5

A two-part circle-cutting jig makes band-sawing accurate curves easy. To make the first part of the jig, cut into a piece of plywood so that its edge is flush with the back edge of the bandsaw table **(8)**. Clamp the plywood to the table and draw a line even with the sawblade teeth down its center. Measuring from the blade, mark the radius of the curve to be cut on that line, and then drill a hole there for a nail or dowel pivot. In this case the radius is 19 in. **(9)**.

Now make the second part of the jig. The first step is to make a thing that looks like a miter gauge **(10)**. Mark its center and the center of the piece you want to cut. Screw the two pieces together, matching up the lines. Mark the radius of the curve to correspond with the radius on the first part of the jig **(11)**.

8

9

10

11

Place the assembly on the bandsaw, align the radii and put a nail through. Start the saw and cut **(12,13)**.

The curve will come out perfectly **(14)**, with no bumps or flat spots. The same jig can be used over again for different radii, so don't throw it away.

For cutting bigger pieces where the full depth of the saw throat is needed, the first part of this jig could be bolted to the bandsaw table. Drill two holes in the left side of the bandsaw tabletop and tap them for two flathead stove bolts.

12

13

14

Now cut the grooves for the slats on both halves of the form, using a table saw with a dado head **(15,16)**. The slats should fit snugly **(17)**. When all the cuts are made, separate the pieces of plywood, keeping them in order **(18)**, and mark all the slats where the ribs are going to be **(19)**. Assemble the form by nailing the slats to the ribs **(20)**. When the slats on the bottom are in, and you're ready to nail on the ones for the edges, make sure the ribs are square **(21)**.

15

16

17

18

19

20

21

Next, put the male and female halves of the form together **(22)**. Make sure the ribs line up with each other. Notice that the curves have different radii **(23)**. Two curves were cut on the block and the waste was removed.

If the curves of a form are not sections of a circle, you will need guide blocks to ensure that the halves of the form fit together properly **(24)**. If the halves do not line up exactly, the form will exert uneven pressure. Glue and screw two blocks or cleats to both ends of one half of the form, and glue and screw one block to both ends of the other half so that it will slide in between the first two.

22

23

Glued and screwed

Glued and screwed

*When a form
is part of a circle, guides
on the form are not necessary;
but if not, guides have to be
used so the male and female parts will fit
together exactly the way they were drawn.*

Forming the bend   Now the form is finished and ready to be used. You should assemble all necessary materials before you start to spread any glue. The selection and use of glue for bent plywood is the same as it is for flat. Once you've gotten the glue on, remember to tack the layers of plywood in the centers of the ends to prevent slipping. Before you clamp up, be certain that the centerlines of the form parts match up.

If you don't have a veneer press, place the form on two heavy planks to keep it from sagging **(25)**. Then put straight 2x4s across it. Here I used four 2x4s on the top and two 2x4s on the bottom, then I put another 2x4 in the center on the top.

Put a couple of pieces of veneer under the center of the 2x4 running lengthwise to make sure that there will be adequate pressure there **(26,27)**. This is faster than tapering (p. 140).

Clamp the top 2x4 first, then put the rest of the clamps on — but don't tighten them too much. Don't put too much pressure on the edges at first, because the glue must have a chance to squeeze out from the center. Work from the center outward, always returning to the center clamps each time you've tightened the outer clamps. Continue until the halves of the form are pressed together tightly and glue is squeezed out along the edges. Make sure that all the clamps have the same amount of pressure.

25

26

27

28

The glue will usually dry after about 24 hours, depending on room temperature. After the clamps come off, transfer the centerline of the form to the piece at both ends before moving it **(28)**. Then draw a reference line for squaring and cutting the piece to width **(29)**. From the reference line, mark both edges **(30)**. With a straightedge, connect the two points **(31)** and bandsaw down the line.

29

30

31

To cut the plywood to width, screw a block of wood to the fence of the table saw for the straight edge to rest upon **(32)**. You can control the angle of the edge being cut by varying the height of the fence block or by tilting the sawblade. Cut the edge oversize, then turn the piece around and cut the first edge to exact width.

To square the end, clamp a thin piece of wood to the concave side of the plywood. Square it up, draw a line **(33,34)**, and bandsaw it out.

Using a table saw, cut the plywood to length **(35)**. Put the end you just bandsawed against the fence and cut the other end, then turn the piece around to finish-trim the squared-up end. If you remembered to make your piece a little longer than necessary, you will now be cutting off the brad marks at both ends.

Use the same methods to apply face veneer to curved stock as to straight. Clamp the 2x4s going lengthwise first, and then slowly apply pressure to the rest of the clamps. Remember, give the glue a chance to squeeze out toward the ends.

If I had to make a large quantity of bent-plywood pieces, I would get them made in a place that specializes in that sort of thing, because it probably would be cheaper than doing it myself. □

32

33

34

35

1

2

3

Sandbag-Veneering

If you don't want to make a two-part form, sandbags can be used to veneer pieces that are not flat. For this operation you need clamps, sandbags and a caul.

A caul is a piece of wood that goes on top of the sandbag (this is also where the clamps go). The caul doesn't have to fit the concavity of the piece to be veneered exactly, as the sandbag will distribute even pressure **(1)**.

With this technique, use hot glue whenever possible. Hot glue is strong and sets fast, and because the veneer is clamped down before the glue starts melting, it cannot expand as it absorbs the moisture.

Put the glue only on the piece to be veneered, not on the veneer. Let the glue cool, and then apply the veneer with a piece of paper on top so the sandbag won't stick to the veneer if any glue bleeds through.

Before putting on the glue, heat the sandbag, half-filled with fine sand, in an electric frying pan or in an oven set to 220° F. Make sure to sift the sand before putting it in the bag. Then place the sandbag on the veneer, spreading out the sand evenly **(2)**.

Put the caul on and clamp it down as quickly as possible **(3)**. As soon as the sand is cold, the glue will hold down the veneer and the clamps can be removed. Scrape with a gooseneck scraper blade and sand using a blackboard eraser for a block, and you are all done.

Sandbags can also be used over convex surfaces and with forms. Large forms can be made out of plaster of paris. □

Inlay
Chapter 7

Inlaying with an Electric Router

Many people confuse inlay and marquetry, but they are two completely different techniques. I like inlay because it is easier than marquetry to design and do, and usually the grain of the wood doesn't have to be chosen as carefully. I prefer to use wood with straight grain for inlay work, because it is less distracting and better emphasizes the shape of the simple forms I like to work with. Marquetry doesn't interest me much, although sometimes I do simple abstractions on the tops of boxes. I am definitely not interested in commercially available pictures such as pretty roses.

When doing inlay work, there are two rules to follow. First, do not inlay solid wood into plywood, as the inlay will crack when it dries and shrinks. Second, when inlaying into solid wood, make sure that the grain of the inlay goes in the same direction as the piece to be inlaid. If you inlay a piece going against the grain or at an angle, the inlay will eventually be pushed out by wood movement.

The oldest way to inlay wood is to make the inlay, put it on the piece to be inlaid, scribe around it, chisel out the recess and smooth the bottom of the recess with a router plane. An easier way is to use a portable electric router with a template guide and a bushing. The idea here is to rout the recess with the bushing pressed onto the template guide, then to remove the bushing before routing the inlay. Thus, provided the walls of the bushing are the same as the diameter of the router bit, recess and inlay will end up the exact same size. The advantage of this method is that the same template makes both inlay and recess. The bit will cut on one side of the line with the bushing on the template guide, and on the other side of the line with the bushing removed. The drawing **(1)** shows the relationship of the template guide, bushing and bit.

For small inlays with fine detail, I use a ⅛-in. router bit. The size of the template guide is not important — I use the smallest one that will fit the bit I am using. Remember that the walls of the bushing must be the same thickness as the diameter of the bit. It is not difficult to make your own bushing nor is it expensive to have one made, but the bushing has to press-fit the guide so it won't fall off when you use it.

The drawback to this technique is that the corners of the inlay can't come to a sharp point, but of course they could be chiseled out afterward and the point of the inlay fitted by hand.

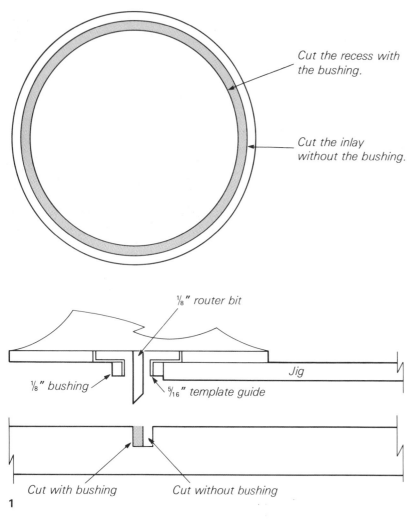

Cut the recess with the bushing.

Cut the inlay without the bushing.

⅛" router bit

⅛" bushing

⁵⁄₁₆" template guide

Jig

Cut with bushing   Cut without bushing

1

Here I am using a ⅛-in. router bit, a ⅛-in. bushing and a ⁵⁄₁₆-in. template guide. This photograph **(2)** shows the template guide without the bushing and this one **(3)** with the bushing on.

To guide the router, you will need a jig that is larger than the inlay to allow for the template guide and the bit **(4)**. I find that ¼-in. plywood works fine for the jig. To determine how much bigger than the inlay to make the jig, measure the distance from the cutting edge of the bit to the outside of the template guide; in this case, ³⁄₃₂ in. Add this measurement to the diameter of the bit, in this case, ⅛ in. The sum is ⁷⁄₃₂ in., so the radius of the jig must be ⁷⁄₃₂ in. larger than the inlay **(5)**.

2

3

4

⅛″ router bit

⁵⁄₁₆″ template guide

Jig

³⁄₃₂″

⁷⁄₃₂″

5

6

After making the jig, clamp it to the board that is going to receive the inlay **(6)**. Put the bushing on the template guide and set the router bit to the right depth, about ³⁄₁₆ in. into the wood. Start the router in about the center of the jig and move out toward the edge until the bushing touches it **(7)**. Then, with the bushing following the jig, cut all the way around. Rout clockwise, so the bit will push the bushing against the jig. If you rout counterclockwise, the bit will push the bushing away from the jig. It's a good idea to rout on a scrap piece first, just to make sure you're going the right way.

After the circle is cut, remove the rest of the wood in the center **(8)**. If the recess is large and there's too much wood to remove with the small bit, use a larger one. If you do this, it's a good idea to cut out the inlay before changing to the larger bit.

7

8

Now cut the inlay. The first step is to remove the bushing from the template guide. Then clamp the jig to the board from which the inlay is going to be cut.

Cutting the inlay usually requires two people, unless you are using a plunge router (p. 163). With the bit retracted, position the router in the jig, holding the template guide against the edge of the jig. Start the router and have somebody lower the bit to the desired depth **(9)**. This is a safe technique, especially when using a small bit. With one person holding the router tight against the jig, it is the same as using a drill press or a plunge router.

Follow the edge of the jig to rout out the inlay. Make sure to move the router clockwise, or else you'll be in trouble. When you are finished, turn off the router and let it stop before removing it.

Here **(10,11)** the inlay is cut and ready to be removed from the board.

9

10

11

12

13

Now mark the desired thickness of the inlay, set the fence on the table saw and cut out the inlay **(12)**. You could also use a bandsaw. Keep the inlay on the outside of the saw so it can fall free after it is cut **(13)**. Never allow it between the fence and the sawblade, where it would be trapped and might get damaged.

Don't try to cut an inlay from a board that is the exact same thickness you want; if you did, the inlay would come loose the minute the cut was completed, and the router bit would chew it up. If you have to use a board of exactly the same thickness, glue it to another board using rubber cement or hot glue with brown paper between.

When the piece is cut out, it should fit perfectly. Just glue it in and sand it flush **(14)**.

This technique has many decorative applications, especially when you use circles of different diameter. I also use inlaid circles to repair imperfections in wood, with the advantage that you can move the inlay around in the recess to match the grain. (For small imperfections, of course, you can use a plugcutter and drill press to cut circles.) ☐

14

Inlaying with a Plunge Router

Inserting a panel into a frame having edges that are not straight is hard to do with hand tools, but with a plunge router, template guide and bushing, it is easy and accurate. Plunge routing lets you begin and end a cut in the middle of a piece of stock without having to lower or lift the base from the work. With the motor running, you can lower the bit into the wood by simply pushing down on the handles.

I finally broke down and bought a Makita 2¾-HP 3600 B plunge router, which I should have done years ago. It has many advantages over other routers I have used and is both well designed and made. The body is attached to the rectangular base by two ⅞-in. diameter steel posts. These fit into sleeves in the body that can slide up and down on the posts (against spring tension) and be locked at any height. The switch can be worked without having to move your hand from the handle **(1)**, but it's not located right on the handle where you might turn it on accidentally while picking up the router. The body is locked on the posts by a latching lever instead of a knob, and you can reach this lever to raise or lower the bit without having to take your hand off the handle **(2)**.

1

2

An adjustable knob on top of the router **(3)** stops the upward travel and also controls the depth of cut for ordinary routing. To set the depth, simply press the button, which is a half nut, and slide the rod to the approximate setting **(4,5)**. For final adjustment, release the button so that the rod can be worked like a screw. The stop block of this router can be set to two different depths **(6,7)**, necessary when making a haunched mortise, for example. But you can control the depth of cut when plunge routing without using these stops. Just turn on the router, release the lock lever, push the bit down to the desired depth and lock it.

This router is also good for mortising, which I explain how to do on p. 167.

3

4

5

The first step in inserting an inlay panel into a frame with curved edges is to make an oversize jig. Here I am using a ⅜-in. template guide and a ¼-in. bit. The distance from the cutting edge of the bit to the outside of the template guide is ¹⁄₁₆ in. This plus the bit equals ⁵⁄₁₆ in., so that is how much bigger than the inlay all around to make the jig.

When the jig is made, nail it at the corners to the piece from which you are going to cut the inlay **(8)**. Keep a piece of plywood underneath the inlay so that you don't cut into the bench. Glue the inlay material to the plywood using rubber cement or hot glue with brown paper between, so when the inlay is cut free it won't slip into the router bit and get damaged.

6

7

8

9

Now put the plunge router (without the bushing) on the jig **(9)**, start it and lower the bit — about ¼ in. into the wood should be safe. Start to cut, making sure to move clockwise **(10)**. (If you were to use a male jig instead of a female jig, you would have to move the router counterclockwise, because you'd be using the opposite side of the router.) Here the inlay is cut **(11)**.

Now place the jig on the frame. Be sure it is positioned properly, so the inlay won't be crooked. Clamp the ends **(12)** and rout the sides first, again moving the router clockwise. Remember to put the bushing on before you do this.

10

11

12

After the sides are routed, move the clamps one at a time and rout the ends **(13)**. Remove the rest of the wood with the plunge router.

Notice how perfectly the inlay fits into the frame **(14)**.

As I have said, the Makita plunge router is also excellent for use as a mortising machine, but a guide base, which is secured with one wing nut, has to be used **(15)**. A mortising machine is a very important piece of equipment, but it usually costs about $2400. By building a simple fixture for holding the stock and cutting the mortises with the router, you can have a mortising setup that works just as well as an expensive machine, but that costs only about $350.

13

14

15

16

The mortising fixture I made looks like a big miter box **(16,17)**. Its length and depth can be varied to suit your needs, but its inside width should not be more than 3¼ in. or the router base will not rest on both sides. Make the bottom of the fixture from two pieces of ¾-in. plywood and make the sides from plywood, too, because solid wood might warp. Install lateral stops on the top edge of the inboard side of the fixture. The stops are slotted strips of wood grooved on their bottoms to fit over and slide along the edge. The slot in each stop rides around a screw, which you tighten when you determine the length of the mortise you want to cut. I use ³⁄₁₆-in. stove bolts to secure each stop. They are engaged by *T*-nuts embedded into the side of the fixture; ¼-in. hanger bolts (bolts having machine threads on one end and wood threads on the other) with wing nuts could also be used.

Use shim to adjust height of wood to be mortised.

Slotted and grooved end stop, one on each end

Glue and screw sides to base.

³⁄₁₆″ *bolt*

½″ *washer*

½″ *dowel*

³⁄₁₆″ *T-nut*

To cut the mortises in a piece of regular dimension, a straight table leg, for example, shim up the workpiece in the fixture so it's almost flush with the top edge **(18)**. Roughly center the area to be mortised in the middle of the fixture and clamp it to the side facing you. Set the stops to contact the router base so the bit can travel the full length of the mortise in one pass. With the fixture held in a vise, or secured to your bench some other way, set the fence on the router the right distance from the bit and butt the base against the left-hand stop.

Switch on the power, release the lock lever and lower the bit into the wood. For a ⅜-in. bit, a ¼-in. depth of cut should be safe.

Then pull the router to the right **(19)**, so the rotation of the bit will hold the fence against the side of the fixture, which will give you a good straight cut. If you were to start at the right-hand stop and push the router to the left, you could get an uneven cut.

Mortising is best done by making several passes to reach final depth, cutting ¼ in. to ⅜ in. deep with each pass, depending on the density of the wood and on the size and kind of bit you're using. All this may sound complicated, but you will be surprised at how fast it works. I think this system is faster and cleaner-cutting than a hollow-chisel mortiser. Here is the finished mortise **(20)**.

18

19

20

For cutting angled mortises in regular stock, like those in chair legs to receive stretchers and rails, you will have to make angled shims that will hold the stock in the right relation to the bit **(21)**, as you would have to for any mortising machine. To mortise curved pieces, a chair back, for instance, bandsaw a piece to fit the side of the curve opposite the cut and use it to support the stock when clamped in the fixture **(22,23)**. You can place the curved shim underneath the stock for mortising on one side. To mortise the adjoining side, support the stock from the inboard side of the fixture, using the same curved shim and a flat support on the bottom. Here **(24)** both mortises are cut.

For general mortising, two-flute straight-face carbide bits will do a good job. High-speed steel bits will work, but will get dull faster and cut a little slower. The Makita plunge router comes with ¼-in. and ⅜-in. adapter sleeves for its ½-in. collet, so you can use different bit sizes and cut mortises of almost any width and up to 2⅜-in. deep. □

21

22

23

24

Finishing
Chapter 8

1

2

Preparation

Finishing is an important part of making fine furniture. You can build a beautiful piece, but if the finish is bad, both beauty and value will be lessened.

Finishing starts the instant you pick up the smoothing plane, which has to be used first if the piece is made of solid wood. (If the wood is curly or bird's-eye maple, use a cabinet scraper, p. 35, instead.) The plane removes the small marks left by jointer and thickness-planer knives **(1)**, which will show up after the finish is on. If the knives are dull, the marks will be even more noticeable.

To demonstrate how knife marks can swell up and stand out, I made three hammer marks **(2)** on the surface of a piece of wood. The two on the left are about $\frac{1}{16}$ in. deep; the one on the right is about $\frac{1}{8}$ in. deep.

I planed the wood **(3)** so that the two marks on the left felt flush with the surface but were still visible, and then I sanded **(4)**. After sanding, the marks on the left were almost gone, but the mark on the right was still half there **(5)**.

3

4

5

6

7

8

Next I applied water to the surface through a double layer of paper toweling **(6)**. (The bottle was filled with water, not rice wine.) Moving a warm iron over the paper toweling created steam **(7)** — remember that moisture and heat expand wood.

As you can see, even though the two $\frac{1}{16}$-in. hammer marks were flush after the board was planed and sanded, the moisture made the wood fibers raise above the surface **(8)**. The $\frac{1}{8}$-in. deep hammer mark, which was not planed flush, raised $\frac{1}{16}$ in. above the surface. The same thing would happen after the finish was put on.

So a good way to remove dents in wood before finishing is to apply steam and then plane the surface with a smoothing plane. Dents can also be raised with warm water put on the surface and allowed to dry, but for deep dents I recommend using steam.

Unless the wood has dents, I usually don't bother to raise the grain before finishing. The only exception is when I am going to use a water stain (p. 182).

After the wood is planed, use a scraper blade to remove the plane marks. This is much faster than sanding. Because the edge of a scraper blade is straight, it will make the surface perfectly level. Most people sand too much and waste time doing it.

When you are working on a piece, try to avoid denting or dropping it. Keep your bench clean; be sure there is no old glue on it, which will definitely dent the wood. Remember that every blemish creates more work for you to do later. □

Sanding

After scraping out the marks left by the smoothing plane, you're ready to sand the surface of the wood. For a sanding block I like to use a piece of cork approximately 4½ in. by 3 in. by 1⅜ in. **(1)**. It fits the hand and is just the right size for a quarter sheet of sandpaper. Cork is light and inexpensive, with a firm and flat, but not hard, surface. Fancy rubber sanding blocks with slots in each end to hold the sandpaper are too heavy and waste too much paper.

Don't use a knife, chisel or scissors to cut sandpaper. Just fold it **(2)** and tear it into quarters on a sharp edge **(3)**. Wrap a quarter of the sheet around the block so that it is off center **(4)**, not as shown here **(5)**. When the portion of the sandpaper you are using dulls, simply move an unused section over into its place. This way, more of the quarter sheet can be used.

1

2

3

5

4

6

Although there are many different opinions on sanding, I prefer to use 80-grit and 120-grit paper for most work. For fine sanding, I use 180 grit. I am not an expert on sandpaper, but I have tried most kinds, and I prefer garnet open-coat D with paper backing. (Open coat simply means that only 60% to 80% of the surface of the paper is coated with abrasives, reducing the paper's tendency to clog. The letter refers to paper weight — D is medium weight.) Always sand with the grain or else scratches will show up when the finish goes on.

I have an oscillating sander **(6)** but hardly ever use it because it makes tiny circular scratches in the wood. Also, its base is soft, which can create an uneven surface. As you can see by the edges **(7)**, the mice like it. This type of sander is fine to use between coats if you have a lot of finishing to do.

7

A belt sander **(8)** is a good investment. It can ruin a piece faster than almost any other tool, but once you've learned how to use it correctly, it can be a big help. Belt sanders have a steel plate on the bottom **(9)** that keeps the surface even, and the mice won't eat it. I use mine all the time and usually can get away without using a smoothing plane first. Using an X-weight 60-grit belt, which is a heavy cloth, I run the sander 45° to the grain in one direction and then 45° in the opposite direction until the surface is flat. Then, using the same grit, I remove the angled sanding marks by going back and forth with the grain. I repeat the process with 80 grit and 120 grit, going with the grain. Lastly, I go over the surface with a sanding block and sandpaper, again using 80 grit first, then 120 grit. I finish up with 180 grit.

When you are using a belt sander, keep it flat on the surface. Rocking it from side to side could result in scratches or dips in the surface, which would show up after the finish has been applied **(10)**.

Make sure to move the sander all the way through a stroke from one end to the other. This is especially important when using the 120-grit belt. Let a third of the sanding plate stick out over the edge of the work before changing directions **(11)**. Going halfway and then turning back could result in scratches in the surface. □

8

9

10

11

1

2

3

4

Filler

I never use commercial filler and sanding sealer because they cloud the wood and usually change color with age. The only time I use filler is to fill imperfections, and when I do, I make my own. Commercial Plastic Wood filler might match the color of your wood in the beginning, but as the wood gets darker, which it normally does, the Plastic Wood will stick out like a sore thumb.

To make your own filler, save the sanding dust from the particular piece you are working on. Then, if you are using a shellac or oil finish, mix the dust with 2-lb. cut liquid shellac so that it is the consistency of putty and use it to fill the imperfection. If you are going to lacquer the piece, mix the sanding dust with thinned lacquer. Or, if you're going to stain the piece, mix the sanding dust with either thin hot glue or Titebond diluted 50% with water.

Put enough filler on so that it can be sanded flush with the surface after it dries. Because the filler is made of the same wood it fills, it will fade with the wood. Making your own filler is cheaper than buying Plastic Wood; you also don't have to store all those cans.

Sometimes a beautiful piece of wood has loose knots or knotholes. To fill them so that they look natural, use stick shellac. It's easy to make stick shellac yourself. I'm sure my son, who is a volunteer fire chief, would not approve of the way I do it in the shop, but I feel it's perfectly safe. Just be sure that the shop is reasonably clean and no sawdust or shavings are next to the fire. Definitely do not make stick shellac in your finishing room.

To begin, put about a handful of orange shellac flakes **(1)** on a flat piece of metal and pour on about one tablespoon of alcohol **(2)**. Move the flakes around to spread the alcohol evenly, then stand back and light it with a match **(3)**. As the alcohol burns, it will melt the flakes. To make sure all the flakes melt, move them around with an old chisel or a piece of metal **(4)**.

When all the alcohol has burned off and the flakes have melted, form the shellac into a stick. Put motor oil on your hands first to protect them **(5,6)** and to prevent hot flakes from sticking to them. Then scrape the shellac off the plate with the chisel and start to form it **(7,8)**. This photograph **(9)** shows the finished stick.

5

6

7

8

9

10

Here is a piece of walnut with a loose knot and a knothole **(10)**. To melt the stick shellac into them, you can use burning-in irons or hot knives, which are best for big jobs. I usually just use a match **(11)**.

While the shellac is still hot, force it all the way down with the back of a chisel or knife **(12,13)**, but moisten the back of the tool first to prevent the shellac from sticking to it. When the shellac has cooled, clean off the excess from the surface of the wood with a sharp chisel **(14)**.

Sand the shellac flush with the surface. When the piece is finished, the knots look natural **(15,16)**.   ☐

11

12

13

14

15

16

Staining

Wood with naturally beautiful color should not be stained. However, some wood can be tinted with a very weak stain to brighten its natural color. Stain is also sometimes used to blend sapwood with heartwood.

A good stain should penetrate the wood and resist fading. It should also be inexpensive. I like to use stains made from about 4 oz. (112 grams) of water-soluble aniline dye powder dissolved in about 1 gal. (3.8 liters) of hot (not boiling) water. Let the stain cool at room temperature before using.

Aniline dye powder is available in many colors, but the two best suited for most hardwoods are bismark brown (reddish brown) and nigrosine jet (black). Keep the powder in an airtight container so that it will not absorb moisture. To dissolve the powder, use water that is as clean as possible and free from iron and calcium — distilled water is safest. It's best to mix the amount of stain you need each time, because liquid stain will lose some of its color if stored too long. Never keep liquid stain in a metal container.

Before using water stain, always moisten the wood with warm water to raise the grain. When the wood dries, sand with fine sandpaper. If you don't do this, the grain will raise when the stain is applied, resulting in a fuzzy surface. Non-grain-raising stains are available in liquid form, and these seem to work fine, but I don't know how much the color will fade over time.

Water stain is fast and easy to apply, and it does not leave a heavy film on the wood. Apply the stain with a brush, after testing it on a scrap piece of wood. After two or three minutes, if you want a light color, wipe off the stain with a dry cloth; for a dark color, even out the stain with a dustbroom.

Don't use an oil finish over a water stain or any stain except a chemical stain, because the oil won't protect it. A shellac, lacquer or varnish finish must be used instead.

In Denmark in the 1930s, stain made from aniline dye powder was widely used, especially on less expensive furniture made of rotary-cut birch plywood. All kinds of tricks were used to disguise the plywood, such as imitating curly birch and maple with stains.

1

Once, when I was still an apprentice, I took a job refinishing a cabinet to make a little extra money. I thought the cabinet was made of curly maple, but when I started removing the finish, I found it was plain maple. You can imagine how I felt. Luckily, I knew an old painter who saved me by teaching me a lesson on how to fake it.

Use a water-based stain and apply it so that the color is fairly even **(1)**. Then take a damp cloth or chamois and twist it. For curly birch, don't twist too hard **(2)**; for curly maple, twist more **(3)**. Roll the cloth over the stain while it is still wet **(4,5)**. The raised part of the cloth will absorb some of the stain. However, in those areas where the cloth does not touch the surface, the stain will remain dark and will appear as curls there.

2

3

4

5

For a bird's-eye effect, dab the end of a sponge cloth, or a damp sponge, onto the surface **(6)**. A nonprofessional will find it very hard to tell if the finished product is real or not.

Another trick is imitating rosewood or other dark, heavily grained wood. Here **(7)**, I used a rosewood-colored, oil-based stain to flood the wood, and painted in the figure with a feather — the wing feather from a goose is best. Oil stain doesn't dry as fast and doesn't flow out as easily as water stain, so it's good for an application like this. But oil stain leaves a heavy film on the wood and usually I don't like to use it.

Alcohol-soluble aniline stains are not very fade-proof and I usually don't use them either. But they can be used to stain shellac and are often used in French polishing. Shellac mixed with nigrosine jet results in a black finishing material that was used in the French polishing of black pianos. When you use stain mixed with shellac for French polishing, however, it can take up to four weeks for the color to fade from your hands.

Chemical stains In the 1930s, staining was also often used for expensive furniture, but the wood was colored by chemical means. At that time, the chemicals were available from special paint stores, but today many of those chemicals are not easy to come by. Whether this is the cause or the effect, chemical staining has become a dying art.

Chemical stains are not stains in the usual sense of the word, because they work through chemical action. Therefore, they leave no film on the wood — a major advantage to using them. Chemical stains are also water-resistant, so you can use an oil finish over them, and they are virtually fade-proof. Chemical stains take more time to apply than stains made from aniline-dye powder, but the results are well worth it — you can get some fantastic colors.

A chemical stain must be applied in two steps. First there is a prestain, or mordant — such as tannic acid, pyrogallol, pyrocatechol or nitroso-b-napthol. The second stain, or afterstain, can be ammonia or salts of iron, cobalt, copper, chromium, manganese or nickel. There are many possible combinations of prestains and afterstains. The chart on the facing page gives some of them and the resulting colors.

Chemical stains take differently on different woods. (They even react differently with the heartwood and sapwood of the same wood.) On woods having tannic acid, such as oak, chemical stains will usually produce a darker color than on woods not having tannic acid. Softwoods take chemical stains well, but it is necessary to apply a wash of ammonia after staining to help the stain penetrate. On hardwoods, a wash of ammonia will often bring out new colors. You can mix ammonia with other afterstains, as long as no sediment results. Always experiment on scrap first.

Apply chemical stain with either a sponge or a brush. If using a sponge, protect your hands by wearing rubber gloves. If using a brush, make sure there is no metal piece holding the hairs.

6

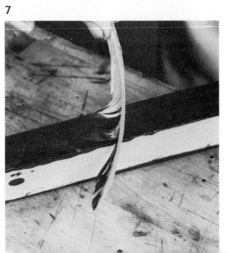

7

Allow at least 24 hours drying time between coats so the chemicals have time to work. It's a good idea to go over the stained surface with a cloth when the stain is dry or to sand it lightly between coats with 320-grit paper, to smooth out the surface. Never use steel wool between coats. Horsehair is good to use, as it is better for smoothing than a cloth and easier to use than sandpaper.

Ebonizing   Here is a great black stain, but it must be used with an oil finish.

Mix together in a clean jar 3½ oz. (100 grams) of copper sulfate, 1¾ oz. (50 grams) of potassium chlorate and 22 oz. (615 grams) of hot distilled water. In another jar, mix 3½ oz. (100 grams) of aniline hydrochloride, 1⅖ oz.

(40 grams) of ammonium chloride and 22 oz. (615 grams) of hot distilled water. To use, mix equal parts of the solutions together, but don't mix any more than you think you will need for each coat. Apply three coats with a sponge or brush, allowing 24 hours drying time in between coats. When the third coat is dry, smooth it with fine sandpaper, using linseed oil as a lubricant.

The first coat of this finish will look a little yellow, the second coat will look a little green, and the third coat will look very green. But don't get nervous, because the instant the oil touches the finish, it will turn a deep, beautiful black. After the stain dries, finish the piece with oil — tung, linseed or penetrating oil is okay.   □

Colors resulting from combinations of prestains and afterstains.

Prestain	Afterstain *	Color
Tannic acid, 1¾ oz. (50 grams) per quart (liter) of hot distilled water	Ammonia	Golden brown
	Ferrous sulfate	Ivory black
	Cobaltous chloride	Golden brown
	Potassium dichromate	Cool brown
	Nickel chloride	Golden brown
Pyrogallol, 1¾ oz. (50 grams) per quart (liter) of hot distilled water	Ammonia	Chestnut brown
	Ferrous sulfate	Greenish black
	Cobaltous chloride	Brown
	Copper chloride	Dark reddish brown
	Potassium dichromate	Dark reddish brown
	Manganous dichloride	Honey brown
	Nickel chloride	Honey brown
Pyrocatechol, 1¾ oz. (50 grams) per quart (liter) of hot distilled water	Ammonia	Cool brown
	Ferrous sulfate	Bluish black
	Cobaltous chloride	Greenish brown
	Copper chloride	Greenish black
	Potassium dichromate	Brownish black
Nitroso-B-naphthol, ⅖ oz. (10 grams), and potassium hydroxide, ⅒ oz. (3½ grams), per quart (liter) of boiling distilled water	Ammonia	Gold
	Ferrous sulfate	Spring green
	Cobaltous chloride	Indian red
	Copper chloride	Burnt orange
	Potassium dichromate	Reddish orange
	Manganous dichloride	Lemon
	Nickel chloride	Orange

* To mix afterstain, dissolve ⅖ oz. (10 grams) of ferrous sulfate, cobaltous chloride, copper chloride, manganous dichloride or nickel chloride in a quart (liter) of hot distilled water. For potassium-dichromate stain, mix ⁷⁄₁₀ oz. (20 grams) of the chemical in a quart (liter) of hot distilled water. Ammonia afterstain is simply 27% ammonia solution (available from chemical supply houses).

Finishing Materials

There are many different kinds of finishing materials. Each has advantages and disadvantages, and certain ones, like lacquer and varnish, are more difficult to use than others. Some finishes sit on the surface of the wood so you have to look through a film; others, such as oil, penetrate the surface of the wood.

Oil   Oil is the easiest material to use and the most practical. Most oil finishes are relatively resistant to heat, water and alcohol, and are easy to maintain and repair. The finish improves with age, too. Never use oil inside a drawer or bookcase, however, or any place where cloth or paper will be stored. Most oil finishes will bleed or sweat on a hot day and cloth and paper will pick up the oil.

Linseed oil, which is made from the seed of the flax plant, is one of the oldest finishing materials, and for many years was the most commonly used. But even after lengthy drying, linseed oil never hardens through completely and, when used by itself, is not a durable finish. For many years I have used a three-step linseed-oil finish that is much more durable than plain linseed. Allow 24 hours of drying time between each coat.

For the first coat, mix half pure raw linseed oil and half pure turpentine. Put on a heavy coat with a rag and allow it to soak into the wood. (In between uses, I keep the rag in a closed container with the linseed oil.)

The next day apply the second coat, using pure boiled linseed oil. Leave it on for two to three hours, then sand the surface with some worn, fine sandpaper and wipe it clean.

On the third day apply the last coat. Mix half boiled linseed oil and half japan drier. When applying the finish, don't cover too large an area at one time. For example, if finishing a cabinet, first put the oil on one side, wait about ten minutes, and apply it to the other side. After ten minutes more, do the top. The reason for allowing the time between is that after a while the finish gets tacky — sometimes after twenty minutes and sometimes after five hours, depending on the drying conditions. When the finish gets tacky, you have to work fast, because it will dry suddenly. If you haven't allowed the ten minutes between areas, the finish on the last area will dry before you have a chance to wipe it off.

When the finish gets tacky, use a piece of burlap to rub the oil into the pores, going across the grain. Then wipe the extra oil off with a clean rag.

To prevent spontaneous combustion, put used burlap and rags in an airtight container or burn them.

On the fourth day, steelwool the surface and wipe it clean with a rag. For a shinier surface, sprinkle on some rottenstone and polish with a piece of leather, going with the grain. Rottenstone is one of the finest natural abrasives for polishing surfaces.

Linseed oil should not be used on eating utensils, but I used the finish just described on our kitchen counters and dining table 24 years ago, and the whole family is still healthy. There are salad-bowl finishes available, approved by the Food and Drug Administration, that are recommended for use on eating utensils.

The oil I use most now is Watco Danish Oil **(1)**, not because I am a Dane, but because it is easy to use and provides a durable finish. The way I use it is not the way recommended on the label, however. I put on a heavy first coat with a rag, but I don't wipe it off after 30 minutes — I leave it on.

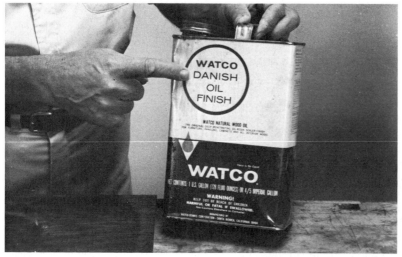

The next day a lot of oil is left dried on the surface. I put on another coat of oil over this, which dissolves the surface residue. After five minutes, I sand with 220-grit paper **(2)**. This results in a thicker oil that helps to fill in the pores. The next day I steelwool with 3/0 steel wool, and the surface is finished.

Of all the different oil finishes, tung oil, which is extracted from the fruit of the tung tree, has the most resistance to water, acid, heat and mildew, but it takes a long time to dry. It is best to rub it into the wood with a small rag. After 24 hours a second coat can be applied. This results in a beautiful finish. All oils darken the wood to which they are applied, but tung oil darkens the wood the least. Linseed darkens wood the most, and Watco is in between tung and linseed.

Shellac　Shellac, an organic material produced from the lac bug found in the Far East, is a good finishing material with several advantages. It's easy to use, is a durable, elastic finish that won't get air bubbles when applied, and dries fast. The disadvantage is that it is not water, heat and alcohol-proof. But it is easy to repair. If a shellac finish is exposed to a lot of sun for many years, it will, like any other finish, fade or change color. Applying thin oil, such as kerosene, to a shellac finish and leaving it on overnight won't damage the finish and will usually result in the return of the original color.

Shellac can be bought either as dry flakes or in liquid form. In liquid form it is sold as 2, 3 or 4-lb. cut, which refers to the amount of flakes dissolved in 1 gal. alcohol. Liquid shellac, especially white shellac, has a short shelf life. White shellac is simply flakes of orange shellac bleached and ground into granules. Even in dry form, white shellac has a shelf life of only three to six months, and I try to avoid using it.

Liquid shellac should have a date on the jar; don't use it after that date because it will never dry, and I mean *never* dry. I once made a cabinet with pull-out trays for canned goods and finished it with old shellac — after eight years, the shellac is still sticky. To get a tray out, you first have to hit it with your hand; then, to get the cans loose, you have to hit them, too. Of course, the advantage is that the cans never fall off the trays.

For best results, make your own shellac. Put some flakes of orange shellac in a jar, then pour denatured alcohol to cover them by 1 in. Immediately shake the jar for three to five minutes to prevent the flakes from gluing themselves together in a big lump. Shake every five minutes after that until all the flakes are dissolved.

Always keep liquid shellac in a glass or plastic jar. If kept in a metal container, the shellac will discolor and get a muddy look.

Shellac can be sprayed (p. 190), brushed or padded on. If you decide to spray, keep the pressure at about 25 lb. Pressure that is any higher will push out the shellac too quickly.

Most craftsmen prefer to apply shellac with a brush because it is not very difficult. Use a good brush that is made especially for applying varnish, enamel and shellac. It will cost a little more to buy but the end result will be well worth it. A 2-in. wide brush is good for all-around use.

If you use 2-lb. cut shellac, it will dry fast and won't leave brushmarks. It's best to brush it on in several thin coats rather than in one or two heavy ones. Apply the shellac going with the grain in long, full strokes. After covering the entire surface, wait five to ten minutes and then sand lightly with fine sandpaper — 220 grit is good. If more than two coats are applied, however, the shellac will take longer to dry.

2

Dry shellac will not stick to sandpaper, so if your shellac does, wait a little longer for it to dry. When sanding, be careful not to go through the finish. After sanding, wipe off the dust and apply another coat of shellac. Never use steel wool between coats: It breaks into small pieces that get stuck in the pores of the wood and make the finish rough. After the desired number of coats are applied, the surface can be rubbed out with 3/0 steel wool or scraped.

You can also pad on shellac for a smooth, shiny open-pored finish. (In French polishing, the traditional shellac finish, the pores are always filled.) Use the same type of pad described for use in French polishing (p. 196), but don't use the same pad for both finishes. This is because pumice and oil are used in French polishing, but not when applying a padded shellac finish.

For a padded shellac finish, first apply two coats of 2-lb. cut shellac with a brush. When the shellac is dry, sand the surface and wipe off the dust with a cloth. Now, put a little shellac into the pad — don't overdo it. Going with the grain, move the pad the full length of the piece, back and forth, over the surface. Continue until the pad is fairly dry. Then, if the surface does not look satisfactory, add a little more shellac to the pad and keep going. Never stop using the pad until it is fairly dry. If the finish is too shiny, wait until the surface is dry and lightly rub with 3/0 steel wool.

Any shellac finish can be removed easily with ammonia. Don't use alcohol because it is messy and will evaporate too fast. Also, ammonia is less expensive than alcohol.

The 4-F Finish An oil-and-shellac finish can be applied quickly and looks beautiful if done right. I first used this finish about 30 years ago, because of an accident. I had a shop with eight people working in it. One day, as we were loading a truck with furniture, one side of a cabinet got badly scratched. The furniture had a four-day oil finish and we didn't have time to redo it. As I was standing there, it occured to me that shellac and oil are used together for French polish, so I decided to take a chance. I scraped and sanded the damaged piece, put oil on and then shellac right over it. When the finish got tacky, I rubbed it out with steel wool and it came out as beautiful as the rest of the furniture. Since then, my students and I have frequently used this finish. When I first demonstrated it to them, the students named it the 4-F Finish: Frid's Fast Fine Finish.

For this finish I prefer to use raw linseed oil or Watco instead of boiled linseed oil, and orange shellac instead of white, because these make it easier to get a smooth finish. If a lot of pieces have to be finished, you could mix the oil and shellac together, but keep shaking the material as you use it. (I don't recommend doing this.)

Here's how to do the work. First put on a nice even coat of oil with a rag **(3)**. Immediately brush on a coat of 3-lb. cut shellac, using a cheap brush or a rag **(4)**. Keep testing the surface as it dries **(5)** until it is tacky. Don't let the surface get too dry or you will really have a problem getting all the shellac and oil off.

3

4

When the piece is tacky, rub it with a pad of 3/0 steel wool going with the grain **(6)** until all the shellac and oil are removed from the surface. If the pad gets saturated, use a new one. Be sure to remove all the oil and shellac from the surface and corners, or else the excess finish will turn gray.

Next wipe the surface clean with a dry cloth. You will have a finish that is as beautiful as a regular oil finish. If you want a higher shine, apply another coat of shellac immediately, but don't use any more oil. This picture **(7)** shows the finished piece.

This finish is best used on small pieces and on pieces that won't come in contact with water, such as chairs and table bases, because it is not waterproof and will spot if water is left on for a while. But this finish is easily repaired. Just put oil on the spot, steelwool or sand lightly and, after the spots disappear, wipe off all the excess oil.

If for some reason the piece gets dry and rough after it has been used for some time, put oil on and sand with 220-grit paper. Then wipe off all the excess oil immediately. If you don't, the finish will get tacky.

Never use an oil-and-shellac finish directly on top of a varnish or lacquer finish. For that matter, never put lacquer over an oil finish because the lacquer won't dry. If lacquer is used over varnish, the varnish will bubble up. If you feel you must put lacquer over an oil or varnish finish, you can use a sealer coat of shellac between the finishes because shellac will dry on any finish. But I don't like to do this.

5

6

7

Lacquer When you want a glossy finish, use lacquer. Lacquer can be sprayed or brushed on and is considerably easier to use than French polish. It is also more resistant to water, alcohol and heat. A lacquer finish is very difficult to repair, but if the damage is simply water spots, these can be removed by moistening the finish with lacquer thinner using an atomizer or spray gun. Don't get the finish too wet — just keep it moist until the spots disappear. Never use lacquer on top of an oil or varnish finish because it will never dry.

Nitrate cellulose lacquer was introduced after World War I and is what most people use today instead of cellulose lacquer, which is made of cellulose dissolved in acetone. Cellulose lacquer will put on only a very thin film, which is fine for use on metal but I don't like to use it on wood. Each manufacturer has its own recipe for lacquer, so it is important to follow the directions for thinning that are given on the can you buy and to use the thinner that is recommended.

It is easier to spray on lacquer than it is to brush it on, but for spraying you need an air compressor, which is an expensive piece of equipment. A good compressor having two pistons will ensure constant pressure. You will also be able to use other pneumatic tools with a compressor, so get a good one. A cheap compressor used to spray a large surface might not be able to keep up the pressure and you'll wind up in big trouble. When you are spraying lacquer, keep the pressure at about 40 lb. to 50 lb.

The proportion of air to lacquer sprayed depends on the work you are doing. For small surfaces, use less air **(8)**; for large surfaces, more air **(9)**. The nozzle of a spray gun has three holes — lacquer is sprayed through the center hole and air through the hole on each side **(10)**. Air flow is regulated by twisting the knob shown **(11)**. This knob **(12)** controls the amount of lacquer. If your gun spits during spraying, check this hole **(13)**, which should be free of lacquer at all times. If the hole is clean and your gun still spits, you might be using lacquer that is too heavy.

Hold the gun about 6 in. to 8 in. away from the surface. Pressure and gun distance vary, depending on the work and the spraying equipment. Experience is the best teacher.

To spray, move the gun first across the grain **(14,15)**, then with the grain **(16)**, continuing the pattern to build up an even coat on the surface. The hardest thing to learn is when to stop spraying. Here's one way to tell. As the lacquer is forced out of the gun in small drops and hits the surface, the surface eventually begins to look like an orange peel. With the application of more lacquer, the orange-peel texture begins to disappear as all the small drops flow together. As soon as the orange-peel texture disappears, stop spraying or the lacquer will begin to run. This, of course, is if the piece is standing on end. If the piece is lying flat, you could apply more lacquer without danger of runs.

If you find some runs after the lacquer is completely dry, use a small mill file to smooth them before scraping. If the scraper were used before filing, it would pull off all the lacquer where the run is.

Many people spray on a coat of sanding sealer to seal the wood and fill the pores before applying lacquer. I never use sanding sealer because it makes you feel as if you are looking at the finished work through a film, and, after several years, there's a good chance that the sanding sealer will make the pores turn white. Depending on how open-pored the wood is, I usually just apply three coats of lacquer, scraping lightly in between coats. For a wood such as oak I'd probably use four coats.

8

9

10

11

12

13

14

15   **16**

17

18

19

Using a brush to apply lacquer is very difficult. The first coat is easy, but because each new coat melts into the previous one, the second and third coats take more skill.

Always use a good-quality brush with soft hair to flow on the lacquer. Never brush it on like paint. Saturate the brush with lacquer, then bring it in like an airplane landing **(17,18)**. Move it all the way to the end of the work **(19)**.

Now reverse the stroke of the brush, moving it down on the surface in the same manner as before **(20)**. Never start the brush at the ends because lacquer will run down along the edges.

After completing the first track (which is the entire width of the brush), start the next one and continue in that way until the whole surface is covered. Never go back over the same track twice. If you do, it's possible that the brush might pick up three coats' worth of lacquer in some places and dump six coats' worth in others.

If the condition of the lacquer is right and it is applied correctly, it should flow out to a smooth finish. Lacquer that is too heavy will not flow out properly and air bubbles might become trapped, resulting in numerous pin holes in the finish. The biggest air bubbles can be removed while the finish is still soft. Puncture them carefully with a scriber **(21)** and the lacquer will flow back together.

Getting the lacquer mixture right takes practice and guesswork and depends on the type of lacquer you use. Once you decide on the type you prefer, you'll figure it out.

To estimate the drying time between coats of lacquer, whether sprayed or brushed, check the can to see what the manufacturer recommends. It's usually about four hours. The last coat should dry for 24 to 48 hours before being scraped and rubbed.

Never use steel wool between coats of lacquer because it breaks into small pieces that get stuck in the finish. And, because of the static electricity put into the steel from rubbing, the pieces will pull the lacquer up into many little pyramids. You could use a flat mill file to remove them, but it's better not to use steel wool in the first place.

Running a scraper blade lightly over the finish is an alternative to using steel wool and sandpaper between coats. Then wipe the finish with a clean rag and apply the next coat of lacquer. Make sure the scraper blade has a fine, smooth burr.

20

21

When I first came to the United States from Denmark to teach woodworking, the first question I was asked is how to finish lacquer. The students and the other teacher were spending a lot of time using wet sandpaper and rubbing the lacquer, but the result was unattractive — the finish still looked uneven, like an asphalt road after a shower. When I explained to them (using my arms and legs instead of English) that I scraped lacquer, they shook their heads and nobody wanted to talk to me. I soon realized that I was not really wanted there. After a couple of months I asked the other teacher if I was going to be sent back to Denmark and he said yes without a moment's hesitation.

After my contract I still had four months left before my departure, so I decided I might as well make some money before I had to leave. I asked if I could borrow a workbench and a set of tools. The next morning, the students helped me to get a plank of mahogany into the workshop before they went to design class (to which I was no longer invited). After four hours I had made a coffee table out of the mahogany. The base was sanded and the top screwed on, and I was sanding the top when the students returned. It was fun to see the looks on their faces when they saw the table ready to be finished; the table would have taken them more than a week to build because they did not know what they were doing. Anyway, I lacquered the table. When the lacquer dried, in front of the students, I scraped and buffed the tabletop in less than half an hour. After that day I never had a dull moment. So because of a coffee table and scraping lacquer, I was never forced to leave this country. Here is the table **(22)**, which my wife won't part with even after 32 years.

When scraping lacquer or shellac, start by going across the grain lightly on both ends first **(23)**, because the ends of a piece are the most difficult to get smooth. When they are smooth, continue scraping the whole surface, going with the grain.

Use the scraper blade in exactly the same way as explained in chapter 2 **(24,25)**. Keep crisscrossing the surface with the blade so that the finish will stay smooth and ungrooved. Before rubbing the finish, use the scraper the full length of the piece going with the grain to remove the marks on the ends made by scraping across the grain.

22

23

24   25

When using the scraper, be careful not to go through the finish. You will know that you have gone too far when you notice a change in color **(26)**. All finishes, including lacquer, darken the wood to some extent, so you know you've gone through when you see a lighter patch in the finish. If you do go through, use a half-dry brush to spot the finish with two or three coats of lacquer. Sand lightly between coats with 220-grit sandpaper, then give the whole surface a light coat of lacquer and scrape it again, which is easy because the surface is smooth and the pores are filled.

After the final scraping, rub with 3/0 steel wool if you want a dull finish. For a glossy finish, make a paste of 4F pumice and mineral oil and rub it on the surface with a felt block. You could also use a commercial rubbing compound. For a really high shine, follow up with rottenstone and oil, but wrap a clean cloth around the felt block to prevent scratches. To remove the oil, use either sanding dust or clean cloths.

There are other types of lacquer available that don't have to be rubbed, but these should be used only on cheap furniture. They are flat, semigloss and rub-effect lacquers. I never use them because they scratch too easily, and you don't get as nice a finish as when you scrape and rub a gloss lacquer. Plus, with these lacquers, you are really seeing the wood through a film, and a good finish should not hide the wood.

For objects such as small boxes, where you want to keep the wood light and just protect it from finger marks, one very thin coat of lacquer is a good finish. When it is dry, steel-wool it. The pores will be open and the surface will look as though it has an oil finish. But the lacquer finish is much lighter in color and will not bleed like an oil finish.

Varnish I hardly ever use varnish, except for outdoor furniture or boat work. There are many different types of varnish available, and each is formulated for a special use. Some are resistant to water, alcohol, heat and scratches.

Varnish is much easier to apply than lacquer because the coats don't melt together, but because it takes so long to dry, dust is a problem. Varnish is also very difficult to repair and it looks like a film on top of the wood. The biggest problem with varnish is discoloration, especially if the varnished piece is exposed to a lot of light and sun.

Many modern synthetic finishes, such as polyurethane, state on the front of the can, in big letters, that they are guaranteed not to discolor for two years. But I certainly don't want to have to refinish my furniture every two years.   □

26

1

2

3

French Polishing

French polish is one of the most difficult finishes to learn to apply and one of the most time-consuming, but if a high-gloss finish is desired, I think a French-polished finish is the most beautiful one. French polishing brings out the beauty of the grain and gives the wood an almost three-dimensional feeling. A disadvantage of this finish is that it is not alcohol, water and heat-proof, but it is as easy to repair as shellac (p. 187).

Materials and equipment　First the pads — you will need at least two, one for polishing and one for clearing the finish of oil afterward. The pad for polishing should be proportionate in size to the area to be polished; for a surface of 3 sq. ft. to 4 sq. ft., the pad should be around 2 in. to 2½ in. in diameter. A smaller surface would call for a smaller pad and a larger surface for a larger pad. The pad for clearing should be about 1 in. in diameter. Any necessary patching or repair work will require a separate pad, which should also be about 1 in. in diameter.

Make each pad from a clean wool rag **(1)** packed into a hard ball. Wool is better than absorbent cotton, which is used when polishing moldings (p. 209), because wool mixes the shellac and alcohol and gives it up better than cotton.

Here is how to make a pad. First fold in all the corners of the rag toward the center **(2,3)**; keep stretching the wool.

When all the corners are pressed in, squeeze the pad into an oval while keeping the corners together in the center with your fingers **(4)**. The pad should be firm and hard **(5)**. Then wrap the pad tightly in a single thickness of colorless muslin or coarse linen **(6,7)**. This cloth is called the cover.

4

5

6

7

8

9

When not in use, keep the polishing pad in an airtight, covered container (**8,9**). The pad will improve with age, becoming harder and keeping its shape better.

For French polishing, use only orange shellac of the highest quality. Orange shellac is even better if it is first filtered through a felt hat. The shellac will take days to go through the hat, but the result is a clear, burgundy-colored shellac with no impurities. It looks like wine, but don't drink it. This shellac will darken the wood very little. Never use white shellac on dark wood, as it will give the wood a gray color.

For solvent, use the highest grade of denatured alcohol you can find, not the ordinary commercial solvent sometimes sold for thinning shellac.

The use of boiled linseed oil as a lubricant, often recommended for French polishing, will cause the finish to sweat and eventually to turn slightly green. The best lubricant is paraffin or mineral oil.

Preparing the surface   Carefully plane, scrape and sand the surface to be French polished. Remove or fill all imperfections, holes and marks. But don't fill the pores, because they will be filled during the first coat with pumice and shellac.

If the surface is to be stained, apply chemical or water stain before beginning to polish, then brush or spray on a sealer coat of 2-lb. cut shellac. This sealer coat is not absolutely necessary on unstained surfaces, but its application will make polishing easier. When thoroughly dry, sand the shellac lightly with 220-grit paper.

If the wood is the type that fuzzes up even after careful sanding, such as butternut, apply a coat of hot glue sizing (p. 135) to the surface and sand it smooth when dry to remove all excess. Don't use a shellac sealer coat if you're going to apply glue sizing. It's also a good idea to put a coat of sizing on veneer that shows any sign of checking.

The strokes A French-polish finish should be stroked on with circular, oval or figure-eight motions. Circles should be approximately 4 in. to 6 in. in diameter, depending on the size of the pad; the strokes should completely cover the surface of the work. Never go over an area with the same stroke twice in a row because this will soften the finish, causing the pad to stick and roughen the area. (This is why it is more difficult to polish a small surface than a large one. On a small surface, the shellac doesn't have enough time to dry and settle into the pores between passes of the pad.)

Stroking too slowly, or stopping the pad for an instant while it is on the surface, may also roughen the finish, as will breaking circular strokes with an angular jag. It's a good idea for beginners to experiment with a dry pad before actually starting to work.

Because beginners tend to build up the center of a surface and neglect the edges and corners, concentrate first on learning how to stroke these areas. Be sure the pad overlaps the edges **(10)** when polishing there.

Corners are the most difficult. I've found that a good system is to hit the corner first at 45°, pushing the pad all the way off the surface **(11)**. The next time go across the grain, again pushing the pad off the surface **(12)**. Go with the grain next and, finally, go in circles.

Don't expect your first attempt at French polishing to produce a perfect finish. Experience and practice are better teachers than even the most detailed instructions.

10

11

12

13

14

15

The first coat The first coat is the foundation of the entire French-polished finish, and great care must be taken to apply it evenly. During the first coat, the pores are filled with pumice and just enough shellac to bind the particles of pumice together.

If a sealer coat of shellac has been applied to the wood, very little shellac should be put into the wool of the pad at this stage. If you're using an old pad, there will probably be enough shellac left in it from the last time you used it. If you're using a new pad about 2½ in. in diameter, put about 1 tablespoon of shellac on the side of the wool that will be the bottom, then add about 2½ to 3 tablespoons of alcohol **(13)**. Put on the cloth cover and hit the pad against the side of your workbench **(14)** to mix the shellac and alcohol and make the polishing surface flat. Always do this whenever you add liquid to a pad. If it becomes too wet, squeeze out the excess liquid by clamping the pad firmly in a vise **(15)**.

If the wood has not been given a sealer coat of shellac, you'll need to put a little more shellac into the wool. About 2 tablespoons each of shellac and alcohol will do for a 2½-in. pad.

Alcohol softens a French-polished finish, and therefore too much pressure with an alcohol-saturated pad will result in an uneven surface. Shellac builds up the finish, but too much shellac will cause the pad to become sticky and prevent smooth polishing. In addition, too much shellac will cause the cover of the pad to become glazed with yellow or brown spots.

To begin polishing, first sprinkle some pumice lightly on the surface **(16)**. Put a small amount of pumice into a piece of linen and tie it into a ball **(17,18)**. This will allow you to shake fine pumice powder onto the wood. Too much pumice will build up in uneven patches and cause burns (p. 207). (If this happens, change the cover on your pad, which will pick up the extra pumice and eventually even out the burns.)

16

17

18

19

20

21

Begin to stroke on the polish, keeping the pad cover tightly over the wool for a firm, smooth polishing surface. Hold the pad in your fist so that pressure is directly under your knuckles **(19)**, not under the extended fingers. In the application of all coats of French polish, only light pressure is required when the pad is wet and the coat is being built up, so use only one hand **(20)**. As the pad dries out, there should be some pull against the surface but not enough to prevent steady strokes. Heavier pressure is required as the pad dries, because then the pad's function changes from building up to smoothing out. Use both hands **(21)**, but increase the pressure gradually — too much pressure when the pad is not dry enough may cause large swirls to stand out, leaving marks on the finish. If continued, this could even cause the finish to burn. Remember never to allow the pad to touch the surface being polished unless the pad is in motion. An instant's hesitation while the pad is in contact with the work might leave an unsightly blemish. Experience will tell you when to add more shellac, alcohol or pumice to the work.

Sometimes a piece of dust gets stuck in the finish **(22)**. Remove it with a sharp chisel while the finish is still soft **(23)** and continue.

The proper temperature for French polishing is 70°F or higher, so if the surface becomes cloudy while you are polishing, the room in which you are working is probably too cold. Never store the work in a cold room.

When all the pores are filled with pumice and shellac, and the pad is half dry, sprinkle on some paraffin oil and continue polishing with the same motions. Paraffin oil is necessary to build up a smooth finish and to help prevent burns, though sometimes, with open-pored wood such as oak, it is better not to use oil in the first coat. When starting the second coat on open-pored wood, don't use oil until the pores are completely refilled.

To apply the oil, dip a fingertip in and shake it here and there over the work **(24,25)**. One sprinkle at a time is enough. Too much oil will cause the pad to ride on an oily surface and lose contact with the work. Too little oil will cause burns.

22

23

24

25

After you start to use oil on the surface, you should no longer apply pumice directly to the work. Sprinkle it lightly on the wool of the pad instead **(26)**.

Apply both shellac and alcohol to the top of the wool, as necessary, so they can work out slowly to the bottom of the pad. Sprinkle on more oil if none shows on the surface when you test it occasionally by wiping it with your finger. An excess of alcohol in the pad will cause the oil to disappear from the surface too quickly.

Application of the first coat is completed when the surface is entirely covered with shellac and is free of swirls and blemishes, and when the pad is half dry. This usually takes about one hour. The application of a coat of French polish — any coat — is not complete until the pad becomes half dry, so when the pad just begins to dry, do not stop polishing. If you put aside the pad to rest or have a smoke, evaporation will dry the pad out in the air instead of on the work surface. So don't rest or smoke.

If, after application of this or any other coat, the surface is rough or uneven, allow it to dry at least one day, then rub it smooth with a felt block, pumice and paraffin oil before applying the next coat. For this you may also use 220-grit sandpaper and paraffin oil. But never use sandpaper, pumice and oil just before the final coat, because scratches will show up.

The second coat After the first coat has been allowed to dry for at least one day, you are ready to apply the second coat. During the second coat you must fill the pores again, because the drying of the finish causes the pores to reappear slightly. After filling them, the idea is to get the surface built up with a thin layer of shellac as quickly as possible. Remember, when the pad is wet it puts on shellac, but as the pad dries out it is primarily smoothing the surface, although it continues to put on a little shellac.

Using the same pad you used for the first coat, add first a little shellac and then a little alcohol to the top of the wool. Sprinkle a little pumice between the wool and the cover. Pumice between wool and cover is necessary during the entire second coat.

Also sprinkle the surface of the work with a few drops of paraffin oil, if oil has been used in the first coat. Keep a little oil on the surface at all times — not so much that the pad will lose contact with the work, but not so little that the surface will scratch.

26

Stroke the pad with firm pressure, using the same motions as before. When the pad is working properly, you'll feel a very slight pull as you move it over the surface of the work and hear a slight rasping noise as the pumice works through the cover. The path left by the pad should be slightly dull, in contrast to the shinier surface that is on each side of the path. If this is not the case, try adding in turn shellac or alcohol until the path looks and feels right.

Keep an eye on the cover of the pad. If it wears out **(27)**, the pumice will come out too fast and damage the surface. If the pad cover turns yellow or becomes too sticky for smooth rubbing, add alcohol to the wool from the top and hit the pad firmly against the bench. Then continue rubbing, adding shellac, alcohol and pumice until the surface is smooth.

This coat, too, is completed when the pad is half dry and when the final strokes of the pad leave no marks on the surface. The finish should be clear and glossy and there should be no imperfections or blemishes. For the beginner, the application of the second coat will take about an hour. If possible, the second coat should be allowed to dry for at least two days.

The final coat   The third coat is usually the final coat. For this coat it's necessary to add a little 2-lb. cut shellac and alcohol to the wool of the pad. If small ridges and depressions appear in the surface as you polish, add a little more alcohol and stroke the surface lightly with the grain. Never use a pad that is too wet for this coat, because it will cause burns and you'll wind up having to apply another coat. Keep a light dusting of pumice between the wool and the cover, and sprinkle paraffin oil on the surface as you work. Work with varying strokes as when applying previous coats. Remember to keep the pad under your fists.

When the coat is built up to your satisfaction, touch the surface with your fingertip and move it lightly across the work to see whether the pad is leaving any marks. This cuts across the streaks. When the process is ended, the surface should have no marks.

To speed up this coat you can sprinkle on oil more frequently than before, after the pad is half dry, but still apply only a little at a time. Using more oil in the final coat than in the previous coats will help prevent scratches.

When the final coat is done, immediately clear the finish.

27

28

29

Clearing The clearing operation removes the oil film from the finish. You will need a fresh pad for this, one that has not been used for polishing. The pad should be about one third the size of the polishing pad and made out of the same material. You may use the clearing pad several times, but there is a limit to its life span. Never use a clearing pad for anything else, and store it in an airtight container when not in use.

To begin, moisten a clean clearing pad with alcohol, but don't get it too wet. Put a clean cloth over the wool and rub the work with long strokes going with the grain. As the pad dries, apply a little more pressure. During this operation, keep moving the cover of the pad over as it becomes saturated with oil, so you present a fresh surface to the work. Continue to move the pad up and down with the grain, running off the edge each time. This operation should remove all oil from the surface and leave a clear, bright finish. Clearing is completed when all oil is removed.

Experienced French-polishers often spit on the finish during clearing to speed it up. If you do this, I advise you not to have a dry martini right before you spit.

Dull finish If a dull finish is desired, two coats of French polish are usually sufficient, and the clearing operation is not required. Keep a light dusting of pumice between the wool and the cover, and sprinkle paraffin oil on the surface as you work. The second coat should be completed when the pad is quite dry. To dull the finish, sprinkle it with pumice and rub thoroughly with a clean shoe brush, always following the direction of the grain **(28,29)**. The pumice will pick up the oil. For a less dull finish, allow the work to dry at least 24 hours before brushing with pumice. □

Burning

The most common defect to appear in a surface being French polished is called burning. This is the buildup of dull, rough spots caused by adhesion of too much pumice to the tacky surface. Burn spots may vary in size from small dots to blemishes that cover the entire surface **(1,2)**. If burning occurs before paraffin oil has been applied to the work (early in the first coat), smooth out the area by rubbing vigorously with a pad moistened in alcohol. When attempting to erase a burn this way, move the cover of the pad frequently so that a fresh surface is always presented to the work to pick up the extra pumice.

If a burn is very heavy, use a sharp chisel to peel off its outer surface **(3)** before using the moist pad to smooth it out completely. But never use a chisel to remove burns in the final coat or after oil has been used. When the burn has been smoothed out, stroke that area more often than the rest of the surface to build up the removed polish.

If oil has been used on the work, apply a little more oil and rub the whole surface with circular and figure-eight strokes, concentrating on the burn until it disappears. If a burn is not removed by this method, leave the work until the next day, then sand the burn off with 220-grit sandpaper lubricated with paraffin oil. Proceed to build up the surface around the burn in the usual manner.   □

1

2

3

Repairing French Polish

If at any time in the French-polishing process you discover small holes or pits in the surface, perhaps spots you didn't notice in final sanding or filling, you should level them immediately with the following technique.

Pour ½ pint of 4-lb. or 5-lb. cut shellac into a clean tin can. Ignite the surface of the shellac and allow the alcohol to burn off until the volume of the liquid remaining is approximately half the original. Extinguish the flame by covering the can. Be careful.

To the remaining heavy shellac, stir in 1⅖ oz. (40 grams) of 4F pumice and 4 teaspoons of paraffin oil. Let the mixture cool. It should be the consistency of thick molasses. You may store it for future use, but if the mixture becomes too thick, add shellac to bring it back to the proper consistency.

Now, get your polishing pad working properly, as in the final coat. Then sharpen a piece of ¼-in. dowel to a pencil point. Dip the point in the mixture and place the drop that clings to its end in the hole to be filled. Take your polishing pad and hammer it down sharply over the drop; at the same instant the pad touches the work, glide off into a French-polishing stroke. Don't let the pad linger, but immediately stroke it over the surface. If you don't quite fill the hole, repeat the process, but do not repeat more than twice without polishing over the entire surface several times.

To erase small dents that have not broken the fibers of the wood on old French-polished finishes, first cover the dent with paraffin oil. Then place a piece of moist paper over the oil to moisten the surface and help raise the dent. Drop hot stick shellac on the paper directly over the dent. Melt the shellac drop from its stick with either a burning-in knife or a match. Repeat, if necessary, until the surface is flush.

To repair large indentations or bruises that are not too deep on old French-polished finishes, again pour paraffin oil over the damaged area. Prepare a small torch by wrapping a piece of cotton around the end of a wire and wetting the cotton with alcohol. Ignite the torch and pass it quickly over the surface of the oil, but be careful not to get the oil so hot that it bubbles up on the surface, because you might burn the finish. If the dents are not filled all the way, level them off with the heavy shellac mixture.

To build up repaired areas or to refinish spots, make up a small pad about the size of a fifty-cent piece, depending on the size of the damage, of course. Use the same material as for a polishing pad. If you are using the pad for the first time, moisten the wool with 2-lb. cut shellac; if you've used the pad before, moisten the wool with alcohol. Dust pumice over the wool before covering it, and follow the regular French-polishing technique, at first confining your strokes to as small an area as possible around the repair. Finish up by widening your circles around the repaired area to blend it into the surrounding area. It's a good idea to French polish a small scrap of wood when the surface being repaired is drying, to keep the pad working. Don't forget to clear the finish of oil, as described on p. 206. If you like, dull the spot with pumice and a shoe brush.   □

French Polishing Moldings

Moldings should always be French polished before beginning the main surface. To do this, use a pad of absorbent cotton without any cover. Pour some 2-lb. cut shellac, alcohol and paraffin oil directly onto the cotton **(1)** and dust pumice over it **(2)**. Squeeze the pad to mix the shellac, alcohol and oil and to remove excess liquid **(3)**.

Now rub the molding with continuous strokes **(4)**. Because of the size of molding, it's possible to use only straight back-and-forth strokes. (The oil prevents the shellac from turning into a sticky mess, so this is why oil is used in the first coat.) As you proceed, the pad will shape itself to the contour of the molding.

1

2

3

4

Slight alterations to this shape may occur when you add shellac or pumice to the pad, but try to maintain the contour as closely as possible to prevent streaking. Apply as many coats of French polish to the molding as you intend to apply to the main body of the work, using the technique just described for each one. Allow drying time of at least two days between coats.

The clearing operation for molding is quite different from that used on the main surface of the work. First, rub the molding with a dry, clean rag to remove as much oil as possible. Next, soak a piece of absorbent cotton with 4-lb. or 5-lb. cut shellac **(5)**. Move the wet cotton along the molding with a single stroke. When dry, the molding is finished. ☐

French Polishing Turnings

To French polish work on the lathe, use the same type of pad and material used for French polishing moldings. Run the lathe at very low speed and apply the polish along the moving surface of the work. Clearing may be done by either of two methods: For a large piece, use alcohol as described on p. 206 or, for small, intricate turnings, use heavy shellac as described in the clearing operation for moldings.

I like to use Qualasole, a padding lacquer especially formulated for use on turnings, as a modern-day French polish. ☐

5

Editor: Laura Cehanowicz Tringali
Designer: Roger Barnes
Layout: Christopher Clapp
Illustrations: Pete Christman, Karen Pease
Cover Illustration: E. Marino III
Editorial Assistant: Deborah Cannarella
Manager of Production Services: Cindy Lee Nyitray
Production Manager: JoAnn Muir
Typesetting: Nancy-Lou Knapp
Darkroom: Barbara Hannah
Pasteup: Jean Zalkind Anderheggen, Johnette Luxeder,
          Kathryn Olsen, Claudia W. Underhill

Typeface: Compugraphic Univers 9 point